I KNOW YOU ARE LYING
Detecting Deception Through Statement Analysis

Mark McClish

Published by
PoliceEmployment.com
Winterville, NC 28590

I Know You Are Lying
Detecting Deception Through Statement Analysis

Copyright © 2001 by Mark McClish
Library of Congress Control Number: 2001117724
ISBN 0-9679998-2-0

Published by
PoliceEmployment.com
P.O. Box 2090
Winterville, NC 28590-2090

All rights reserved. No part of this publication may be reproduced without the prior permission of the publisher except for brief quotations and as provided by the United States copyright law.

Printed in the United States of America.
Third printing 2005

DEDICATION

This book is dedicated to my father and mother, Alan and Diane McClish, who taught me to tell the truth.

The opinions and techniques expressed in this book do not necessarily reflect the views of the United States Marshals Service or the Department of Justice.

For more information on Statement Analysis, visit our web site at **www.StatementAnalysis.com**

CONTENTS

Introduction 7

Part I Preparing For The Interview 11
   Chapter 1 Nonverbal Communication vs Statement
               Analysis 13
   Chapter 2 Liar Liar Pants On Fire 19
   Chapter 3 Watch How You Phrase Your Questions 23

Part II Detecting Deception In A Verbal Statement 29
   Chapter 4   Look At The Language 31
   Chapter 5   Examine All Of The Pronouns 43
   Chapter 6   Check The Verb Tenses 51
   Chapter 7   Order Is Important 55
   Chapter 8   Pay Attention To Time References 61
   Chapter 9   Words And Phrases That Indicate Deception . 65
   Chapter 10 Did The Subject Answer The Question? 69
   Chapter 11 Did The Subject Answer The Question
              With A Question? 77

Part III Detecting Deception In A Written Statement 81
   Chapter 12 Did The Writer Cross Out Any Words? 83
   Chapter 13 Look For Unnecessary Words 87
   Chapter 14 Internal Dictionary 91
   Chapter 15 What Is The Breakdown Of The Story? 95

Part IV Some Final Thoughts 99
   Chapter 16 What Hasn't The Subject Told You? 101
   Chapter 17 A Quick Review 105

Part V Case Analysis 111
   Chapter 18 The Oklahoma City Bombing 113
   Chapter 19 The Nicole Brown Simpson And Ronald
              Goldman Murders 119
   Chapter 20 Sexual Molestation Allegations Against
              Michael Jackson 147
   Chapter 21 The Assassination Of Dr. Martin Luther
              King, Jr. 159

Chapter 22 The Lindbergh Kidnapping And The Trial
               Of Bruno Richard Hauptmann 177
Chapter 23 President Clinton And Monica Lewinsky
               Scandal 199
Chapter 24 The Murder Of Marilyn Sheppard 219
Chapter 25 The JonBenet Ramsey Murder 227

Notes 263

Introduction

I began my law enforcement career in 1983 with the United States Secret Service Uniformed Division. I was stationed at the White House during President Regan's first term in office. Like all new recruits, before I could assume my role at 1600 Pennsylvania Avenue I had to complete training. The first part of my training was conducted at the Federal Law Enforcement Training Center (FLETC) in Glynco, GA. Nearly all federal law enforcement agencies conduct part, if not all, of their training at the FLETC. After attending eight weeks of police training at the FLETC, I then completed my training at the U.S. Secret Service Training Academy in Beltsville, MD. Two years later I found myself again attending training at the FLETC when I switched to the U.S. Marshals Service. It was during my second stay at the FLETC that I decided I wanted to teach in a training environment. After spending five years in Springfield, Illinois as a Deputy U.S. Marshal, I was able to obtain my goal. In November of 1990, I was promoted to the position of Inspector/Instructor at the U.S. Marshals Service Training Academy located at the FLETC.

I stayed at the Marshals Service Training Academy for nine years before returning to the field in December 1999 as a Supervisory Deputy U.S. Marshal in Greenville, North Carolina. As an instructor I was responsible for three areas of instruction: defensive tactics, physical conditioning, and interviewing techniques. Having a Bachelor of Arts degree in Physical Education and a Black Belt in the martial arts, I was fully prepared to teach in the matroom. However, I wasn't as comfortable teaching interviewing techniques in the classroom. Over the years, I had conducted many interviews in looking for fugitives. I was confident I could tell if someone was lying to me, but I wasn't sure if I could teach others how to recognize deception. Many times you may sense someone is lying, but you can't identify exactly what it is that's telling you he is being untruthful.

Before teaching interviewing techniques I attended several courses on the subject. Classes such as nonverbal communication, linguistics, response analysis and scientific content analysis gave me a better understanding of what to look for during an interview. I now had enough information to write a lesson plan on interviewing. However, I decided to take my teaching responsibilities one step further. Instead of just sharing this knowledge with the students, I wanted to find out if these techniques actually worked.

For nine years I conducted my own research on how people answer questions. There were three groups of individuals that I used in my studies. The first group consisted of recruits who were attending basic Deputy U.S. Marshals Service training. A typical class consisted of 48 students. Over a nine year period there were plenty of classes for me to observe. I would analyze the type of language the students used in the various reports they had to write. I also conducted blind studies with them. I would have the class write a story about something they did or something they experienced. Half of the class had to write a truthful story. The other half had to make up a story that was completely false. The papers on which these stories were recorded were coded so I could tell which ones were truthful and which were false. As I read their statements I could see several patterns emerging. Those students who were purposely lying would lie in the same way. Likewise, those students who were truthful would tell the truth in a similar fashion.

The second group I studied was an outfit called Role Players Inc. The Marshals Service Training Academy as well as the FLETC uses semiprofessional actors to play various roles in the practical exercises the students must complete. This helps to create realistic training. When the students knock on a door during a practical exercise, it will be answered by an individual they have never seen before. These actors had various roles to play. Sometimes they were an innocent neighbor, a sympathetic family member, or the bandit himself. These role players were given a short description of the scenario and told to either lie or tell the truth when interviewed by the students. What we did not tell them was how they should lie. Those role players who were being deceptive could lie in any manner they chose. As I watched over one hundred role players answer the students questions, I found they too would lie in a similar fashion. When being deceptive, they would use some of the same words and phrases.

The third group I studied and continue to study is prominent people in the news. Whenever an incident occurs, the press will hound someone for an interview or a statement. Often I will detect deception or additional information in these statements. Usually this goes unnoticed by the media and the general public. Sometime after the statement has been given, my findings will be confirmed when the person involved in the incident admits he withheld information or misled the interviewer.

The techniques I am about to share with you are referred to by several names such as "Word Analysis" and "Response Analysis." I prefer to call it "Statement Analysis." These techniques are based on my research as well as the research conducted by other experts in the field of interviewing. What you will find though is most of these techniques need no verification. That's because we are talking about the English language. Every word has a meaning. When you combine this with the fact that people mean exactly what they say, it then becomes possible to determine if a person is being truthful or deceptive.

Part I
Preparing For The Interview

Chapter 1

Nonverbal Communication vs Statement Analysis

When we communicate with those around us we usually do so by vocalizing our thoughts and feelings. However, verbalization only makes up about half of the communication process. We also convey our true feelings through our body language. Our nonverbal communication can sometimes speak just as loud as our words. People may be verbally telling us one thing, but displaying conflicting nonverbal signals. We can sometimes use these nonverbal signals to detect deception.

For most people, knowingly telling a lie creates some degree of stress. This stress will usually surface in the form of a body movement. This is similar to the principle that governs a polygraph test. A polygraph will measure a person's heart rate, respiratory rate, blood pressure and perspiration. When abnormal changes occur in these areas it is a sign that the person is under some stress. Even though the subject may claim he didn't do it, the polygraph is detecting stress which indicates he may be lying. While you cannot detect someone's heart rate just by looking at them, there are other nonverbal signals you can recognize which may indicate a person is being untruthful.

One of the easiest ways to detect deception through nonverbs is to watch the person's hands. Many times when a person tells a lie one of his hands will go towards his mouth. This is usually a subconscious gesture of wanting to cover the mouth. The speaker is attempting to mask what he is saying because he knows it not to be true. How much of the mouth is covered by the hand depends on the age of person. When a child tells a lie he may cup his hand or hands completely over his mouth. He is signaling he knows he just told a lie. When a teenager tells a lie the hand may come to the face but it usually will not cover the mouth. Instead he may gently rub his lips with his fingers. When an adult tells a lie, experience has taught him not to bring his hands to his mouth. However, it can be very hard for him to fight that instinctive response to cover the mouth. Therefore, he will usually touch his nose instead of his mouth.

Another gesture that indicates stress and possible deception is when an individual begins to adjust his clothing or touches his hair. This is known as grooming. He may begin to tuck in his shirt or play with the buttons on his shirt even though his shirt doesn't need any adjusting. His hair may be perfectly combed, but he will run his fingers through his hair to make sure they are all in place. This type of person wants to make sure he is looking his best. Subconsciously he is thinking that if he looks good, then his deceptive answers will look good.

When some people tell a lie they begin to blush. Their face will turn light red in color revealing they are uncomfortable. For those individuals who are able to avoid this blotchy redness, the stress caused by telling an untruth is sometimes manifested as a tingling sensation in the facial and neck area. This will cause the person to rub the back of his neck. The person may even unconsciously tug on the collar of his shirt. This gesture is an attempt to circulate air around the neck area in order to cool down.

The hands can also tell us if a person is being open, or if he is being closed off and withholding information. During an interview if a person has his arms folded across his chest, this is an indication of tension. He is not relaxed and not open to what is being asked of him. The interviewer may have to draw the information out of him. A person who has his hands resting on his lap is displaying an attitude of being open to the interviewer's questions. This type of person is more likely to give truthful answers.

Aside from the hands, the eyes can also give away a person's true feelings. Studies have shown that during a conversation most people will maintain eye contact about 50% of the time. It is natural to occasionally look away for a brief moment when speaking with someone. After glancing away, a person will then focus his attention once again on the speaker. Any extreme deviation from this 50% ratio is an indication of deception. For example, a person may continually look away when being questioned. He will stare at the ground or he will look up in the air.

He will maintain very little eye contact with the speaker. This can be perceived as a sign that the person is not interested in what the speaker is saying. In an interview setting, this is an indication that his answers will be deceptive. This is a typical response of a young child. He cannot look his parents in the eyes and tell them a lie.

As a person gets older he learns how to lie. He knows that he should maintain eye contact when speaking with someone. Therefore, he will make a conscious effort to not look away. This type of deceptive person will sometimes make the mistake of maintaining too much eye contact. He will literally stare at you while you are speaking with him. He is making his best effort to convince you he is interested in what you are saying, and that you should believe what he is telling you. An honest person will be attentive, but he will not stare you down.

When a person does look away, it is important to recognize which way he looks. Studies have shown that a right handed person who looks to his left while thinking about his answer, will probably give a truthful answer. He is using the part of his brain that stores memory. His answer is based on his memory of what happened. However, if this same person looks to his right, he is now relying on the creative part of his brain. This is the part of the brain that makes up stories. Therefore, he will probably give a deceptive answer.

Despite it's usefulness, there are several reasons why I feel an interviewer should not focus on a person's nonverbs. If your attention is drawn to the interviewee's body movements, then you probably are not listening to everything the person is saying. This is important because people's words will betray them. It may only be one or two words that will let you know this person is being deceptive. If you focus on their hands, feet, and eyes, then you may miss these few words that reveal their true thoughts.

In order to interpret nonverbs effectively you first have to establish the normal body movements for the person being interviewed. This is done at the beginning of the interview when you are asking the person questions he should be answering truthfully. Questions such as, "What is your name?" "What is your address?" "What is your telephone number?" should not be stressful questions. As the person answers these questions look to see what type of actions he is displaying. Later on when you start asking more sensitive questions you then look for any abnormal movements. When the hands start to move or the eyes suddenly look away this can be a sign of deception. Establishing normal body movements at the beginning of the interview is the key to reading nonverbal signals. A problem arises when you do not have a chance to establish the norms. For example, you may turn on the television and watch a news reporter interview a prominent person. Many times the actual interview will be one hour in length. However, for the television broadcast the interview will be edited to fifteen minutes. The editors will delete some of the nonessential questions and answers. They will only televise the responses that deal with the incident at hand. As the interviewee displays various nonverbal signals you cannot say his actions indicate he is being deceptive. You do not know what is normal for him because you were not able to watch him during the first part of his interview.

With Statement Analysis, you do not have to establish any norms. Most of the time you can look at one question and one answer and determine if the person is answering the question truthfully. You can take one statement and obtain additional information from that statement. This is all possible because people mean exactly what they say.

Another problem I have with nonverbs is that the information conveyed through nonverbal communication is not specific. Let's say you do establish the norms for the person you are interviewing. You ask this person if he performed a certain act and he denies doing it. However, while making his denial he performs the abnormal movement of rubbing the back of his neck. Does this mean he is lying? The bottom line is you do not know. This nonverbal cue probably means he was asked a very sensitive question. Despite his nervous actions, he could be answering the question truthfully. Nonverbs can tell us if a person is under some stress. However, this stress does not always equate to deception.

Statement Analysis is usually very specific because people mean exactly what they say. If a person says he is "thinking about buying a car," that is exactly what he means. He has not told you he did buy a car. He has not told you he will buy a car. All he has stated is that he is considering buying a car. Now that example may seem rather simplex, but the same rule applies when the question is asked, "Do you know who did it?" and the person answers, "I can't think of anyone." This answer may sound good, but the subject has not told us he does not know of anyone who would do this. All he is saying is at this present moment in time he cannot think of anyone. Perhaps with a little prodding he may have a better recollection.

My final argument in support of Statement Analysis is that in order to read nonverbal signals, the subject must be present. You have to visually watch him to see what he is telling you through his body movements. With Statement Analysis the subject does not have to be present. You can use Statement Analysis when speaking with someone on the telephone. You cannot do that with nonverbs. With Statement Analysis you can take a written statement and determine if the subject is being truthful or deceptive. Again, you cannot do that with nonverbs. With Statement Analysis, you do not have to see the person, hear the person or know anything about the person in order to determine truth or deception.

When we compare nonverbs with Statement Analysis, we find the following differences:

Nonverbs	vs	**Statement Analysis**
Establish norms		No norms
Not specific		Very specific
Presence required		Presence not required

Whether you are conducting an interview or just speaking with someone, your main focus should be on the person's language. Listen to what people are telling you. Your secondary concern should be the nonverbal signals displayed by the interviewee. Nonverbs should be used in conjunction with the Statement Analysis. If a person displays an obvious nonverbal signal, then take note of it. However, if you concentrate on the nonverbs you will miss what the person is telling you.

Chapter 2

Liar Liar Pants On Fire

You have probably heard the children's rhyme "Liar liar pants on fire." This clever piece of poetry is sometimes proclaimed when a person has been caught telling a lie. While it may sound cute, this saying is a complete misrepresentation of reality. It leads us to believe that it is easy to determine if someone is telling an untruth. However, recognizing deception is not always easy. As we all know a person's clothes do not burst into flames when he or she tells a fib.

There is also a second falsehood in this phrase. It is the words "liar liar." The truth is most people who have something to hide will not lie about. In an open statement in which a person can say anything he wants to, most people will not tell a lie. They will tell you what they saw or what they did. What they will not tell you is anything that is in incriminating. In other words, they will not tell you everything they saw or everything they did. They will give you a lot of truthful statements and leave out the damning information.

The reason people choose not to lie is because knowingly telling a lie causes stress. As mentioned in chapter one this stress may surface in the form of a body movement. When some people lie they become fidgety. They begin to squirm in their chair, rub the back of their neck, run their fingers through their hair, or look away when speaking. People know these nonverbal signals may give away the fact they are lying. Therefore, out of fear of having their emotions betray them, most people will choose not to tell a lie.

Another reason people choose not to lie is because they do not know what you, the interviewer, know. If they tell you a lie and you have information that directly contradicts that lie, then they are in big trouble. They have just placed their head into the noose. So, the safest way for them to play it is to not tell any lies. Instead, they will give you a bunch of truthful statements. Although they haven't lied they are still being deceptive because they are withholding crucial information. They are leading you to believe they are innocent.

Keep in mind that we can force people to lie. If you back a person into a corner and leave him no options, he may choose to lie. For example, "Did you do it? Yes or no?" is a terrible way to begin an interview. This type of question forces the person to give a direct answer. Since an answer in the affirmative would be admitting to the crime, the deceptive person's only choice, if he doesn't want to get caught, is to answer "no." The interviewer now has to decide if the person is lying or telling the truth. If the question was phrased, "Did you do it?" the person now has more options as to how he will answer the question. Even though the question still requires a "yes" or a "no" answer, he may choose not to directly answer the question. Instead, he may give an answer that only sounds like a denial. By analyzing his answer you will see he hasn't denied committing the crime. Therefore, you cannot believe he did not do it.

What all of this means is we have to change our way of thinking. A lot of times when we speak with someone who we suspect is lying we look for the lies. We want to catch him making a false statement. However, since people rarely lie you probably will not find any lies in their statements. Because you are focusing on trying to detect lies that do not exist, you miss important information the subject provides. You conclude the interview without having gained much knowledge. The key is to believe what people tell you. Don't assume they are lying, but believe they are telling you the truth. If a person says, "I did not do it" believe him. He probably didn't do it.

For example, consider the bomb that went off at the Olympics in Atlanta, Georgia on July 27, 1996. In a matter of days, security guard Richard Jewell became a prime suspect in the bombing. On July 30, 1996, reporters asked Jewell if he had planted the bomb. His response was "No, sir I didn't. I'm sure they're investigating everyone who was in the area."[1] Jewell makes a strong denial that he did not plant the bomb. The next day reporters again were questioning Jewell about his possible involvement in planting the bomb. Jewell responded by saying "I'm innocent. I didn't do it."[2]

There we have it again. The words "I didn't do it." Jewell claimed he was innocent as many people often do. After all, a person is innocent until proven guilty. However, unlike those people who are guilty, Jewell backs up his claim of innocence by saying "I didn't do it." In September 1996, Jewell was interviewed by Mike Wallace for the CBS news program *60 Minutes*. In the transcript of the interview released by *60 Minutes*, Jewell is quoted as saying, "They don't have anything to arrest me on, and they never will because I did not do it."[3] There we have it once again. Richard Jewell telling us, "I did not do it." He starts out saying, "They don't have anything to arrest me on, and they never will." This statement by itself is the type of statement a lot of guilty people will make. Even though they committed the crime, the statement is true. The police do not have enough evidence to make an arrest. Because the perpetrators feel they have covered up their tracks, the police will never have enough evidence to convict them. However, this statement alone is not a denial. Therefore, Jewell goes on to say, "I did not do it." Unfortunately for Richard Jewell, it took three months before the press and law enforcement officials finally listened to what he was saying. On October 26, 1996, federal prosecutors stated that Jewell was no longer a suspect in the bombing.

Rarely will a guilty person state "I did not do it." This is because people do not want to lie. They do not want to deal with the internal stress caused by lying. Instead, they will usually say something that sounds like a denial such as "I wouldn't do that." Remember to believe what people tell you. If someone says, "I wouldn't do that" believe him but recognize he hasn't denied doing it. All he has stated is that this is something that he wouldn't do. This is a truthful statement. Normally this person wouldn't commit such an act. However, we have all done things we thought we would never do. The same thing applies to the statement, "I couldn't do that." Although it may sound like a good answer again the person hasn't denied doing it.

The first step in detecting deception is to listen to what people are telling you. Don't let their words go in one ear and then out the other. Pay attention to what they are saying. The second step is to believe what people tell you. Don't assume they are lying because they are probably telling the truth. You will get a lot more out of the interview, and you will discover people's true thoughts if you believe what they are saying. The final step to detecting deception is to analyze what people are saying. If they are being deceptive, they may tell you the truth but not the whole truth. Through careful analysis we can determine exactly what they are telling us, and what they are not telling us.

Chapter 3

Watch How You Phrase Your Questions

Before we begin our analysis of a statement, let me briefly address how you should phrase your questions. Sometimes we make it easy for people to be deceptive by the way we ask our questions. A mistake made by some interviewers is to ask a compound question. Compound questions make it easy for the interviewee to be deceptive. The interviewer will ask two questions, but the subject will only answer one of them. The interviewer focuses on the answer given and may move on without realizing the person didn't answer the second part of the question. Therefore, the subject gets away with not answering one question. For example:

> Question: "Have you ever smoked marijuana or used cocaine?"
>
> Answer: "When I was in college at a fraternity party, someone was passing a joint around. Everybody was taking a puff so I took one too. It was the only time in my life that I tried the stuff and I didn't like it. I was young and I didn't use good judgement."

The person appears to be honest and open about his drug usage. Many people may relate to the situation he was in. He takes responsibility for his actions when he tells us he used poor judgement. Most importantly he tells us it only happened once. This type of lengthy answer can deceive an interviewer into thinking this person has completely answered the question. What this person has neglected to comment on is his possible cocaine usage. He gives the appearance he is talking about cocaine when he uses the word "stuff." The fact is he never mentioned cocaine. He did not tell us that he has never used cocaine. Compound questions should be converted into two questions. First ask, "Have you ever smoked marijuana?" Listen to his answer. Probe a little into his marijuana use if necessary. Then ask the next question, "Have you ever used cocaine?" and listen to his answer to that question.

Many journalists will ask compound questions. This is because their questions are not designed to necessarily seek the truth, but to be more entertaining. On April 12, 1997, Larry King interviewed James Earl Ray, the convicted killer of Dr. Martin Luther King, Jr., from a prison hospital on his *Larry King Live Show*. At one point in the interview, King asked Ray a compound question:

King: "OK, what are you doing? Were you on that ledge at the motel across from where Dr. King was standing?"
Ray: "Ledge?"
King: "I mean wherever the shooting occurred from. Did you hold a rifle that day? Did you shoot a rifle that day?"
Ray: "No. I think that is one of the main issues before the courts now, about who shot the rifle, and whether it was — that was the rifle used. There is another issue that hasn't been brought up regarding this rifle. And that is, whether it was ever — what you call — been sighted in."[1]

Larry King asked four questions:

1. "OK, what were you doing?"
2. "Were you on that ledge at the motel across from where Dr. King was standing?"
3. "Did you hold a rifle that day?"
4. "Did you shoot a rifle that day?"

Ray responds with a "No." What is Ray saying "no" to? Being on the ledge? Holding a rifle? Shooting a rifle? Based on his answer it appears he was saying he did not shoot a rifle that day.

However, we really don't know since several questions were asked.

Another mistake sometimes made is the interviewer will not ask specific questions. Specific questions probe certain areas within a person's story to obtain additional information. However, when asking probing questions interviewers sometimes do not specifically ask what they want to know.

One rule we have at our house is we do not park bicycles behind the van in the garage. To do so is an accident waiting to happen. One day my wife Pam was getting ready to leave in the van when she noticed a bike parked behind the van. She immediately yelled out, "Who was riding the bike?" Now she really wasn't concerned with who was riding the bike. What she wanted to know was who parked the bike behind the van. She assumed and rightly so that the rider was the guilty party. However, because she did not specifically ask, "Who parked the bike behind the van?" our youngest son, Mitchell, was able to honestly reply, "I rode it this morning." Although Mitchell knew what his mother was referring to, he was able to tell the truth without admitting he had done something wrong. As for my wife she still did not know for certain who parked the bike behind the van. The reason for her uncertainty is she did not ask specifically what she wanted to know.

When you do not ask the right questions, people will use this to their advantage when answering your questions. They will give you truthful answers making it appear they do not know what you are talking about. Let me refer to my family again. We have a pool in our backyard. One day both of our sons, Michael and Mitchell, were playing in the pool. I looked out the window and saw Michael go into the garage and get the beach umbrella. He then took the umbrella into the pool. After they were done swimming, the beach umbrella was left outside. That night the wind blew it around and damaged it. The next day I told Michael he would have to buy a new umbrella. He replied, "I didn't break it." I asked, "Who broke it?" He responded, "I don't know." I then asked, "Who took it outside?" He said, "I did." So far, my son can easily give truthful answers. I then told him the umbrella was left outside and the wind damaged it. I then asked him, "Who was responsible for the umbrella breaking?" He did not want to answer that question because a truthful answer would incriminate him. Get to the point by asking specific questions.

Another inappropriate question is one that answers itself. For example, "You don't know who did it do you?" This is a terrible question. The answer is actually contained within the question. This type of question tells the subject that he (the subject) does not know who did it. The only question being asked is, "Do you?" This form of questioning makes it very easy for the interviewee to answer with a "No." Since he has been given the answer, this makes it difficult to decide if he is lying or telling the truth. Your questions should always be straight forward. Ask exactly what you want to know. "Do you know who did it?" This way the person has to decide for himself how he will answer the question.

Another mistake people sometimes make is they will ask a question, and then they will answer the question before the interviewee finishes his answer. The subject will begin to give an answer and then will hesitate. During this moment of silence, the interviewer will verbally finish the answer for him.

Question: "How did the window get broken?"
Answer: "Well, we were playing baseball and...."
Question: "The ball went through the window?"
Answer: "Yes."

Here the person who is asking the question also answers the question for the subject. Based on his partial answer of playing baseball it can be deduced that the baseball probably went through the window. This was then confirmed by the subject. The problem is we do not know what the subject would have said had he been allowed to finish his answer. Maybe he was going to say, "Well, we were playing baseball and *Bobby hit the ball through the window.* "We now have more information. We now know exactly how the ball went through the window and who did it. All this potential information is lost when the interviewer answers the question for the subject.

Answering the question for the subject occurred when the Los Angeles Police Department first interviewed O.J. Simpson on June 12, 1994 concerning the murders of his ex-wife, Nicole Brown Simpson, and her friend Ronald Goldman. LAPD Detective Philip

Vannatter asked Simpson questions about his relationship with his ex-wife.

Vannatter: "How long were you together?"
Simpson: "Seventeen years."
Vannatter: "Seventeen years. Did you ever hit her, O.J.?"
Simpson: "Ah, one night we had a fight. We had a fight, and she hit me. And they never took my statement, they never wanted to hear my side, and they never wanted to hear the housekeeper's side. Nicole was drunk. She did her thing, she started tearing up my house, you know? I didn't punch her or anything, but I ......"
Vannatter: "Slapped her a couple of times."
Simpson: "No, no, I wrestled her, is what I did. I didn't slap her I mean, Nicole's a strong girl. She's a ... one of the most conditioned women. Since that period of time, she's hit me a few times, but I've never touched her after that, and I'm telling you, it's five - six years ago."[2]

Simpson hesitates after saying, "I didn't punch her or anything, but I ....." Vannatter answers the question for Simpson by stating, "Slapped her a couple of times." Simpson then tells us he only wrestled with Nicole. We must remember that when the police are interviewing a prime suspect, they want to get a confession. Therefore, they will sometimes try to extract a confession by suggesting certain things to subject. They want to make it easy for the subject to state what happened. However, it is better not to suggest anything or answer the question for them. Allow them to tell you what they want. If they hesitate, wait for them to finish their answer. If it is a very long pause, then tell them to "Go on" or state "I am listening." It is possible Simpson was going to say that he did slap Nicole. However, because the detective suggested it maybe he felt he shouldn't admit to it. We will never know.

Sometimes people ask questions that are so poorly worded no matter how the person answers it there is little information to be gained. The April 15, 1996 issue of *TIME* magazine reported an interview they conducted with then accused Oklahoma City bomber Timothy McVeigh. In this interview, we find the following question and answer:

> TIME: "You have been painted as a kid from a working-class family who somewhere along the line became disenchanted with the government and became involved in the bombing. Are you the killer people think you are?"
>
> McVeigh: "If it means that I was angered at Waco and I enjoy guns as a hobby, I do go to gun shows, and I follow the beliefs of the Founding Fathers. If it means that I was involved in the bombing, then that means about a billion other Americans were involved as well. I don't think it is right to take someone's beliefs and convict them because of those beliefs."[3]

The question posed to McVeigh is, "Are you the killer people think you are?" This is a lousy question. A suspect could have killed thousands of people, and still truthfully answered this question with a "no." The suspect may be a killer but not the kind people are thinking of.

When interviewing someone think about how you are going to word your questions. Do not ask compound questions. Compound questions make it easier for a person to avoid answering a question, and harder for you to recognize he did not answer a question. Your probing questions should be specific and to the point. When you ask questions that only allude to something, you give the person the opportunity to give you an honest answer without supplying the information you wanted. If the interviewee gives a partial answer, show a little patience. Do not finish the answer for him. Finally, do not give him the answer within the question. Asking the right kind of questions is very important in determining if a person is telling the truth.

Part II

Detecting Deception In A Verbal Statement

Chapter 4

Look At The Language

To detect deception in a statement, you must be a good listener. One of the first things you want to listen for is the specific words used in a conversation. Everything a person says has a meaning. When you combine this with the fact that people mean exactly what they say, you can begin to recognize what a person is really telling you. To the untrained listener, it may sound like this person is innocent. However, the attentive interviewer hears a different story. Ask yourself, "What is this person telling me based on the language he is using?" This will help you to determine exactly what someone is saying.

As a Deputy U.S. Marshal, I have the collateral duty of being a recruit interviewer. Several other deputies and myself will interview applicants for the position of Deputy U.S. Marshal. I remember one applicant who had a questionable incident in his background. The incident alone would not disqualify him. However, the panel wanted to know if the applicant had a pattern of participating in this activity or was this an isolated incident. I asked him if there was any other time he had engaged in this activity but didn't get caught. Now the only good answer to that question is "no." However, the word "no" was not in his lengthy response. He was doing his best to lead us to believe he had only done this one time.

At this point, the room became quiet as we were writing down the information we had received. Silence is a good interviewing tactic. Some people feel they need to say something to break the silence. That is exactly what this applicant did. He blurted out, "You know, I am trying to be as honest as possible." Now think about what he said. What did this applicant tell the panel with his unsolicited comment? Look at the words he used. There is one word I have a big problem with. It is the word "trying." What does the word "trying" mean? It means to attempt; failed; did not succeed. The applicant told us he was not being truthful in his answers! He was only attempting to tell us the truth. The words "as possible" also jumped out at me. Here the applicant was telling me that his honesty has a limitation. He can be honest with the interviewing panel up to a certain point. Upon hearing this, I continued to question the applicant about this incident. He finally admitted there was another time when he engaged in this activity but wasn't caught. Now we have him changing his story. Needless to say he didn't pass the interview.

We see this same use of language with former President William Clinton. On August 17, 1998, the President appeared before a grand jury at the request of independent counsel Kenneth Starr. Starr was investigating whether or not the President had lied during his testimony in the Paula Jones litigation. The independent counsel wanted to know if the President understood that during his testimony in the Paula Jones deposition he was under oath and obligated to tell the truth. The President responded by stating, "I swore an oath to tell the truth, and I believed I was bound to be truthful, and I <u>tried</u> to be."[1] The President told the independent counsel's office and the members of the grand jury that he failed to tell the truth in his Paula Jones deposition. I wonder how many of them actually heard what he was saying!

These are two examples of listening to what a person is telling you. Ideally you want to pay close attention to each word that is spoken. However, that is hard to do. Therefore, focus on the major words in a sentence. Remember to ask yourself, "What is this person telling me?" Let us look at some more examples of analyzing a person's words.

In July 1999, Mark Barton went on a shooting rampage in Atlanta, Georgia. When the shooting stopped, nine people were dead. Barton had also killed his wife and two kids. Instead of surrendering to the police, Barton ended his life with a self-inflicted gun shot wound. Barton had been a suspect in the deaths of his first wife and her mother who were murdered years earlier. People felt he had gotten away with the crime because the police did not conduct a thorough investigation. Barton had left a suicide note and in it he denied killing his ex-wife and mother-in-law. The note read in part, "There may be many similarities between these deaths and the death of my first wife Debra Spivey. However, I deny killing her and her mother."[2] This is a very strong denial especially coming from a suicide note. However, he does not tell us he did not kill his first wife. He never says, "I didn't kill her" or "I didn't do it." All he says is, "I deny killing her." The word deny can mean to refuse to accept the truth. When someone is an alcoholic but will not admit to it we say this person is in denial. He refuses to accept the fact that he is an alcoholic. Mark Barton could be saying the same thing. He refuses to accept the fact that he killed his first wife and her mother.

In 1992, Arkansas Governor William Clinton was running for President. At the time, he was the front-runner to receive the Democratic presidential nomination. However, his campaign stalled when a former television reporter, Gennifer Flowers, stated she had an affair with the governor. In an effort to salvage his campaign, on January 26, 1992, Governor Clinton and his wife Hillary appeared on the CBS news program *60 Minutes*. Governor Clinton described his relationship with Flowers as being "very limited."[3] He then went on to say, "She left our state, and for years, I didn't really hear from her and know what she was doing."[4] Question: Did Governor Clinton hear from Gennifer Flowers after she had left the state of Arkansas? The answer is yes. He did not tell us he "didn't hear from her." What he said was he "didn't really hear from her." By using the word "really" he is qualifying his statement. This also applies to knowing what Flowers was doing. The President didn't want to tell a lie. That is why he did not say, "I didn't hear from her." On the other hand, he did not want to tell us he did periodically keep in touch with Flowers. Therefore, he used the word "really" to give the appearance he did not have contact with her.

Let's look at a statement given by Colin Powell. Powell was the chairman of the Joint Chiefs of Staff from 1989 - 1993. In this position, he successfully directed the Persian Gulf War in 1991. When he retired from military service in September 1993, there was speculation he may go into politics and perhaps the presidential race in the year 2000. His popularity was at an all-time high. His independent standing allowed him to be courted by both

Democratic and Republican parties. In an interview published in the April 14, 1997 edition of *U.S. News & World Report* magazine, Powell stated, "I'm very happy in private life and I have no plans to run for political office."[5]

Ask yourself, "What is Colin Powell telling me?" He is telling you exactly what he said. He has no plans to run for political office. So, what does this mean? Does it mean he will never run for political office? Look at the language he is using. The key word is "plans." Colin Powell is saying that right now he does not plan to run for a political office. When people make plans it is not always a sure thing. Sometimes they change their plans. This is a good political answer given by Powell. He is telling us he is not considering politics at this time, but he is open-minded to the possibilities. If Powell knew for certain he would not pursue a political career, he would have told us "I will not run for political office."

We see a similar use of this language with Marv Albert. In 1997, Marv Albert was a distinguished sportscaster for the National Broadcasting Company. Known as the voice of the New York Knicks and the New York Rangers, he was famous for his "Yesss" exclamation whenever a key play was executed. Albert's straight arrow image was tarnished on March 20, 1997, when he was indicted and charged with forcible sodomy and assault and battery.

His accuser was Vanessa Perhach, a 41 year old hotel receptionist, who had met Albert in 1986. Albert has stated that, "Vanessa and myself had a ten year relationship. We would see each other once or twice a year. It was purely a sexual relationship."[6] According to Perhach, on February 12, 1997 Albert invited her to his room at the Ritz-Carlton Hotel in Arlington, VA. Albert allegedly became angry with Perhach because she would not participate in three-way sex. He allegedly began biting her on the back ten to fifteen times and forced her to perform oral sex. After the alleged incident, Perhach called 911 to report the crime.

From the time of Perhach's report, Albert denied any wrong doing. In March of 1997, Albert stated, "I categorically deny these charges and intend to vigorously defend myself against these allegations. I am confident that I will be completely exonerated when these allegations are addressed in a public courtroom."[7] However, on September 25, 1997, Marv Albert surprised many people by pleading guilty to misdemeanor assault and battery charges stemming from this incident. His plea bargain wouldn't have shocked anyone if they were listening to what Marv Albert was saying.

Look again at Albert's statement given in March 1997, "I categorically deny these charges and intend to vigorously defend myself. I am confident that I will be exonerated when these allegations are addressed in a public courtroom." The first question I want you to answer is, "Will Marv Albert vigorously defend himself?" Most people answer that question with a "yes." Look at the language used. What did Marv Albert say he was going to do? He said, "I.... <u>intend</u> to vigorously defend myself." People have great intentions. We usually see a lot of these intentions at the beginning of a new year. People intend to lose weight, get in shape, get good grades, make more money, etc. While intentions may serve as a good motivator, using the word intention does not mean the person is going to absolutely carry out the task or fulfill his goal. People often don't live up to their intentions. Marv Albert wanted to make a strong statement that would give the appearance he was innocent. However, by using the word "intend" he was telling us he may or may not vigorously defend himself. As an innocent person, I would have said "I will vigorously defend myself."

Let's examine the rest of Albert's statement. "I am confident that I will be exonerated when these allegations are addressed in a public courtroom." Does Marv Albert believe he will definitely be exonerated when these issues are addressed in court? No. He is only "confident" he will be exonerated. When someone says he is confident that something will happen, there is still the possibility in his mind it will not happen. An innocent person would have said, "I will be exonerated." That is a stronger denial and a more positive attitude than just being confident.

I once read an article in the newspaper about a young child that had been beaten to death. The prime suspect was the child's father. As the police conducted their investigation they uncovered more evidence implicating the father. Eventually, the father confessed to beating his son and causing his death. In describing the beating, the father stated, "To me, it wasn't that violent." The father was trying to downplay the severity of the beating he administered. He was trying to tell us it wasn't that bad. However, he actually tells us this was a very violent beating. The first thing we notice is he says, "To me, it wasn't that violent." He is telling us that to you, to the police, to the coroner, this beating may be considered very violent. It just didn't seem that violent to him. The second thing to consider is he tells us "it wasn't that violent." In other words, it was a violent beating. It just wasn't "that" violent. When you first glance at his statement, it appears he is telling us this beating wasn't severe. However, if you listen to what he is saying, he tells us this was a very brutal beating.

Consider the Tonya Harding and Nancy Kerrigan scandal. On January 6, 1994, figure skater Nancy Kerrigan was preparing for the U.S. National Figure Skating Championship in Detroit, Michigan. After finishing her practice session, an unidentified assailant struck Kerrigan above the right knee with a metal police baton. The injury was severe enough to keep Kerrigan from competing in the competition.

Days after the attack the hit man was identified as Shane Stant. An investigation discovered that Stant had been hired by two individuals, Shawn Eckardt and Jeff Gillooly, to carry out the attack. Eckardt was the bodyguard for skater Tonya Harding and Gillooly was Harding's ex-husband. The plan was to ensure that Harding would win the national championship and make the other skaters fear for their safety. The conspirators hoped to prosper by being hired as bodyguards for the fearful skaters. Everyone speculated whether or not Tonya Harding had anything to do with the attack.

On January 11, 1994, Tonya Harding gave a statement in which she said, "I didn't do anything wrong and neither did anybody else. I don't know anything. I don't know for sure anything about what's going on at all."[8] What is Tonya Harding telling us? She tells us three things. First, she "didn't do anything wrong." While this is a denial, we do not know what she considers to be right and wrong. Secondly, she says "neither did anybody else." We do not know for sure whom she is referencing. We do know that someone did do something wrong. After all, Nancy Kerrigan was assaulted. Thirdly, she tells us she doesn't know anything about the assault. However, she then qualifies this statement with "I don't know for sure anything about what's going on at all." Miss Harding was telling the whole world that she knew something. She just didn't know "for sure" all the details. Sixteen days later, after some pressuring, we found out what she knew. On January 27, 1994, Harding admitted "I am responsible, however, for failing re—for failing to report things I learned about the assault when I returned home from Nationals."[9]

If any good reporters were listening to Harding's statement on January 11, they should have stated to her, "Miss Harding. Tell us about the things you are not sure of in respect to this incident." More than likely on January 11 and not two weeks later, she would have told us that she failed to report things. However, people were not listening to the words she was using. We saw this on the CBS news program *Eye to Eye with Connie Chung*. On February 10, 1994, the program did an exposé on the Tonya Harding and Nancy Kerrigan scandal. After airing Harding's statement "I don't know for sure anything about what's going on at all" which she gave on January 11, host Connie Chung stated in a voice over, "Words she later contradicted with her own damaging admission."[10] CBS then played the statement Harding gave on January 27 in which she admitted she failed to report things. The problem is Harding never contradicted herself. By stating she didn't know "for sure," she was telling the truth, and she was telling everyone she did know something about the assault.

On November 17, 1999, a Clemson University football player was shot in the head. The shooting occurred in Pendleton, South Carolina so the Pendleton Police were conducting the investigation. In commenting on the shooting, Pendleton Police Chief Robert Griffin stated, "All I can say is it happened in the city of Pendleton and our investigator is out working on it."[11] There is a difference between the phrases "all I can say" and "all I know." In both statements, the person is telling us he is limited in the information he can provide. When a person says "all I know" he is limited in his knowledge about the situation. In most cases, this person will share with us the information he has. When a person says "all I can say" he is restricted by something other than his knowledge. In the example above, the Police Chief has more information. However, he is probably abiding by standard procedures that only allow for a brief comment until the investigation produces more substantial information. When a person uses the phrase "all I can say" he is telling us he has additional information. He may not want to provide the information because it is incriminating.

We see a similar use of this phrase in the Rae Carruth murder trial. Carruth played football for the NFL's Carolina Panthers. On November 16, 1999, his pregnant girlfriend, Cherica Adams, was shot and killed while driving in her car. The gunmen had fired several rounds from a car as they passed Adams' car. Carruth and several other men were arrested for her murder. Prosecutors said that Carruth hired the men to kill Adams because he did not want to pay child support. Nearly a year would pass before Carruth would go on trial. On January 3, 2001, Carruth's attorneys rested their case without calling the former NFL player to the stand. Defense attorney David Rudolf stated that they did not need Carruth to testify about the shooting because "Rae wasn't there so he can't say what happened between the two cars."[12] Notice that Rudolf did not state that Carruth does not know what happened between the two cars. He only tells us that Rae "can't say" what happened. On January 18, 2001, Carruth was found guilty of conspiracy to commit murder. He was sentenced to serve 19 to 24 years in prison.

You often see good examples of people trying to deceive you on television. Pay close attention to commercials and especially info-commercials. I recently saw an info-commercial for a psychic hotline that used astrology. By reading the stars and planets, they can tell you just what type of day you are going to have. Of course this information wasn't free, you had to call their 900 number. They concluded their advertisement with the following statement: "See how accurate reading the stars can be." Their conclusion sounds good and probably entices a lot of people to pick up the phone and call. However, in their concluding statement they tell us the truth about astrological readings and predicting the future. "See how accurate reading the stars <u>can be</u>." They are not telling us that reading stars is accurate. They did not say, "See how accurate reading the stars will be." They are only telling us it "can be" accurate. Sometimes it is accurate and sometimes it is not. It may not be accurate when you call, but I am sure every once in awhile they get lucky in their predictions.

The latest commercial I saw which craftily used the English language related to ceiling fans. There are several features people look for in a ceiling fan such as color and size. When it comes to quality probably the biggest consideration is quietness. Nobody wants an irritating clanging fan. In an attempt to sell you their fan, this company used the phrase, "Possibly the quietest fan." The key word is "possibly." They did not tell us their fan is the quietest fan although they would like for us to believe that. All they told us is that it is "possible" their fan is the quietest fan. This of course leaves the possibility their fan is not the quietest fan on the market.

Often when we converse with people, we have the tendency to interpret what they are telling us. This is especially true if we are writing down someone's statement. Instead of writing down word for word everything they say, we paraphrase what they are saying. Paraphrasing makes it easier to record their statement. However, when you paraphrase you leave out some of the information they are giving you, and you interpret what they are saying. By interpreting, you are placing words in their mouth. You are crediting them with things they didn't say. You are visualizing them doing things they never said they did. This makes it harder for you to tell if they are being deceptive or telling the truth. Remember people mean exactly what they say. Don't interpret.

For example, consider the investigation of money stolen from a company safe. The police interviewed the security guard who discovered the money was missing. The security guard began his statement by saying, "I work the 12 pm to 8 am shift. I am the only guard on duty during that shift." Question - When the security guard said, "I am the only guard on duty during that shift" what did he mean by that? Some people would say he told us he was the only person there that night. Others might say he is telling us he was the only guard there that night. However, both of these interpretations are wrong because that is not what he said. The guard stated, "I am the only <u>guard on duty</u> during that shift." This leaves the possibility other people were there who were not guards. It also leaves the possibility there were other guards there who were off duty. If he was there all by himself, he would have said, "I was the only person there." Do not interpret what people are telling you.

Statement Analysis is not limited to interviews concerning an actual event. You can also use it when watching a fictional television show. Many times in the first fifteen minutes of the show, you can figure out who did it by using Statement Analysis. This is because the writer of the show knows which character is guilty. When this guilty person is interviewed by the police, the writer has him respond in the same manner that a deceptive person would answer the question. Recently I was flipping through the television channels and I came across the show *Walker Texas Ranger* staring martial artist Chuck Norris. I paused before moving onto the next channel because I saw that Walker was conducting an interview. He and his partner were speaking with a business owner about a former employee. The owner said the employee had worked for him for two months, but he had to let him go. Walker then asked the owner about another man:

Walker: "Have you seen Chico Gonzales?"
Owner: "Chico Gonzales. I can't say that I have."[13]

In the 30 seconds I was watching the show, I could tell this business owner was being deceptive. Look at his answer. He did not state he has not seen Chico Gonzales. All he said was he could not tell Walker he has seen Chico Gonzales. He didn't say, "No I haven't seen him" because the show's writer did not want him to tell a lie. As soon as Walker and his partner left, the owner walked into another room and guess who was there? Chico Gonzales.

On a recent episode of *Law And Order*, the police were looking for the killer of a young boy. In tracing the boys steps on the day he was killed, they discovered he had been looking at girly magazines in a local store. Because he was under age, the store's security guard told him to leave the premises. The police asked the security guard which direction the boy went when he left the store. The security guard paused to think about his answer and then responded, "It must have been right."[14] I asked myself, "What kind of answer is that?" The security guard did not tell the police he is certain the boy went to the right. He did not say, "He went right." Instead he said, "<u>It must have been</u> right." The words "must have been" tell us the security guard is thinking about something that leads him to conclude the boy took a right hand turn as he exited the store. Maybe he is thinking of a reason why the boy could not have gone left. Therefore, it "must have been right." Perhaps something else is on his mind which caused him to not answer the question directly. Based on his answer, the police should have asked additional questions which they did not. I said to myself, "He did it." Sure enough, fifteen minutes later he confessed to the murder.

The key is to carefully listen to what people are saying. You have to focus on, analyze, and think about everything a person says. Too often though, we skim over what people tell us. We think they have told us one thing, when in reality they have told us something completely different. Do not interpret what people are saying for they mean exactly what they say. By listening to the words they are using, you can determine what people are really telling you, including if they are being truthful or deceptive.

Chapter 5

Examine All Of The Pronouns

Another thing you want to listen for in a statement is the use of pronouns. Pronouns can give us a lot of information. We know that if someone uses pronouns such as "we" "us" "they" or "ours" it indicates more than one person was involved. Pronouns also show possession. If a person says, "I left my car in the parking lot," he is telling us the car belongs to him. However, if a person states, "I left the car in the parking lot," he is not claiming possession of the car. He may be telling us the car does not belong to him. He may also be distancing himself from the car. If the car belongs to him but will not start, many people will refer to it as "the car." They do no want to take possession of it because it will not operate. When a husband refers to his wife as "the wife," he is creating distance in the relationship. Perhaps in his mind, she is not operating properly!

To detect deception using pronouns, first look to see if the person is taking responsibility for his actions. If an individual has done something wrong and states, "we messed up," he is not claiming full responsibility for what happened. He is blaming others for a mistake he has made. Sometimes the pronouns will show us a person is taking no responsibility even though he is trying to convince us he did perform a certain act. I recently saw an interview with a man who said that he and his wife were attacked and then gunned down by two men. His wife died but he survived the shooting. In describing what happened, he said that as soon as his wife was shot, "Grabbed the gun and tried to take it away from him. The man shot me and they ran down the street. Chased after them but I could not catch them." The problem with his statement is that the pronoun "I" is missing. He does not tell us who grabbed the gun. Who tried to take it. Who chased after them. He should have said, "I grabbed the gun." However, since he did not grab the gun, and he did not chase after them, he couldn't use the pronoun "I." He unknowingly let the truth slip out. He was later convicted of killing his wife and making it look like a robbery.

When a person uses the pronoun "you," he is not talking about himself. In the statement, "You do the best you can" the person is telling us that doing your best is something other people would do. He did not state, "I do the best I can." Remember the applicant's statement mentioned in chapter four? "You know, I am trying to be as honest as possible." We saw deception with the words "trying" and "possible." We also see deception with the pronoun "you." The applicant stated "You know..." The problem is we do not know if he is being honest. He has to tell us he is being truthful. Even if he were to say, "You know I am being honest" we still have a deceptive statement. He has not told us he is being honest. He expects us to take his honesty for granted. Believe what people tell you. If he tells you he is being honest, believe him. If he doesn't tell you he is being honest, you have to believe that too.

Sometimes people will take responsibility for their actions without realizing it. They will slip up and use a pronoun that will reveal an admission. O.J. Simpson did this. On June 12, 1994, Simpson's ex-wife Nicole Brown Simpson and her friend Ronald Goldman were brutally murdered at Nicole's Los Angeles home. O.J. Simpson became the prime suspect in their deaths. To raise money for his defense, Simpson wrote a book entitled, "I Want To Tell You." On page 13 of his book, we find the following:

> "I am grateful that even those who believe in my guilt also believe that I should have my day in court and have agreed to let their words be published in this book."[1]

Here we have a confession by Simpson that he committed these murders. "I am grateful that even those who believe in my guilt." "My" is a possessive pronoun. When people use this pronoun, they are taking possession or responsibility. Simpson is taking responsibility for the murders by referring to the guilt as being "my guilt." An innocent person would not have said it that way. An innocent person would have said, "I am grateful that even those who believe I am guilty...." In this sentence, the accused is not saying he is guilty. He is only saying there are people who believe he is guilty. In Simpson's statement, he is saying there are people who believe in something that has already been established, "my guilt." Guilt is something you personally feel. Simpson shows us that by using the pronoun "my." In this same statement, Simpson refers to "<u>my</u> day in court." Everyone has gathered together in the courtroom for him. No one else will have their case heard because this day belongs O.J. Simpson. Just as that was his day in court that was also his guilt.

Perhaps you are not convinced this is a confession. Five days after these murders Simpson made an obvious confession that can be detected by looking at the pronouns. On June 17, 1994, O.J. Simpson was to be arrested via voluntary surrender. Instead of surrendering, Simpson and his friend, Al Cowlings, got into Cowling's Ford Bronco and, according to Simpson, headed for the cemetery to visit Nicole's grave. Because of a police presence at the cemetery they were unable to visit her grave site. Simpson then claims Cowlings noticed that Simpson had a gun. Fearing Simpson might shoot himself, Cowlings called the police on his cell phone and told them he had Simpson, and he was taking him back to his house. What followed was the infamous slow speed Bronco chase which was televised to millions of viewers. During the chase, detective Tom Lange spoke with Simpson on the telephone. Simpson was huddled in the back seat of the Bronco with a gun in his hand. Lang spends the entire conversation trying to convince Simpson to throw away the gun. At this point in time, Simpson is suicidal. Let's take a look at some excerpts from this taped conversation.

Simpson:	"I just need to get to my house. I can't live with (unintelligible)."
Lange:	"We're going to do that. Just throw the gun out the window."
Simpson:	"I can't do that."
Lange:	"We're not going to bother you. We're going to let you go up there. Just throw it out the window. Please. You're scaring everybody. O.J., you there?"

Simpson:	"—-for me. This is not to keep you guys away from me. This is for me."
Lange:	"Okay. It's for you, I know that. But do it for....."
Simpson:	"This is for me, for me. That's all."²

There is no doubt Simpson is contemplating suicide. He tells us the gun is not to keep the police away but it is for him. We see further evidence of his suicidal state when later in the conversation he makes the statements, "Ah, just tell them I'm all sorry." "I've said goodbye to my kids."³ What follows is his confession.

Lange:	"Don't do this. They love you. Don't do it, O.J. It's going to work itself out. It's going to work. Its going to work. You're listening to me, I know you are, and you're thinking about your kids right now, aren't you? Aren't you?"
Simpson:	"Ah –"
Lange:	"They're thinking about you. They're thinking about you."
Simpson:	"Ah –"
Lange:	"So is your mother. Your mother loves you. Everybody loves you. Don't do this."
Simpson:	"Ooh –"
Lange:	"I know you're thinking."
Simpson:	"Oh –"
Lange:	"Man, just throw it out the window."
Simpson:	"Ah –"
Lange:	"And nobody's going to get hurt."
Simpson:	"I'm the only one that deserves it."
Lange:	"No, you don't deserve that."
Simpson:	"I'm going to get hurt."
Lange:	"You do not deserve to get hurt."
Simpson:	"Ah –"
Lange:	"Don't do this."
Simpson:	"All I did was love Nicole. That's all I did was love her."
Lange:	"I understand."⁴

Did you see the confession? It occurs right after Lang tells Simpson, "nobody's going to get hurt." Simpson responds by saying, "<u>I'm</u> the only one that deserves it." The murder of his ex-wife has placed Simpson in this suicidal situation. It is in this setting he tells us he is the only who deserves to die. If these murders were committed by someone else, wouldn't they be worthy of death? There is only one killer and "only one that deserves" to die for this crime; O.J. Simpson.

The second thing to look for in a statement is consistent use of the same pronouns. If a person is telling a story that is stored in his memory, he will continually use the same pronouns. This is because his memory is a reflection of reality. However, if he is making up the story then he does not have a memory he can draw upon. As he tells his tale he is making it up as he goes. Many times deceptive people will change the pronouns in their statement without realizing it. Let's say a mugging victim refers to his attacker as a male using the pronoun "he." However, later in his story of the assault, the victim refers to the assailant as "she." We now have a problem. Was the attacker a male or a female, or is the victim fabricating this story of being assaulted? When people start to change their pronouns, it is an indication they are not speaking from memory and are being deceptive.

We see this change of pronouns in the Susan Smith murder case. On October 25, 1994, in Union, South Carolina, Susan Smith reported that she was car-jacked by a black male in his late 20's to early 30's. The car-jacker not only stole her Mazada Protege, but he also drove off with her two boys, Michael, age 3, and Alexander, age 14 months, who were in her car. The Union County Sheriff's Office along with the F.B.I. spent the next week searching for the two boys as well as the car.

On November 2, 1994, Susan Smith made a public plea to the kidnapper. In part of her statement she said, "I would like to say to whoever has my children, that they please, I mean please, bring 'em home to us where they belong."[5] Look at the pronouns Susan Smith used in her statement in referring to the kidnapper. She referred to the kidnapper as "whoever" and "they." This does not make sense. If the last picture you had of your kids was the two of them being driven away by a male suspect, you would constantly refer to the kidnapper as "him" or "he" or "this man." This is how she described the kidnapper in her earlier statements. However, now she is telling us a different story. First she says, "Whoever has my children." By saying "whoever," she is acting like she has absolutely no idea who abducted her kids. However, she supposedly does know a little about the kidnapper because she was able to give a description of him. Even though she does not know the kidnapper's name, she should still refer to him as a male suspect. Secondly, she refers to the kidnapper as "they." Allegedly, one man abducted her kids. So where does the "they" come from? It comes from her deceptive mind. Because she is making up the story she cannot relate to it. She cannot see one man driving away with her kids because it never happened. Therefore, she slips up and uses the pronouns "whoever" and "they."

As the days went by without any sightings of her children or her car, police officials began to suspect Susan Smith may have been responsible for the disappearance of her two boys. By listening to the statements Susan Smith made, we can see that law enforcement authorities were on the right track. On November 3, 1994, the day after giving her deceptive statement, Susan Smith confessed she drowned her two boys by driving her car into John D. Long Lake. A search of the lake revealed that she finally did tell the truth.

After finding her car in the lake, Susan Smith continued to be deceptive. Even in her confession she was misleading the police. We can see this deception with changing pronouns. In her confession, Smith stated,

> "When I was at John D. Long Lake, I had never felt so scared and unsure as I did then. I wanted to end my life so bad and was in my car ready to go down that ramp into the water, and I did go part way, but I stopped. I went again and stopped. I then got out of the car and stood by the car a nervous wreck."[6]

Look at the pronouns Smith uses in reference to her car. "I wanted to end my life so bad and was in <u>my</u> car ready to go down that ramp into the water.......I then got out of <u>the</u> car and stood by <u>the</u> car a nervous wreck." Smith starts out by saying "my car" and then changes it to "the car." What does it mean when she goes from "my" car to "the" car? It means she no longer wants to take possession of the car. She is distancing herself from the car. We would expect to see this if she was describing the car going into the water. There were two boys trapped in the car who were drowning. Nobody would want to take possession of that car.

Everyone would refer to it as "the" car. However, in her statement she is not talking about the car going into the water. She is talking about getting out of the car and standing next to it. She is trying to convince us she was contemplating drowning all three of them. At the last minute she bailed out and somehow her car went into the water. If that were the case, she should have said, "I then got out of my car and stood by my car a nervous wreck." By changing it to "the car" it tells us she knew exactly what she was going to do. As she stood next to "the car" she was visualizing "the car" going into the water. She was thinking of drowning her two boys and not herself. In the end, that is what the jury decided.

Let's take a look at one more example of detecting deception through changing pronouns. It has to do with the JonBenet Ramsey murder and it could have changed the outcome of the investigation. JonBenet Ramsey was the six-year-old daughter of John and Patsy Ramsey who resided in Boulder, Colorado. On December 26, 1996, Patsy Ramsey woke up around 5:45 a.m. As she walked down the stairs to the first floor she found a three-page handwritten note at the bottom of the staircase. The note was addressed to John Ramsey and stated that JonBenet had been kidnapped. Upon reading that her daughter had been kidnapped, Mrs. Ramsey ran to JonBenet's bedroom only to find she was indeed missing. She then awakened her husband and called 911.

The Boulder Police arrived shortly after the 911 call. The ransom note demanded $118,000.00 in cash and stated, "I will call you between 8 and 10 am tomorrow to instruct you on delivery."[7] The police were checking on any leads they had and were waiting for the kidnappers to call. At around 1:00 p.m., a detective at the house asked John Ramsey and one of his friends to check the house to see if anything had been taken or was out of place. The two of them started their search in the basement. John Ramsey opened the door to a small room and turned on the lights. There he found JonBenet on the floor. Her wrists were tied above her head. A piece of duct tape was covering her mouth and a cord was wrapped around her neck. John Ramsey removed the duct tape from her mouth and picked her up. He quickly carried her upstairs and emergency medical services were called. The discovery of JonBenet was too late. She had been dead for several hours.

Because of the ransom note, when the Boulder Police arrived at the Ramsey house they treated JonBenet's disappearance as a kidnapping. However, the first officer on the scene within two minutes could have recognized that this ransom note was bogus just by looking at the pronouns in the note. The ransom note started out saying, "Mr. Ramsey. Listen carefully! We are a group of individuals that represent a small foreign faction. We respect your business but not the country that it serves. At this time we have your daughter in our possession."[8] Clearly the writer of the note was trying to convince the police that a group had kidnapped JonBenet. The note also contained the following statements: "She is safe and unharmed and if you want her to see 1997, you must follow <u>our</u> instructions to the letter." "Follow <u>our</u> instructions and you stand a 100% chance of getting her back."[9] However, the writer slips up and the truth comes out when he or she wrote "Any deviation of <u>my</u> instructions will result in the immediate execution of your daughter."[10] If this kidnapping/murder was carried out by a group, then the writer would have a group mentality. He or she would consistently use plural pronouns because he or she is part of a group. This change in pronouns shows us this was not a terrorist group. The note also contains the phrase "<u>we</u> might call you" and "<u>I</u> may call you."[11] Again we have the shift from plural to singular. One person and perhaps an accomplice committed this crime. Had the police recognized this at the time the note was discovered the investigation may have been approached differently. JonBenet's body may have been discovered sooner. The police would have controlled the crime scene and perhaps discovered additional evidence.

People's words will betray them and sometimes it is through the pronouns they use. Look to see if the person is taking responsibility for his actions, or is he being deceptive and passing the blame. If he does take responsibility, see if this is an admission. Focus on changing pronouns. When a person changes his pronouns he is telling us something. Maybe he is letting us know that someone else was present. Or, he may be unknowingly telling us that he is being deceptive. Be certain to examine all of the pronouns in a statement. If you are reviewing a written statement, circle all of the pronouns. This will make it easier to identify them and recognize what the person is saying.

Chapter 6

Check The Verb Tenses

When analyzing a person's words you also want to pay attention to the verb tenses they use. Obviously, if they are speaking in the past tense they are referring to something that occurred or perhaps didn't occur in the past. A problem arises when people are questioned about their past actions, but they give answers which are in the present tense. Consider the following exchange:

> Question: "Have you ever used illegal drugs?"
> Answer: "I don't use illegal drugs."

The answer is a very strong denial and is probably a truthful statement. The person is telling us he does not take illegal drugs. However, the question encompasses the person's entire lifetime, "Have you <u>ever</u> used illegal drugs?" The answer is given in the present tense. The interviewee is telling us at the present moment he does not use illegal drugs. He does not answer in the past tense because that would be a lie. Since people rarely lie he chooses to answer the question in the truthful present tense. The subject may have smoked a joint five minutes ago. However, he can honestly say he doesn't use illegal drugs because five minutes ago he quit! An hour later he may be high as a kite, but at the time he gave his answer it was a truthful answer. We can see this person is being deceptive because his answer does not address his entire life. Therefore, he has not answered our question. We would continue to ask him questions about any previous drug usage.

There have been many missing children cases solved by looking at the verb tenses used by the parents or guardians. Most child abductors are not strangers. Therefore, whenever a child disappears everyone who had contact with the child is a suspect. This even includes the parents. As a grieving parent you of course would want your child returned unharmed. When interviewed by the media you would plead with the kidnapper to release your son or daughter. When talking about your child you would refer to him or her in the present tense. "She's a great kid. If anyone has seen her, please call the police." However, if a parent caused the death of a child then that parent knows the kid is no longer living. This fact will usually be revealed because people's words will betray them. When talking about their missing kid this parent will do his or her best to refer to the child in the present tense. However, the knowledge that their kid is dead will eventually slip out. The guilty parent will make the mistake of referring to the child in the past tense. "She was a great kid." Investigators will pick up on this, and will focus their attention on the suspected parent. We saw this in the Susan Smith case. After her two boys were allegedly kidnapped by a male suspect, Smith told reporters, "My children wanted me. They needed me. And now I can't help them."[1] Smith spoke in the past tense because she knew her kids were dead. This was in contrast to the boys' father, David, who believing Susan's story always spoke of the kids in the present tense: "They're okay. They're going to be home soon."[2]

Joey Buttafuoco played the tense game. In May 1992, someone walked up to the Buttafuoco residence in Massapequa, New York and knocked on the door. When Buttafuoco's wife, Mary Jo, opened the door she was shot in the face. Fortunately, she survived the assault. The investigation into her attempted murder led to the arrest of a 17-year-old named Amy Fisher whom the press would dub as the Long Island Lolita. Fisher told the police she and Buttafuoco were having an affair, and that Buttafuoco wanted her to kill his wife. Fisher went on trial for the shooting of Mary Jo Buttafuoco. She was found guilty and sentenced to five to 15 years in prison. Joey Buttafuoco plead guilty to statutory rape and was given a 6-month sentence.

At the onset of the investigation, Buttafuoco denied any sexual involvement with Fisher. In 1992, he stated, "Let me tell you something. I don't cheat on my wife. No. Oh, no. Oh, no."[3] However, on October 5, 1993 when Joey pled guilty to statutory rape, he stated that he had sexual relations with Amy Fisher at the

Freeport Motel. We know by his own court admission he had an affair with Amy Fisher in 1991. So how can Joey Buttafucco in 1992 make a statement denying an affair? It is because in 1992 he was telling the truth. He didn't say, "I have never cheated on my wife." He didn't say, "I didn't cheat on my wife." All he said was, "I <u>don't</u> cheat on my wife." This reply is in the present tense. With all the publicity he was getting, he probably wasn't cheating on his wife in 1992. However, he did not tell us he never cheated on his wife. Buttafuoco only tried to deny he had an affair.

There was a man who had allegedly drowned in the ocean. His family wanted to collect on his life insurance, but the insurance company did not want to pay because the man's body was never found. The authorities also suspected that this reported drowning may be a scam. The police had discovered the missing man had a friend who years earlier had drowned in a similar accident. It took several weeks before the friend's body was discovered. The authorities felt this friend's drowning may have given this man the idea to stage his own death.

In an effort to have his father declared dead and to satisfy the police, the man's son testified at a deposition. At the hearing, the prosecutor asked the son about the family friend who had drowned. He specifically asked if his father knew about the friend's death. The son replied, "Yeah, he, he knows about that drowning." The son slipped up and spoke about his father in the present tense. His words show us he knows his father is still alive. Several years later the father was found alive and well.

One way that people's words will betray them is through verb tenses. Typically the question will be asked in the past tense, but the person will answer in the present tense. It may also be that by talking in the past tense a person will reveal he is being deceptive. Listen to the verb tenses used in a statement. Inconsistencies in verb tenses can show you what a person is really saying.

Chapter 7

Order Is Important

In a story, people will sometimes mention several names, items, or things they did. The order in which they list these names or events is important. We can sometimes gain additional information based on this order. For example, if a person said "I went bowling with Craig and Bob" there is absolutely a reason why he mentioned Craig's name first and Bob's name second. Chances are he is telling us he likes Craig more than Bob. However, it maybe that Bob is his best friend but Craig is the one who invited him to go bowling. The point is there is additional information to be gained by the fact he mentioned Craig's name first. As an interviewer it is up to you to discover this information.

Play It Again Sports is a chain of sporting goods stores located throughout the country. I recently drove by one of their stores and happened to notice their advertising sign. This sign was not your standard company neon sign that is usually mounted above the front door. This sign appeared to be hand-painted, probably by the manager, and was displayed in front of the store close to the street to draw attention. The sign read, "Play It Again Sports, Used and New Sporting Goods Equipment." The sign tells us this business is a sporting goods store that sells used and new athletic equipment. However, the sign also provides us with some additional information. Because the word "used" was mentioned first, it tells us that although they have new equipment they predominately have used sporting goods equipment. If you go into any of their stores, you will find this to be true. The person who created this sign didn't ask himself, "Should I write New and Used or Used and New?" He automatically wrote what he knew to be true.

This past Christmas season I went out to my mailbox and pulled out several Christmas cards. As I was looking through them I noticed that one of them was addressed to "Pam and Mark McClish." Now I am use to seeing "Mark and Pam McClish" or "Mr. and Mrs. Mark McClish." However, this person chose to put my wife's name first and my name second. When I opened the card I found that it was from a friend of ours, but it was from a friend my wife grew up with. She has known him all her life. I have only known him ever since we were married. When our friend addressed this envelope he didn't stop to think should I write "Mark and Pam or Pam and Mark?" Without giving it any consideration he automatically wrote what was in his heart. Since he is better friends with my wife, he wrote her name first.

One Christmas my family made a trip to Ohio to visit with my folks. As usual there were lots of presents under grandma's Christmas tree. On Christmas morning my two boys, Michael and Mitchell, got busy opening and handing out (notice the order) Christmas presents. When they got down to the last present, Michael handed it to me and said, "Here dad this is for you and mom." I looked at it and noticed that it was not addressed to "(me) and mom" but it was addressed to "Pam and Mark." My own mother put my wife's name first and my name second! Now I must give you a word of caution. If you use Statement Analysis on family and friends, there is a good chance you won't have any family and friends! When you use it on people that you know, you always run the risk of it becoming personal. You may read into things. You may look for things that just aren't there. You are not as objective as when you are interviewing someone you don't know. In the story of my Christmas present, it would be easy for me to think that my mother likes my wife more than me. However, I knew that is not what my mother was saying. By putting my wife's name first, it told me that what was in the box was meant more for my wife than me. So, I handed it to me wife and said, "Here honey you open it up." It turned out to be a toaster oven. My mother didn't think, "Should I put Mark's name first or Pam's name first?" She knew the gift was meant more for my wife, so she automatically put my wife's name first. Had there been a cordless drill in the box I am absolutely certain my name would have been first.

By analyzing the order that names or items are mentioned in a story, you can obtain additional information. You can also detect deception using this same technique. One of the oldest examples of Statement Analysis can be found in the Bible, and it has do to with order. I must give credit to Avinon Sapir from the Laboratory of Scientific Interrogation in Phoenix, Arizona for finding this superb example. Mr. Sapir has done a lot of research in word analysis.

The story takes place in the days of King Solomon. The Bible tells us that King Solomon was the wisest man to ever live. One of the more famous displays of his wisdom centered around two women who lived in his kingdom. The women lived together in the same house and they both had infant children. One night while sleeping one of the mothers rolled on top of her child and accidentally suffocated it to death. She woke up in the middle of the night and found that her baby had died. She then switched babies with the other woman. When the other woman woke up in the morning she recognized the dead baby lying next to her wasn't her baby. She accused the other mother of swapping kids and demanded her baby back. The deceitful mother denied she had done such a terrible thing. So, they took the matter to King Solomon to decide who was the rightful mother of the living child.

You may recall how King Solomon decided who was lying and who was telling the truth. He commanded that the living baby be cut in half. One half of the baby would be given to one mother, and the other half given to the other mother. Upon giving this decree, one of the mothers spoke up and asked for the baby not to be killed. She agreed to let the other woman have custody of the child. At this point King Solomon awarded the baby to the mother who had requested the child not be put to death. This was the true mother for she would rather see her child live with someone else then to be killed.

Let's play what if. What if the deceitful mother was deceptive but not to the point of death. In other words, what if the deceitful mother was the one that requested the baby not be killed. Then the king might have given the baby to the wrong mother! Not so, because King Solomon knew who was lying and who was telling the truth before he ever brought out his sword, and he did it with Statement Analysis!

The Bible tells us in I Kings 3:16-28 that when the women came before the king one of them told her side of the story. As soon as she was done the other woman responded, "No! But the living one is my son and the dead one is your son." The other woman quickly fired back, "No! But the dead one is your son and the living one is my son." (KJV) The Bible then tells us that King Solomon repeated their statements. He said, "The one says, 'This is my son, who lives, and your son is the dead one'; and the other says, 'No! But your son is the dead one, and my son is the living one.'" (KJV) King Solomon was analyzing their statements. He then brought out his sword to display his wisdom and for our edification. Based on these two statements we can tell who is lying and who is telling the truth. It sounds like the women were saying the same thing. Both were claiming possession of the living baby. However, what is different in their statements is the order in which they talked about the living and dead baby. The first woman mentioned the living baby first because all she cared about was getting her son back. Therefore, the first words out of her mouth were, "The living one is my son." What was heavy on the second woman's heart is that her son had just passed away. Therefore, she talks about the dead baby first. The order in which these women talked about the living and dead babies showed King Solomon and us their true feelings.

Deception can sometimes be detected by looking at the order of events listed in a story. We would expect these events to be in chronological order. However, if a person is making up a story then he may slip up and mention something that appears to be out of order. Several years ago there was a man who was convicted of federal income tax evasion. He was sentenced to prison but allowed to self surrender to the institution. Two weeks before he was to report to prison his son told the police that his dad was missing in a scuba diving accident. When the father failed to report to prison, a warrant for his arrest was issued. The U.S. Marshals Service started looking for him. My colleagues were able to obtain written statements from the three men who witnessed the alleged accident. They sent me their statements for analysis.

Two of the men had remained on the boat while the father and son went diving. Based on their written statements, I felt the men on the boat were being truthful. All they knew was the father and son went diving and the father never surfaced. The son's written statement showed deception. According to the son he and his father went diving around an oil rig. They split up and agreed to meet at a certain spot in five minutes. When the son returned to this location his father was not there. He waited a couple of minutes for his dad, and then surfaced and asked the two men on the boat if his father was with them. They responded they had not seen him. The son then dove again looking for his dad. When he ran out of oxygen the son was forced to surface. The son then mentions he had 2,000 pounds of air in his tank. He asked his dad how much air he had and his dad responded he too had 2,000 pounds of air. His story goes onto say they searched for his dad and called the Coast Guard to help in the search.

In analyzing the son's statement, look at the order in which the events occurred. You will find he mentions one thing which is out of order. After the father has run out of air and presumably drowned, the son tells us he spoke with his dad! He asked him how much air he had in his tank. We know why he put this in his story. He wants us to know they had the same amount of air. When the son ran out of air the father must also be empty and therefore presumed drowned. However, he should have mentioned this earlier in his statement. Perhaps when they first entered the water he could have told us they both had 2,000 pounds of air. That too would have set the stage for this drowning. This out-of-order statement tells us the son knows his father is alive. It also tells us the son has spoken with his father in the time period between the alleged drowning and when he wrote his statement. The reason the son slips up is because to him his story makes sense. He knows his dad is alive and he has spoken with him. Therefore, it goes unnoticed by him that he mentions talking to his dad after he allegedly drowned. To the reader, this out-of-order statement should jump out at you. I shared my findings with the deputies working the case. I told them the son was lying and pointed out other areas in his statement that needed further questioning. Eventually the father was found, very much alive, and arrested.

People's words will betray them. Sometimes this will occur in the order in which they list certain things. Analyzing the order may provide additional information. Clarifying this information may require further questioning. Sometimes this information will reveal to us they are being deceptive. Listen to what people are telling you and listen to the order in which they tell it.

Chapter 8

Pay Attention To Time References

As people tell us their story of what happened or what they did, they will sometimes mention the times that certain activities occurred. We can use these time references to see if the subject is withholding information and thereby being deceptive. Consider the following answer to the question "What did you do from the time you woke up to the time you went to bed?"

"At 8:30, I woke up and made breakfast. As I ate breakfast I watched the morning news on tv. At around 10:00 I mowed the yard and cleaned around the house. At 11:30, I drove to Raleigh to meet Mike Sharp. I met Mike at the Carolina Sports Bar just after noon. We had lunch together and watched the baseball game on the big screen tv. Mike and I talked about going hiking next month. I left the bar around 2:30 and returned home. At 6:00, I called Jeff Wolf to see what he was doing. I invited him over and he arrived at my house just before 7:00. We ordered a pizza and watched a movie. Jeff left around 10:00. I watched tv for about another hour and then went to bed."

What we are looking for in this statement is missing time. In the answer given, we have the following time references: 8:30, 10:00, 11:30, noon, 2:30, 6:00, 7:00 and 10:00. The subject left his house at 11:30 in the morning and arrived in Raleigh just after noon. We can presume it takes about 30 to 45 minutes to drive to Raleigh. He tells us that he left the bar at 2:30 and returned home. Assuming that he went straight home, this would place him at his residence at around 3:00 to 3:15. The next time reference he mentions is 6:00. We have to ask ourselves, and more importantly the subject, what was he doing between 3:00 and 6:00? He has three hours of missing time in his story. If we were investigating a crime, it may be that during this time period is when he committed the crime.

Another thing to look for is time references that are out of place. In his story, the subject will miscalculate his time. We see this in a statement given by a man concerning his girlfriend who was found murdered in her house. In his written affidavit, he mentions several time references.

> "The first time I called her was around 10:00 pm and she did not answer the phone. I then called her at 11:00 pm and at 12:00 am. At 12:15 am I went to her house. I knocked on the back door and blew my horn. I then went to the front and blew the horn again. I left Susan's house and went to Billy Adams house. I called Susan's mother from Billy's around 1:30 am to ask if she had any keys for Susan's house. I wanted to get in the house to check on her. I then called Susan again around 1:00 am, 2:00 am, 3:00 am and the last time was at 4:00 am."

The subject states that he called Susan's mother at 1:30 a.m. He then states, "I then called Susan again around 1:00 am." If he was speaking from memory and giving us a chronological order of what he did, he should have stated that he called Susan at 1:00 a.m. and then called her mother at 1:30 a.m. When a person is making up a story he will sometimes forget what he previously stated. This deception is sometimes unveiled with out of sequence time references.

You should also look to see if the time references add up. Is it possible for the subject to have done what he said he did in the amount of time he said he did it in? Consider the following statement of a man who said that he was car jacked:

> "Last Friday at 7:15 p.m., I left my house and got into my car. I was hungry so I decided to go out and get something to eat. My plan was to eat at Burger King on Memorial Drive. While driving to Burger King, I stopped at the light at the intersection of Memorial Drive and 10th street. It was now 7:30 p.m. and

fairly dark outside. I was listening to some music in my car waiting for the light to turn green. All of the sudden my door opened and a man pointed a gun at me. He grabbed me and told me to get out the car which I did. He then jumped into my car and drove away. I ran to the gas station on the corner of Memorial Drive and 10th street. I told the person working there to call the police because my car had been stolen. Approximately five minutes later the police arrived at the gas station. I gave them a description of my car and of the thief."

The subject said that he left his house at 7:15 p.m. His car was stolen at the intersection of Memorial Drive and tenth street at 7:30 p.m. We should look to see how long it takes to drive from his house to the intersection of Memorial Drive and tenth street. If it only takes five minutes, then we need to find out what he was doing during the other ten minutes. If it takes longer to get to this intersection, then we have to wonder how he could have gotten there so quickly. If the time references do not add up, then something is going on. Either he did something else that he hasn't told us, or he is making up the story.

Nobody is going to tell you absolutely everything they did or every little thing that happened. Whether through deceit or just condensing their story, people will leave out certain information. Sometimes, you can find this missing information by comparing the time references mentioned in a story. If there are time references that don't add up, this may be an indication the person is being deceptive.

Chapter 9

Words And Phrases That Indicate Deception

In an effort to get you to believe their answer, people will sometimes use words or phrases designed to emphasize their truthfulness. However, studies have shown that when people use these words or phrases, they may be giving you a deceptive answer. The following is a list of some of the more common deceptive words and phrases:

"Honest to God."   "Truthfully"
"To be honest."   "I swear to God."
"To tell the truth."   "I swear on my mother's grave."

Chances are you probably have heard several other phrases that could be added to this list. When you hear these words or phrases in a statement that lightbulb in your head should go off. You should pay even closer attention to what the person is telling you.

A few years ago there was a sheriff who was indicted for coercing female prisoners to perform oral sex on him. His response to the press about the pending charges was, "I swear to God I ain't never touched no inmate." The first thing we notice is he begins his statement with a phrase which indicates deception, "I swear to God." Therefore, we should suspect he is being untruthful. We should continue to question him about the alleged incident. The other thing we see is this sheriff used a triple negative, "<u>aint' never</u> touched <u>no</u> inmate." This too should lead us to believe he is being deceptive. Two months after giving this statement, he was convicted of these charges. Remember people will rarely lie. In his mind, the sheriff is telling the truth. He was not charged with rape.

Therefore, he can deny he touched any female prisoners. Technically he is correct. They did all the touching!

On March 18, 2001, the CBS News program *60 Minutes* did a story titled "Jailhouse Scientists." If featured Anthony Turner who had been arrested in Milwaukee, Wisconsin near the scene of a rape. Turner's DNA which was found at the crime scene was run through the Wisconsin State Crime Lab's DNA bank to see if it matched any unsolved rape cases. There were three hits which made Turner a serial rapist. While awaiting trial for these four rapes another rape was reported in Turner's neighborhood. This rape was very similar to the rape charges Turner was facing. Turner wrote to the Wisconsin State Crime Lab and told them he had heard of a similar rape in his neighborhood. He wanted the crime lab to do a DNA test on this recent rape. He also wanted them to compare his DNA with the DNA found in the new rape case. The testing was done and it showed that Turner's DNA was a perfect match with the DNA found at the recent rape crime scene. With Turner locked up in jail, it appeared the DNA had come from another suspect. There has never been a case of individuals possessing identical DNA except in the case of identical twins. Turner doesn't have an identical twin. The police knew that something was amiss for two people to have the same genetic profile, and for both of these individuals to live in the Milwaukee area. Therefore, police detectives interviewed the latest rape victim. It didn't take them long to get her to confess that her reported rape was a hoax. Turner had smuggled out his semen in a ketchup condiment. He sealed the small package with tape, flattened it, and mailed it to his mother. It was then given to the recruited victim who placed it on her inner thighs and panties and called the police. When confronted with this evidence Turner confessed that he did participate in this hoax. However, he told *60 Minutes* that he wasn't trying to mislead anyone to gain his freedom. "I wasn't really trying to fool anyone. I was trying to find out the truth."[1] Most people probably believe Turner was trying to fool law enforcement officials into releasing him from jail. We can see his deception in his statement. According to Webster's Dictionary, the word "really" means truly or genuinely. When Turner says he wasn't "really" trying to deceive anyone, this is very similar to saying he "truthfully" wasn't trying to fool the officials.

Words that indicate deception may appear anywhere within the statement. In July 1995, there was speculation the NFL football team the L.A. Raiders might move back to Oakland, California. On July 22, 1995, owner Al Davis was asked about the possible move. His response was "I don't know what's going on, so help me God."[2] Mr. Davis started to give us a great answer. There is not much you can do with "I don't know what's going on." He would have been telling us he has no information about the move. However, that would be a lie. So, Al Davis adds the phrase "so help me God" which shows us he does have some knowledge about a possible move. On the very next day, July 23, Al Davis signed the paperwork for his team to move back to Oakland. He knew what was going on, and he told us he knew what was going on by adding the phrase "so help me God."

There may be times when a person uses one of these words or phrases and is not being deceptive. When looking for fugitives, I have had people tell me, "Honest to God I don't know where he is." Some of these people I believe were telling me the truth because this was the only sign of deception they displayed. However, for most people this is an indication the person is being deceptive because people have a hard time telling a direct lie. Listen for these words and continue to ask additional questions to ascertain the truth.

Chapter 10

Did The Subject Answer The Question?

Most of the time when we seek information people will answer our questions and tell us what we want to know. However, when people do not want to tell us certain things they may avoid answering the question. Common sense tells us if people refuse to answer our questions, there must be something they do not want us to know. Maybe it would be embarrassing for them to answer the question. Maybe an honest answer would incriminate them. Perhaps they are protecting someone by withholding information. The bottom line is, if they were willing to speak freely and tell us everything they know, they would answer our questions. By not answering the question they are being deceptive.

The problem is we sometimes do not realize a person did not answer our question. If he refuses to talk to us, or he tells us he is not going to answer our question, it is clear he is withholding information. For example, when Oklahoma City bomber Timothy McVeigh was asked by *Newsweek* magazine if he had been through Oklahoma City with Michael Fortier, McVeigh replied, "I think I'd rather not answer that."[1] Obviously there is something he doesn't want to tell us. What we have to watch for are those people who give us an answer which appears to answer our question. They are very sly in that they will respond to the question, and try to make it look like they gave a satisfactory answer. The reality is they have not answered the question.

Take for example the child who took a cookie from the cookie jar. When his mother asked him if he took a cookie he replied, "I don't like those kinds of cookies." That may be a truthful statement, but he did not answer the question. The question requires a "yes" or "no" answer. He gave neither. Sometimes people want to explain themselves or expound upon their answer. That's fine, but they still have to answer the question. "No. I don't like those kind of cookies" would be a good answer. Since he did not answer the question about taking a cookie, we know there is something he does not want to tell us. If we continue to question him, the truth will eventually come out that he did sneak a cookie.

It all gets back to listening. Did this person answer your specific question? If he didn't, then he is hiding something from you. I once had a woman approach me after I gave a presentation on Statement Analysis. She wanted to let me know she completely understood this deceptive technique of not answering the question. She shared with me that she recently had forgotten to telephone a friend. Her husband asked her if she had made the telephone call. She did not want to lie to her husband, but she did not want to admit she had forgotten to make the call. So, she replied, "I haven't been able to get a hold of her yet." She gave a truthful answer, but she did not answer her husband's question.

You find plenty of examples of people not answering the question when you watch TV journalists conduct interviews. Unfortunately you find many of these journalists not recognizing that their questions haven't been answered. On November 22, 1992, Steve Kroft interviewed Woody Allen on the CBS news program *60 Minutes*. Allen was in the middle of a custody battle with the mother of his three children, Mia Farrow. Complicating matters was the fact that Allen admitted to having an affair with 21-year-old Soon-Yi Previn the adopted daughter of Mia Farrow from a previous marriage. Farrow accused Allen of molesting their seven-year-old daughter Dylan. The incident allegedly occurred in August of 1992 at Farrow's home in Connecticut. Dylan had told a doctor about the alleged molestation. Therefore, the authorities were required to investigate the case.

> Kroft: (Voiceover) "It is that investigation and the attendant publicity that convinced the reclusive Allen to sit down with us in his Manhattan apartment and discuss the situation no holds barred."

Kroft:	"The allegations are that you took Dylan into an attic or crawl space...."
Allen:	"Mm-hmm."
Kroft:	"...that you touched her in her private part."
Allen:	"Mm-hmm. Mm-hmm."
Kroft:	"Is there any truth to that at all?"
Allen:	"Well, be—be logical about this. I'm—I'm 57. Isn't it illogical that I'm going to, at the height of a—a very bitter, acrimonious custody fight, drive up to Connecticut where nobody likes me in a house—I'm in a house full of enemies, I mean, Mia was so enraged at me and—and she had gotten all the kids to—to be angry at me, that I'm going to drive up there, and suddenly, on visitation, pick this moment in my life to become a child molester? It's just—it's just incredible. I could have—if I wanted to be a child molester, I had many opportunities in the past. I could have quietly made a—a—a custody settlement with Mia in some way and done it in the future. I mean—you know, it's so insane."[2]

Woody Allen never answers the question, "Is there any truth to that at all?" Allen gives a rather lengthy answer, but he never says, "No, there is no truth to that." He asks us to think about it, "Isn't it illogical...." Yes Woody, it is illogical, but is there any truth to the allegation? Refusing to answer the question does not necessarily mean Allen is a child molester. It does mean there is something he isn't telling us.

When *TIME* magazine interviewed Oklahoma City bomber Timothy McVeigh, they asked him "Have you ever built a bomb?" McVeigh responded, "I've never had my hand on one. I used to watch other people do it. I won't go into that. There were plastic soda bottles. They would put vinegar and baking soda in and screw the cap on, and it would burst."[3] McVeigh gives what appears to be a good answer, "I've never had my hand on one." However, the question requires a "yes" or "no" answer. McVeigh never says "yes" or "no." He doesn't answer the question. Therefore, he is withholding some information.

It is hard to believe a former military person could make a statement that he never had his hand on a bomb. After all, the military has all kinds of ordinances. You would think at some point in his training or military service he would have touched a hand grenade. McVeigh's answer is probably based on his definition of the word "bomb." When most people think of a bomb they picture sticks of dynamite tied together, or perhaps the large devices dropped from planes during war time. They usually visualize the main ingredients of a bomb being gun powder. Now think of what the Oklahoma City bomb looked like. It was a large truck packed with barrels of fertilizer and fuel oil. This is not what most people would consider to be a bomb. Since it didn't look like a bomb, McVeigh can say he never had his hand on one.

On May 1, 1997, John and Patsy Ramsey gave an interview to seven members of the press. The interview centered around the murder of their daughter JonBenet. In this interview, we find the following questions and answers:

> Question: "John, would you recommend the death penalty for the person convicted of killing JonBenet?"
> J. Ramsey: "I would absolutely want the most severe penalty to be brought."
> Question: "Patsy?"
> P. Ramsey: (Nods silently with tears in her eyes.)[4]

John Ramsey gives a stern answer to this question. However, he does not answer the question. He does not tell us he wants the death penalty for the person convicted of killing JonBenet. Why didn't he say "Yes" or "Absolutely, I want the death penalty?" It is possible that John Ramsey does not believe in capital punishment. He is now faced with a dilemma with the murder of his daughter. Personal convictions will not allow him to ask for the death penalty. Public opinion will not allow him to say he does not want the death penalty. So, he doesn't answer the question. We should look to see if he opposes capital punishment.

Another possible reason why John Ramsey did not answer the question is because he knows who the killer is and he doesn't want this person to be put to death. Remember, when people do not answer a question they are withholding information. We get this same impression from Patsy Ramsey who answers the question by only nodding her head. Why doesn't she vocally proclaim she wants the death penalty for the person who killed her child?

On February 28, 1997, two suspects robbed the Bank of America in North Hollywood, California. Armed with assault rifles and wearing body armor, the bank robbers got into a shootout with officers from the Los Angeles Police Department. The gunman fired over 1200 rounds injuring 18 people, 11 of which were police officers. One gunman was killed and the second gunman, Emil Matasareanu, was cornered by the police. Having been shot 29 times, Matasareanu decided to surrender. As Matasareanu laid on the street bleeding, it took over an hour before an ambulance arrived. By the time emergency medical services had gotten to him, Matasareanu had bled to death. Many people believe the police prevented Matasareanu from receiving medical treatment. Perhaps the police were administering some street justice for the eleven officers who had been wounded.

On June 18, 2000, CBS's *60 Minutes* did a story on the L.A. shootout. Host Steve Croft interviewed the Los Angeles city attorney who was representing the Los Angeles Police Department in a lawsuit that had been filed by Matasareanu's family members.

Croft: "Did Mr. Matasareanu ask for an ambulance? Did he ask for medical attention?"

Attorney: "As a matter of fact he asked to be shot in the head. (Pause) And nobody obliged him."[5]

The city attorney does not answer the specific question. If he doesn't know if Matasareanu had asked for an ambulance, he should have told us, "I don't know if he asked for an ambulance." Instead he gives a rather cute non-answer. Even in his response we can gain some information. When people don't answer a question, they usually give an answer that infers they have answered the question. For example:

Question: "Did you do it?"
Answer: "I couldn't do that."

In this answer, the person leads us to believe that he didn't do it. However, he hasn't told us that he didn't do it. What is the city attorney inferring in his answer? He won't tell us if Matasareanu asked for an ambulance. However, he does tell us that Matasareanu asked "To be shot in the head and nobody obliged him." He could be telling us that no matter what Matasareanu asked for the police wouldn't do it. His answer "and nobody obliged him" may apply to Matasareanu's request for medical treatment.

When you place a camera in front of people they sometimes do not want to give short "yes" and "no" answers. They want to explain and comment on their actions or the situation. There is nothing wrong with that but they still need to answer the question. Hillary Rodham Clinton gives us a good example of answering a yes or no type question with a lengthy answer. On January 27, 1998, Matt Lauer interviewed the first lady on NBC's *Today* show. He asked her about the charges that the President had an affair with White House intern Monica Lewinsky.

> Lauer: "So these charges came as a big shock to you as anyone?"
>
> Clinton: "And to my husband. I mean, he woke me up Wednesday morning and said, you're not going to believe this but——and I said, 'What is this?' So yes, it came as a very big surprise."[6]

At first, it appeared Mrs. Clinton was not going to answer the question. She began by telling us the President was surprised by the charges. She then tells us how she found out about the alleged affair. However, at the end of her answer she does answer the question, "So yes, it came as a very big surprise."

When people do not answer your question you need to not only recognize it, but ask the question again. This will help you in obtaining more information and make it easier to determine if they are continuing to withhold any information. On May 11, 1997, CBS's *60 Minutes* broadcasted a segment entitled "The Court-Martial Of Lt. Flinn." Kelly Flinn was a lieutenant in the Air Force. In 1995, she was the pride of the Air Force when she became the first female B-52 bomber pilot. However, her career became marred when it was discovered she had an affair with a married man whose wife was enlisted in the Air Force. The Air Force charged Lt. Flinn with adultery and making false statements to investigators. All of which are punishable with a prison sentence under military law.

60 Minutes host Morley Safer interviewed Flinn. Flinn admitted to the sexual relationship stating she believed the man was legally separated at the time of their affair. Flinn believed the Air Force was singling her out because she was a woman. Safer looked into this targeting when he interviewed Colonel Robert E. Reed who is the chief of the Air Force's military justice division.

Safer: "Tell me, Colonel, in—in your 25 years, do you know of any colleague, any officer who committed adultery, fraternized and got away with it?"

Reed: "The point is we have established professional relations, responsibilities that go across the board Air Force-wide for men, for women, overseas, in the United States."

Safer: "I understand...."

Reed: "....under all circumstances."

Safer: "I understand. Do you know of any who did it—in other words, broke the rules and got away with it?"

Reed: "What we are concerned with here is commanders dealing with professional responsibilities as they are met."

Safer: "Again, I ask: Any colleague of yours in all those years you spent in the Air Force, back when it was pretty much a boy's club—any guys who engaged in adulterous relationships?"

Reed: "I can't think of any."[7]

Unlike a lot of reporters, Safer recognized the Colonel did not answer his question. Therefore, he asked the question again. The Colonel again does not answer the question. Safer is persistent. He asked the Colonel for a third time if he knew of any men in the Air Force who committed adultery and got away with it. The Colonel knows he has to give a better answer, or Safer will keep asking the question. So, he answers with "I can't think of any." For a third time he didn't answer the question. He did not tell us, "I do not know of anyone." He only stated he could not think of anyone. Because the Colonel refused to answer the question three times, we are assured there is something or someone he does not want to tell us about. If we did some digging, we would probably find there was someone, whom the Colonel knew, that had committed adultery.

Listen to what people are telling you. Listen to see if they answer the question. If a person has not told you that he didn't do it, then you cannot believe that he didn't do it. If people don't answer the question, there is something they are hiding. If you are asking the questions, then repeat the question. Often a person will provide you with more information if you are persistent in your questioning.

Chapter 11

Did The Subject Answer The Question With A Question?

Another tactic people will use to avoid telling you certain things is to answer your question with a question. By asking you a question, they have not answered your question. As we saw in chapter ten, this means they are withholding some information which may be incriminating. For example, a person suspected of stealing money is asked, "Did you take the money?" Some deceptive responses would be, "Are you accusing me of stealing?" "You think I took the money?" "Don't you know me better than that?" In each reply, the person answered the question with a question. He cannot deny taking the money because he would be telling a lie. Therefore, he is hoping the interviewer will accept his answer/question as a denial. Let's go back and look at Woody Allen's answer to the question concerning allegations of child molestation.

> Kroft: "Is there any truth to that at all?"
> Allen: "Well, be—be logical about this. I'm—I'm 57. Isn't it illogical that I'm going to, at the height of a—a very bitter, acrimonious custody fight, drive up to Connecticut where nobody likes me in a house—I'm in a house full of enemies, I mean, Mia was so enraged at me and—and she had gotten all the kids to—to be angry at me, that I'm going to drive up there, and suddenly, on visitation, pick this moment in my life to become a child molester?"[1]

We noted that Allen never answered the question which indicated he was withholding something. We also see he answered the question with a question which further shows us there is something he does not want to tell us.

On October 24, 2000, Larry King interviewed Paula Jones on his show *Larry King Live*. During this interview we find the following question and answer:

> King: "Are you still friends with Susan Carpenter-McMillan?"
> Jones: "Well, I considered myself, you know, still her friend, but I don't know – yes, I'm – I think so, I'm still her friend, I consider myself her ...."
> King: "Have you heard from her since the 'Penthouse' thing?"
> Jones: "Well, have you heard from her, Larry?"
> King: "No. But she isn't my friend, she's your friend." (Laughter)
> Jones: "I thought maybe you knew something I didn't. I thought maybe you heard something."[2]

When Larry King asked Paula Jones if she had heard from Susan Carpenter-McMillan, Jones answered his question with the question "Well, have you heard from her, Larry?" Since Jones did not answer the question, we can presume that Susan Carpenter-McMillan has not contacted her since Jones posed for Penthouse. If she did call her, Jones would tell us that. Look at Jones's answer to the question, "Are you still friends with Susan Carpenter-McMillan?" It is all one sided. Jones states, "I considered myself, you know, still her friend." "I'm still her friend, I consider myself her ..." All Jones tells us is how she feels. She does not state, "We are friends." This is further evidence that Jones has not heard from Susan Carpenter-McMillan.

Sometimes after answering your question with a question, people will then give you an answer.

> Question: "Did you take the money?"
> Answer: "Did I take the money? No."

This is a delay tactic which gives the person time to think about his answer. Typically a person will do this by repeating the question. However, asking any question is a sign they are thinking about their answer. The question you should be asking yourself is, "Why does this person need to think about his answer?" "Why can't he give me an immediate straight answer?" It is because he has information he does not want to share with you. Therefore, he stalls for time to think about how he should answer your question.

One day at work I had a practical joke played on me. One of my co-workers had placed some petroleum jelly on the doorknob to my office door. When I opened my door I got a sticky surprise. I had my suspicions as to who was responsible for this prank. I asked this person "Did you do it?" His response was, "Did I do it? No." Although he denied doing it, he answered my question with a question. He did not wait for me to answer his question. Therefore, he was not looking for clarification. His answer is a truthful answer. He did not put the petroleum jelly on my door knob. However, he could not immediately answer my question with a "no." He was stalling to think about how he should answer my question. I asked myself, "What is there to think about? Either he did it, or he didn't do it." This mystery wasn't too hard to figure out. My co-worker knew who was responsible for the practical joke. He just wasn't sure if he should give that person up. Therefore, he had to pause and think about his answer.

After being asked a question, some people may respond by saying "Could you please repeat the question?" or "What did you say?" They are giving the appearance they did not hear the question. Recognize they answered the question with a question. You will have to decide for yourself if this person is only seeking clarification, or if he is stalling for time.

Quite often people will answer a question with a question. Many times this means they have not answered the question and are withholding some information. If their question proceeds their answer, they are thinking about how to answer the question. The reason for their delay in responding may be because they are guilty of something. If they are innocent, this delay may be telling us they have some additional information they do not want to share. If you are asking the questions, probe this area to find out what else this person knows.

Part III
Detecting Deception In A Written Statement

Chapter 12

Did The Writer Cross Out Any Words?

A written statement is the best kind of statement to have because you can take your time analyzing it. You can underline, circle, and highlight words or phrases to help you identify what the person is saying. Everything mentioned in the previous chapters can be applied to written statements. There are also a few other techniques which may be hard to use on a verbal statement that you can apply to written statements to detect deception. One of these techniques is to look for any crossed out words. In order to utilize this technique, you should give the person writing the statement a pen. If you give him a pencil, he will have the ability to erase. Anything he erases is lost information. Therefore, give him a pen and tell him if he makes a mistake to draw a single line through it. That way you can read what he had written.

Sometimes people will misspell a word. They will cross it out and write it again correctly. Most of the time this is an insignificant error. We all make mistakes. However, sometimes people will begin to write the truth. They will realize this could be incriminating so they stop writing. They cross it out and they go on with their deceptive story. We can sometimes learn they are being deceptive or gain additional information by analyzing the crossed out portion of their story. I once read a report in which a gentleman claimed that while he was changing his clothes in a locker room someone stole his wallet. One of the first things I noticed in his short statement was that he had crossed out a word. His statement read:

"On May 12, 1998 at around 6:30 pm, I was in the locker room sitting at my locker. As I was getting dressed a man ~~ask~~ was standing by my locker when I had my backed turned. When I turned around he seemed startled and asked for change for a dollar. I told him that didn't have any change. He then left and I then got dressed. As I was leaving the gym I noticed my wallet was missing."

We can see the writer had crossed out the word "ask." He was about to tell us the truth. As he was getting dressed a man asked him for change. He then realized he needed to set the stage for a theft. So, he crosses out the word "ask" and tells us the man was standing behind him and when he turned around the man was startled. After mentioning this, he then proceeds to tell us the man asked for change. When I interviewed the alleged thief he confirmed what I had expected. He stated that he needed change to use the vending machine. He saw the gentleman sitting in the locker room, so he asked him if he had change for a dollar. The man stated he did not have any change, so he asked another guy in the locker room for change. He did not take the man's wallet.

In chapter seven, I mentioned the story of the man who was sentenced to prison and allowed to self surrender to the institution. Two weeks before he was to serve his sentence, he disappeared while scuba diving with his son. The son's story about his dad's disappearance showed deception in that he had a statement which was out of order. We see further evidence of deception in that his statement contained some crossed out words.

"I descended again to look for him. By now I only had about 300# of air. I only had enough air to search for a minute. I looked but did not see an him anywhere."

The son wrote, "I looked but did not see an." He then crosses out the "an" and writes, "him anywhere." We have to wonder what he was thinking about when he wrote the letters "a-n." These letters may be the word "an" or they may be the beginning of a word such as "anything." This crossed out word tells us that something else was on his mind when he wrote this statement. Towards the end of his statement we find another crossed out word.

"We continued searching until about 11:00 pm. ~~He~~ We were forced to stop because we were out of fuel."

The father and son entered the water at 6:00 p.m. Approximately fifteen minutes later, the father was missing. It is now 11:00 p.m. At this point in his statement, the father is presumed drowned. In talking about looking for his missing father, the son appears to use the pronoun "he." This is a reference to his father. It sounds like the son was about to tell us what his father was doing. How could he be doing anything if he is dead? If the son knows he is alive, then we can see how he could start to mention this. It is possible the son was going to write, "He <u>had not surfaced</u>." If that is the case, then he should have finished his sentence. That would not be an incriminating statement.

Even if you cannot read what the writer has crossed out, it may still be helpful. You may be able to determine what the writer was about to say, or you may see a change in thought. Most of the time when people cross out a word, they will write something else. However, there are times when they will simply cross out a word or words without adding anything to it. One of the most obvious and blatant examples of this can be found in a letter written by O.J. Simpson concerning the murder of Nicole Brown Simpson. On the day of infamous Bronco chase in which Simpson was suicidal, a letter written by Simpson was found. It read like a goodbye letter to all of his close friends. It would later be dubbed as the "suicide letter." The letter printed in the press and read on national television stated, "To whom it may concern: First, everyone understand I had nothing to do with Nicole's murder." The problem is that this is not what O.J. Simpson wrote. The actual handwritten letter reads "To whom it may concern: First, everyone understand ~~I had~~ nothing to do with Nicole's murder."[1] In his letter, Simpson crossed out the words "I had." Some believe he crossed out the words "I have." Since he did a good job crossing out the two words it is difficult to determine exactly what he had written. The point is he didn't write anything in addition to this. He simply crossed out the words. What does it mean when a person crosses out certain words? It means the writer does not want to say that. This is important because Simpson is taking himself out of this denial. He wanted to tell us he had nothing to do with Nicole's murder, but he couldn't bring himself to say that. Remember people will rarely lie. All Simpson tells us is that someone or something had "nothing to do with Nicole's murder."

It is interesting that after the criminal trial Simpson blamed the press for making him look guilty. Yet here the press was making him look good. Every time I have seen his letter in print or heard it read on television, it always includes the words "I had." That is because with the "I had" missing, it sounds funny and doesn't make much sense. However, from a Statement Analysis point of view, it makes a lot of sense.

Even if Simpson had left in the words "I had," he still isn't telling us he didn't do it. That is what an innocent person would say, "I didn't do it." "I had nothing to do with" sounds pretty convincing. After all, if a person truly had nothing to do with the murders, then how could he have committed them? Somehow in his mind he can justify saying, "I had nothing to do with Nicole's murder." However, in the end Simpson could not even make that statement because took himself out of the denial.

Crossed out words can sometimes reveal a person's true thoughts. In a written statement, be sure to analyze these words. Did the person misspell a word, or is he withholding information. Perhaps he started to write what actually happened before he realized what he was about to say. If you can read what the writer has crossed out, see if you can finish the sentence for him. If you cannot read what he has crossed out, you may be able to recognize a change in thought. This too can sometimes show us deception.

Chapter 13

Look For Unnecessary Words

Sometimes you will find in a person's statement unnecessary words. These are words that can be taken out of the statement without significantly changing the content of the statement. The statement will still make sense without these words. Unnecessary words may be hard to detect in a verbal statement, but they are easy to find in a written statement. To the reader, these words are unnecessary, but to the writer they are very important. These extra words mean the writer is giving us extra information. For example, consider the statement "I saw Bob in his blue Camaro." The word "blue" is an unnecessary word. Without it the statement is still grammatically correct and all of the key information is there. You should ask yourself why did the writer include the word "blue?" He of course is telling us the color of Bob's car. However, there is additional information he is providing. He may be telling us that Bob has more than one Camaro. Perhaps he has another one that is red. Therefore, he distinguishes between the two of them. What if Bob doesn't have another Camaro? What additional information could the writer be giving us? He may be telling us that his (the writer's) favorite color is blue. If Bob drove by in a red Camaro, the writer probably would not have mentioned the color of the car. Since blue is his favorite color, he chose to put it in his story.

Unnecessary words provide you with additional information. Sometimes this additional information can show you the person is being deceptive. Look at the following question and answer:

Question: "Do you know where Bob is?"
Answer: "I don't really know where he is."

The word "really" is an unnecessary word. Remove it and you still have a good answer, "I don't know where he is." What is the person telling us by including the word "really?" There is a very good chance the answer "I don't know where he is" would be a lie. Since people don't want to lie, the interviewee chooses not to answer the question that way. Instead he includes the word "really" which qualifies his answer. "I don't really know where he is" is not a lie. With this answer he is telling us he has an idea of Bob's location, but he is not absolutely certain of his whereabouts. As mentioned in chapter nine, the word "really" means truly and can fall into the category of words that indicate deception. This is further evidence this person knows where Bob is probably staying.

There was a mother who was hiding her fugitive son in her house. When the police went to her door and interviewed her, she stated, "The last time I actually saw him was a week ago." "Actually" is an unnecessary word. The answer, "The last time I saw him was a week ago" would be a great answer. However, it would also be a lie since her son is currently hiding in her house. To this mother, the word "actually" probably means spending some quality time with her son. It may have been a week ago when she spent some valued time with him. When her son is hiding from the police, she does not consider that "actually" being together. When the police searched her house they found her son hiding in the closet. Technically the mother did not lie to the police, but she was being deceptive.

I recently asked a friend what her plans were for the weekend. She responded, "Actually, I am going to a birthday party." She did not place any emphasis on any particular word. She gave her answer using the same tone of voice. However, I noticed she used an unnecessary word. She could have said, "I am going to a birthday party." In order to find out why she used the word "actually," I asked her some additional questions. It turned out she didn't mind going to the party, but she had planned to do something else. In this case, the word "actually" tells us she is going to the birthday party, but it was not her first choice. If her weekend was completely open and she had no plans, she would not have used the word "actually."

I once saw an interview with a prisoner who was discussing how he and his cell mate were scheming to make some money. In the interview he said, "My a cell mate was laying up one night in the county jail. He looked up, it was over crowded so they doubled you up, he was on the floor, I'm on the bunk of course, and he said I got a way where we can get some money." We can consider the words "of course" unnecessary words. They are not needed except to tell us that the prisoner being interviewed is the dominant prisoner. That is his cell. Therefore, he is going to make the other guy sleep on the floor. Had he not included these extra words, we would not know who was doubled up with whom. Perhaps the prisoner living in the cell allowed his guest to sleep in his bed while he slept on the floor. The words "of course" let us know who is in charge of that cell.

Unnecessary words appeared in the JonBent Ramsey murder. In the ransom note left at the Ramsey house, we find the sentence "The two gentlemen watching over your daughter do not particularly like you so I advise you not to provoke them."[1] The writer of this ransom note could have stated, "The two gentlemen watching your daughter." However, he or she added the word "over." What is the difference between watching someone and watching over someone? The best example I can think of is in reference to God. If I say that God is watching over me, I visualize God keeping his distance. He sees me, but he also sees the entire world at the same time. He can see me because I am part of the world. While He is watching over me He is also watching over others. The word "over" means that God is spreading His watchful eye upon the earth. However, if I say that God is watching me it becomes more personal. Even though He can see the entire world, He is focusing His attention on me. Another example would be if a friend asked you to "watch over" his house while he was out of town. In this case, he probably wants you to stop by every once in a while and make sure everything is ok. Maybe you will pick up his mail and water his plants. However, if he asked you to "watch" his house, he probably wants you to house sit. He wants you to be there where you can keep a close eye on things.

In a kidnapping, the kidnappers should be "watching" the abductee. They will want to keep a close eye on her. They want to make sure she doesn't escape or alert someone that she needs help. They will want to make sure she doesn't harm herself if her being alive is dependent upon them receiving the ransom. When the writer of the ransom note said they were "watching over" JonBenet, he or she was telling us they were not keeping a close eye on her. There are only two reasons why you would not closely watch your hostage: 1. You know for certain she was alright and could not possibly escape; 2. You know she was dead. Since a dead body isn't going anywhere, it is something you "watch over." Through Statement Analysis the police could have presumed that JonBent was dead hours before they discovered her body.

Look for any unnecessary words. It is possible to find them in verbal statements, but you may have to use this technique solely with written statements. Unnecessary words reveal to us additional information. Sometimes we can use this extra information to determine if the person is telling the truth.

Chapter 14

Internal Dictionary

According to Avinon Sapir from the Laboratory of Scientific Interrogation, everyone has what he calls an internal dictionary. My research has found this to be true. Certain words mean certain things to people. What comes to your mind when you see the word "girl?" You may picture a female about nine-years-old. I may picture a female about sixteen-years-old. Someone else may visualize an older female. We all realize the word "girl" represents someone of the feminine gender. However, we all have our own specific definition for the word "girl." We can detect deception by analyzing a person's internal dictionary. If the person is telling the truth, his internal dictionary will remain consistent. Take a look at the following story.

> "Last Thursday I got into my vehicle and started to drive to Jacksonville, Florida. As I was driving down Interstate 95 I heard a sound in the right rear of my car. I pulled my vehicle off the highway and onto the shoulder. I got out of my car and saw that I had a flat tire. I opened the trunk of my vehicle and found that my spare tire was flat. I left my car parked on the shoulder and walked to the nearest gas station to use a telephone."

In this story, the writer refers to his automobile as a "vehicle" and as a "car." By calling it two different things, this is an indication of deception unless there is a justification for the change in language. If he was speaking from the heart, he would consistently call it either a "car" or a "vehicle" but not both. If his internal dictionary says this is a "car," then it should always be a "car" in his story. When a person is making up a story, his internal dictionary may not remain constant. He may refer to things by several names because he is not speaking from the heart. Let's take a look at the same story but worded differently.

> "Last Thursday I got into my <u>car</u> and started to drive to Jacksonville, Florida. As I was driving down Interstate 95 I heard a sound in the right rear of my <u>car</u>. I pulled my <u>car</u> off the highway and onto the shoulder. I got out of my <u>car</u> and saw that I had a flat tire. I opened the trunk of my <u>car</u> and found that my spare tire was flat. I left my <u>vehicle</u> parked on the shoulder and walked to the nearest gas station to use a telephone."

In this story, the writer consistently refers to his automobile as a "car" until he gets to the end of his story. Again, this is an indication of deception unless there is a justification for the change from "car" to "vehicle." In this case, there is a justifiable reason for the change. To this person, the word "car" means operable and the word "vehicle" means disabled. He is driving his "car" down the road. He pulls his "car" off the road. He leaves his "vehicle" parked on the shoulder. This writer is speaking from his heart and we can see that by looking at his internal dictionary. As soon as the car becomes disabled, he refers to it as a vehicle.

I read a lot of reports written by police officers. I can usually see their internal dictionary at work by the way they refer to their firearm. The words "gun" "pistol" "firearm" "handgun" "revolver" all have different meanings. In a shooting situation, a typical report may contain the phrases, "I drew my gun. I pointed my gun. I fired my weapon. I holstered my gun." This is a truthful story. To this officer, the word "gun" means the firearm hasn't been discharged. The word "weapon" means the gun has been fired. As soon as he stops shooting he goes back to calling it a "gun." His internal dictionary is consistent because we have a justifiable change in the language. Another officer may write that he drew his "gun," pointed his "gun," and fired his "pistol." To this officer, the word "pistol" refers to a weapon that is being discharged. He has a different internal dictionary.

How a person refers to a firearm is not limited to police officers. Several years ago there was a man who reported his wife had committed suicide. In his written statement, he said that she "picked the pistol up from her dresser. She put the gun to her head and started teasing him. The gun then went off." When we look at his internal dictionary we see that he first called the firearm a "pistol." Then he called it a "gun." Now if to him that firearm was a pistol, then he should have continually called it a pistol. If it was a gun, he should consistently refer to it as a gun. I see no justification for one time calling it a pistol and then calling it a gun. The only reason he referred to it by two different names is because he is making up the story. After further questioning by the police, he eventually confessed that he shot his wife.

We cannot take anything for granted because people have their own language. We saw this with O.J. Simpson. In 1995, Simpson wrote a book entitled *I Want To Tell You*. Simpson was facing a murder charge so he wrote the book to raise money for his defense fund. Before we even open the book, we see a problem with the title of the book. Simpson is not saying, "I am going to tell you" or "Let me tell you." All he is saying is he wants to tell us something. We can presume he wants to tell us he did not kill his ex-wife and her friend. However, he never states that in his book. As indicated by the title of his book he only alludes to his innocence. In his book he states,

> "I am one hundred percent not guilty. In my open letter read on television on June 17, 1994, by my friend Robert Kardashian, I said I was innocent. When asked at my arraignment, where the charges against me were first formally stated in court, I said, 'I am one hundred percent not guilty.' I said it again in Judge Ito's chambers and I say it again here."[1]

This sounds like a very strong denial. However, as mentioned in chapter twelve Simpson did not state he was innocent because he took himself out of the story by crossing out the words "I had." We also have a problem with his statement "I am one hundred percent not guilty." Most people believe 100% is inclusive of everything. If Simpson is 100% not guilty, then he must be 0% guilty. However, we must remember that numbers go on for infinity. There are different rating systems that we use. Sometimes we rate things on a scale of 1 to 10. Other times it may be on a scale of 1 to 100. So, what scale is Simpson using? Later in his book, Simpson talks about Nicole as a caring mother. "I had one thousand percent faith and trust in Nicole's decisions about the kids."[2] We see that Simpson also rates things on a scale of one thousand. Simpson has more confidence in Nicole's decisions about the kids then he does in his own innocence. Based on his scale of 1,000, Simpson is 100% not guilty and 900% guilty!

Everyone has their own internal dictionary. There are no synonyms in Statement Analysis. Every word has its own meaning even if it's just slightly different from a similar word. In a written statement you should analyze a person's internal dictionary to see if he is being truthful or deceptive. If he is speaking the truth, his language will be consistent. He will constantly use the same words when describing certain things. If he is being deceptive, he may use a variety of words in his description. This is because he is not speaking from the heart but is making up the story. You should look to see if there is a justification for the change in language. If you cannot find a justification, then you can conclude he is being deceptive.

Chapter 15

What Is The Breakdown Of The Story?

Every story has a before, during, and after incident segment. The writer will start out telling us what was going on before the incident occurred. He will then provide us with the details of what happened. Once the incident is over, he will continue on with his story telling us what he did in the aftermath. We can determine if a story is truthful or deceptive by examining the length of these three segments.

Whether they are being truthful or deceptive, people usually will not begin their story by describing the incident in question. Instead, they will set the stage for the event. The writer will tell us what he was doing before the incident. Perhaps he was watching tv or driving in his car. Maybe it was raining or the wind was blowing. These events which may be non-related to the incident will appear at the beginning of the story. In a truthful story, the before incident segment will be approximately 25% of the entire story. A deceptive story will also have a significant beginning comprised of about 25 to 40%.

The writer will then describe the incident. He will provide a lot of details concerning the actual events. The majority of his story will center on what happened to him or what he witnessed. In a truthful and deceptive story, the during incident segment will be approximately 50% of the story.

After the incident is over, the writer will then describe what happened next. It is this portion of the story that lets us know if a person is being truthful or deceptive. In a truthful story, once the incident has ended there will always be something else going on that effects the person involved. If he experienced a crime, he will probably call the police. When the police arrive he will tell them what happened. He may have to go to the police station with them to look at photos and sign a complaint. He may experience some emotions of anger or fear because of the incident. All of these things will appear in the after incident segment of a truthful story. In a deceptive story, the writer will usually fail to include details of what happened after the incident. As he makes up his story he will be sure to tell us what he was doing before the incident. He will then provide a lot of information about the incident itself trying to convince us this actually happened. However, his story will end very quickly because in his mind the incident is now over. Since he is not drawing from his memory of what happened or the emotions he experienced after the incident, he will forget to include these details in his deceptive story. The key is a truthful story will have a significant ending comprised of about 25% of the entire story. The after incident segment of a deceptive story will be less than 25% of the entire story.

Let's breakdown the segments to the following story:

"On June 12, I was working security from 3:00 pm to 11:00 pm. By 6:00 all of the employees had left the building and I was there by myself. At 8:00 I made my rounds throughout the building making sure everything was secure. I was done with my rounds at 8:30. I then turned on the radio and listened to the Indians baseball game. At around 9:30 I saw on the video monitor a small truck pull up to the back gate. I went out the back door and asked the driver what he was doing. Another man got out of the passenger side of the truck and pointed a gun at me. He told me to open up the gate or he would shoot me. When I opened the gate the driver drove the truck into the complex. The man with the gun told me to get back in the building. The two of them tied me up and told me they would not hurt me if I gave them no problems. I could hear them moving around some of the offices but I did not know what they were looking for. About 15 minutes later I heard them leave the building and start the truck. I freed myself and looked at the video monitor to see if they were still around. I then called 911 and notified the police we had been robbed."

This story is comprised of 19 lines and can be broken down with the following segments:

Before	5.5 lines	29%
During	11 lines	58%
After	2.5 lines	13%

We see this story has a substantial beginning (29%). The bulk of the story talks about the incident. However, the ending is somewhat short comprising of only 13% of the entire story. After the robbers leave, the security guard "looked at the video monitor" and "called 911." That is all he did or at least that is all he told us he did. There is no mention of him looking around to see what had been disturbed or taken. There are no emotions in the story. He does not tell us he was afraid or he feared for his life. Because of the short ending, we should suspect he is being deceptive as to what happened that night.

When analyzing a written statement you should look at the before, during and after incident segments. As you read the story draw a line when you get to the end of the before and during segments. This will help you identify the breakdown. If the story has a very short ending, this is an indication the person is being deceptive.

Part IV
Some Final Thoughts

Chapter 16

What Hasn't The Subject Told You?

As we have seen, people do not want to lie. When giving a statement they will usually tell you the truth. However, deceptive people will withhold certain information. Therefore, it is important to ask yourself not only what is this person telling me based on his language, pronouns, internal dictionary, etc., but what hasn't this person told me. When we already have an idea of what has happened it becomes very easy for us to unknowingly interpret what a person is saying. Often times when I am speaking at a law enforcement conference, officers will ask me if I would look at a written statement given to them by a suspect. As they hand me their statement they will begin to tell me about the person who wrote the statement. I always stop them and tell them I don't want to know anything about the case. This allows me to be more objective in my evaluation of what the person is saying. Once I have completed my analysis, I will call the officer and discuss the case with him. Remember people mean exactly what they say. If they haven't told us something, then we cannot believe it has happened. Take for example the following employee's statement about money that was stolen from a safe in his boss's office.

"I arrived at work at 7:45 am. When I entered the building I noticed that Mr. Johnson's office door was opened. I know that he locks his door when he leaves in the evening. I thought that maybe he had come to work early so I looked into his office. I did not see Mr. Johnson but I saw that the safe in his office was opened. I looked around but did not see anyone. I knew that my boss would be arriving soon. As soon as he arrived at work I reported the theft to him. My boss then called the police."

Did you figure out what the employee hasn't told us? Look at his statement line by line. He arrived at work at 7:45. He saw the office door open. He looked into the office. He saw the safe was open. He did not see anyone. He reported the theft to his boss when he arrived. What did he tell us about the money? Nothing! He did not tell us the money was missing. All he said was he found the safe opened. When you read his story did you envision the safe being empty? If you did, it is because I told you this statement was about money that had been stolen from a safe. Therefore, when he says he found the safe opened, it is very easy to assume the money was missing from the safe at that point in his story. However, he did not tell us that so we cannot believe it. In this case, he did get to work early. He did see the office door opened because he opened it. He did look into his boss's office. He did not see anyone around the office. He saw the safe opened because he opened it. He took the money and notified his boss when he arrived. Technically, he never lied in his story.

Let's look at another example. In September 1959 in a Canadian courtroom, 14-year-old Steven Truscott was found guilty of raping and murdering his classmate 12-year-old Lynne Harper. Sentenced to death, Truscott became the youngest person to sit on Canada's death row. His death sentence was eventually commuted to life in prison. Truscott has always maintained his innocence. He claims that on June 9, 1959, he was riding his bicycle when he met Lynne Harper near the school. She asked him for a ride to the highway because she wanted to see the man who kept ponies at his house. Truscott gave Harper a lift on his bike and dropped her off at the highway. As he was cycling back he saw a car stop where Harper was standing. She got into the car and the car drove off. Harper's body was found the next day not too far from where Truscott dropped her off.

In 1969, after serving ten years in prison, Truscott was paroled. He took on an alias and maintained a private life for thirty plus years. Recently Truscott has made a public appeal in the hope his case will be reopened. In April 2000, he participated in TV program that re-examined the case. Many people feel he had been railroaded, and the evidence which would have vindicated him was overlooked. There have been several web sites devoted to seeing this injustice set right.

Since the crime occurred over 40 years ago, it becomes difficult to sort through all of the facts. Some of the evidence has been destroyed. Some of the people involved in the investigation are no longer living. However, there is one document we can review that is a very good source of information as to what happened on that June evening in 1959. In 1971, Pocket Book published "The Steven Truscott Story" by Steven Truscott as told to Bill Trent. In his book, Truscott talks about how thrilled he was when he received a stay of execution. Let's see what Truscott has to say about this or more importantly what he does not have to say.

> "This was the first news I received that a stay of execution had been ordered. I often wonder when I would have been told, had it not been for that guard. I was dazed and it was some time before the full significance of what had occurred got through to me. I wasn't going to die! Hastily, I qualified my jubilance. I wasn't going to die as soon as I'd expected. But Pop used to say, 'Where there's life there's hope', and I was alive! Perhaps there would be yet another miracle – an appeal, a new trial, even an acquittal."[1]

After receiving his stay of execution, Truscott hopes for another miracle. He then lists three things he would like to see happen: "an appeal, a new trial, even an acquittal." An appeal would allow new evidence to be presented which would possibly lead to a new trial. He is then hopeful a new trial would win him his freedom. However, what is Truscott not telling us? If you were an innocent person sitting on death row, what would be the greatest miracle of all that would give you your freedom? It would of course be that the person who killed Lynne Harper was caught and confessed to the murder. You would be set free and completely exonerated. That is much better than receiving a new trial. Yet Truscott never asks for that. It never crosses his mind that the best thing would be for the killer to be found. To him this isn't an option because he knows he killed Lynne Harper.

If you want to get the most out of an interview, listen and believe what people are saying. Remember not to interpret what they are saying. People want you to believe certain things.

However, if they haven't told you something, then you cannot believe it occurred. This is why you need to ask yourself, "What is this person telling me?" and "What is this person not telling me?" in order to see the truth.

Chapter 17

A Quick Review

Everyone has the capability of determining if someone is being truthful or deceptive. In order to become proficient at discerning the truth, you must listen to what people are saying. Let's look at one more case which serves as a good review of what to look for in a statement.

Kevin Ryder and Gene "Bean" Baxter are disc jockeys for radio station KROQ in Los Angeles, CA. Several years ago on their show they had a comedy segment called "Confess Your Crime." People would call in and confess they had stolen their boss's coffee mug or had played a practical joke on a co-worker. One day they received a call in which the caller confessed to murdering his girlfriend. The Los Angeles Sheriff's Department spent over 100 man hours investigating the case. They didn't find a murderer and they didn't find a victim. This led to speculation the call may have been a hoax perpetrated by the two DJs to boost their ratings. The television show Un*solved Mysteries* interviewed the two DJs in regards to the mysterious telephone call. *Unsolved Mysteries* asked them if the call was a hoax created to boost their ratings. They responded with the following answers:

> Ryder: "Um, there are, there are real definite lines that you do not cross. Um, obviously everybody's you know trying to get ratings, trying to get noticed, trying to be this and that, but there are lines that you just don't cross and that's one of them. I, I, I don't know that anyone could sit down and say someone confessing to murder will make our ratings go up."[1]

Baxter: "Um, you know all we can say is you know the ex, the experts feel this guy was legitimate. It is no one we know and as you know far as we're concerned that, that's his story. We certainly hope it's not true. You know I'd trade whatever publicity we got from it for you know the story not to be true because it is pretty grim, really."[2]

The show ended with this mystery still unsolved. Several months later, this episode of *Unsolved Mysteries* aired again. This time the show ended with an update. The call was indeed a hoax arranged by the two DJs. It shouldn't have taken months to solve this mystery because the DJs themselves tell us this call was a hoax.

Did the subject answer the question?
One of the first things we notice is that neither of these DJs answered the question. *Unsolved Mysteries* asked them if the call was a hoax created to boost their ratings. This question requires a "yes" or "no" answer. The words "yes" or "no" never appear in their answer.

People will usually give an answer when asked a question. Look to see if they answered the specific question. If they didn't answer the question, there is something they are hiding. If you are the interviewer, ask the question again. Do not let the person get away with not answering the question. Keep asking questions and you will obtain more information from the person.

Look at the language
Gene Baxter starts out his statement by saying, "all we can say." He is telling us they can only provide a certain amount of information. However, they are not limited by their knowledge (all we know), but are choosing to withhold information from us.

Do not interpret what people are saying. People mean exactly what they say. Look at the specific words they are using. Ask yourself, "What is this person telling me?" If someone says, "I think I went to bed at 10:00," recognize he did not tell you he was in bed at 10:00. Also, look to see if people are specifically addressing the issues at hand, or are they talking about something else in an effort to lead you away from the truth?

Examine all of the pronouns

Kevin Ryder states, "There are real definite lines that you do not cross." "There are lines that you just don't cross." Ryder tells us there are lines that YOU wouldn't cross. This is a truthful statement. Most people wouldn't cross that line. However, he didn't say he wouldn't cross that line. He didn't say the two of them (we) wouldn't cross that line. All he is doing is pointing the finger right back at you.

Both Ryder and Baxter use the phrase "you know." The problem is we do not know. Instead of telling us what they know, they want us to assume they are being truthful.

You can learn a lot by looking at the pronouns in a statement. Pronouns give us responsibility, and will sometimes show us a person is admitting to performing certain act. If an individual uses the pronoun "we," he is not taking full responsibility for his actions. The lack of the pronoun "I" in a statement is an indication the person hasn't done what he wants us to believe he did. Also look for consistency in the pronouns people use. If people are telling you the truth, they will use the same pronouns throughout their story. When people change their pronouns, there is the possibility of deception.

Words and phrases that indicate deception

Gene Baxter ends his statement by saying, "I'd trade whatever publicity we got from it for you know the story not to be true because it is pretty grim. Really." As mentioned in chapter 9, the word "really" means truly. Baxter is telling us this story is "pretty grim (truthfully)." This is very similar to saying "Honestly" or "To tell the truth."

In trying to convince you they are being truthful, people will use certain phrases as an added emphasis. However, phrases such as "I swear to God" or "To tell the truth" indicate the person is being deceptive.

Look for unnecessary words

Kevin Ryder ends his statement using some unnecessary words. "Um, I, I, I don't know that anyone could sit down and say someone confessing to murder will make our ratings go up." Most people would say, "I don't know that anyone could say someone confessing to murder will make our rating go up." It turned out the caller in this hoax was another DJ. When the three DJs got together to plan this publicity stunt what do you think they were doing? They were "sitting down." When Ryder was questioned about the call he could see the three of them sitting there planning it. That information surfaced in his statement when he added the words "sit down."

We also see unnecessary words in the form of stuttering. Both of these DJs used the word "um" and repeated a couple of other words. Since these guys speak live on the radio, we can presume they probably do not stutter. Stuttering when answering a sensitive question is an indication of deception.

Unnecessary words can be taken out of the statement and the statement will still make sense. These extra words provide us with additional information. This information may show us the person is being deceptive.

What hasn't the subject told you?

By not answering the question, neither DJ told us this was not a hoax. Baxter tells us the "experts feel this guy was legitimate." However, he does not tell us that he feels the caller is for real. Also by using the pronoun "you" they haven't told us they would not participate in such a publicity stunt.

People will leave out certain information from their story. This information may be incriminating or it may indicate that the person wants us to believe something that never occurred. Listen but do not interpret what people are saying.

Remember people's words will betray them. As we saw with these two DJs, it will usually betray them in several ways. Although they did not show up in their statement, there are also several other things you want to consider in a person's statement.

Check the verb tenses

Look at the verb tenses used in a statement. Recognize if the person is talking about the past or the present. When a person uses the word "never," he is accounting for his entire life. However, if he uses the words "I do not," he is only talking about the present. If someone is questioned about his past, but he gives an answer in the present he is being deceptive.

Order is important
There is always a reason why a person will list things in a certain order. Finding out why he chose that order will give you some additional information. This information may show you if his answers are truthful.

Pay attention to time references
Time references help us to account for everything a person did. Look to see if the person has some missing time. He may be purposely leaving this out of his story. Inquire what he was doing during this time period. This withheld information may be what you are looking for. Also check to see if there are any time references that are out of order. This is an indication the person is making up the story.

Did the subject answer the question with a question?
This indicates the person is thinking about his answer. He has information to tell, but he is uncertain how much he should tell you. Therefore, he may repeat the question to buy himself some time to think of a good answer. If you do not ask the question again, he will get away with not answering the question. Even if he eventually answers the question, you know he is withholding some additional information.

Did the writer cross out any words?
Crossed out words mean there is something the person does not want to tell you. He may not want you to know he misspelled a word. It could also be there is some information he doesn't want to share with you. This information may show you what really happened.

Internal dictionary
Everyone has their own internal dictionary. Certain words mean certain things. In a truthful statement, their internal dictionary should remain constant unless there is a justification for change. In a deceptive story, they may use a variety of words to describe something because they are making the story up.

What is the breakdown of the story?
Every story should have a before, during and after incident segment. The breakdown of these segments in a truthful story will

be approximately 25% before, 50% during, and 25% after. Any significant deviation from this formula is an indication of deception. This deception is usually seen in the story's short ending.

Watch how you phrase your questions

Do not ask compound questions. Compound questions make it easy for the person to withhold information. He may not answer one of the questions and you may not recognize this. Ask your questions one at a time. Also do not give them the answer within the question. "You didn't do it, did you?" is a terrible question. Never answer the question for them and do not anticipate what their answer will be. Allow them to state whatever they want to say.

How would you answer the question?

Finally, ask yourself how you would answer a certain question, or how you would respond to a certain allegation. By comparing your answer with their answer, you can sometimes gain insight into what people are telling you, and what they are not telling you. Ascertaining the truth can be easy if you listen to what people are saying.

Let's examine some famous and controversial cases. By applying the Statement Analysis techniques, we can see who is being deceptive and who is telling the truth.

Part V
Case Analysis

Chapter 18

The Oklahoma City Bombing

On the morning of April 19, 1995, a rented Ryder truck pulled up in front of the Alfred P. Murrah Federal Building in Oklahoma City, Oklahoma. After parking the truck, the driver lit a fuse, exited the truck, and walked away. At approximately 9:02 a.m., the truck exploded ripping away half of the federal building. Nine floors and the offices they contained came tumbling down forming a pile of rubble. Almost immediately cries for help could be heard from those individuals who were trapped in the debris. Rescue workers quickly arrived and began sorting through the wreckage trying to save as many lives as possible. Sadly, 168 people died in this terrorist attack on the United States.

    U.S. intelligence and law enforcement agencies quickly went to work trying to find the perpetrators of this crime. There was speculation that foreign terrorists had come to America. Using the Vehicle Identification Number from a piece of the truck, the police were able to identify the exact truck used in the bombing. The Ryder rental agent gave law enforcement officials a description of the man who rented the truck. The police were also able to identify the main ingredients of the bomb: ammonia nitrate and fuel oil. On the same day soon after the bombing, a trooper with the Oklahoma Highway Patrol pulled over a car that did not have a license plate. The lone occupant of the vehicle was taken into custody. Just before he was to be released on April 21, the police recognized he fit the description of the man who rented the Ryder truck used in the bombing. The police now had a suspect in custody. His name was Timothy McVeigh.

From the time of his arrest, things did not look good for Timothy McVeigh. A picture of him being a home-grown terrorist was starting to come into focus. McVeigh was a Gulf War veteran who had left the army in December 1991. He had expressed a dislike in the way the F.B.I. and the federal government had handled the Branch Davidian tragedy several years earlier in Waco, Texas. He owned a copy of the "Turner Diaries" an anti-government publication which storied a plot to blow up the F.B.I. Headquarters in Washington, D.C. It was believed he had ties to a militia group, and traces of the explosive were found on his clothes. He was also identified as the person who rented the truck used in the bombing.

As he sat in jail, McVeigh was not granting many interviews with the press. He was abiding by his attorney's good advice to keep quiet. Finally after two months in jail, McVeigh decided to tell his side of the story. Along with his attorney, Stephen Jones, he granted an interview with *Newsweek* columnists David H. Hackworth and Peter Annin. The following are excerpts from the interview:

Newsweek:	"What about the recent claims from Fortier that you allegedly cased the federal building together last December?"
Jones:	"Now, wait a second. I don't know that Fortier's made any such claims. That's a report."
McVeigh:	"I've been through Oklahoma City."
Newsweek:	"With Michael Fortier?"
McVeigh:	"I think I'd rather not answer that."[1]

McVeigh has a chance to deny casing the federal building in Oklahoma City. So, why didn't he say, "Those claims are false. I did not case the federal building with Michael Fortier." The reason he doesn't say that is because it would be a lie, and like most people he doesn't want to lie. So he doesn't answer the question. All he tells us is that he has been through Oklahoma City. When specifically asked if he was with Michael Fortier in Oklahoma City, McVeigh tells us he does not want to answer that question. This blatantly shows us there is something he does not want us to know.

Compare his answer about casing the federal building with the following answers he gave during the interview:

Newsweek:	"There is a report that you've confessed to the crime."
McVeigh:	"I can clearly deny that."
Newsweek:	"There are reports that you've been a member of the Michigan Militia."
McVeigh:	"Those reports are false reports."[2]

McVeigh can "clearly deny" that he did not confess to this crime. He can also tell us that reports of his Michigan Militia membership "are false reports." However, he will not deny the claim that he cased the federal building with Michael Fortier.

Newsweek:	"This is the question that everybody wants to know - Did you do it?"
McVeigh:	"The only way we can really answer that is that we are going to plead not guilty."
Jones:	"And we're going to go to trial."
Newsweek:	"But you've got a chance right now to say, 'Hell no!'"
Jones:	"Well, but that...."
McVeigh:	"We can't do that."
Jones:	"And if he says, 'Hell, no!' the government isn't going to just [say] 'Well, OK, that settles that.'"[3]

The interviewers prep McVeigh by telling him, "This is the question that everybody wants to know." By doing this they are telling McVeigh this is a very important question. All this does is put the interviewee on guard and makes him concentrate on his answer. It makes it easier for him to lie. Fortunately for us, McVeigh chooses not to lie. Instead he doesn't answer the question. There is no "yes" or "no" in his answer. Pleading not guilty is not saying, "I didn't do it." This means there is something McVeigh doesn't want to tell us. *Newsweek* even points this out to him. "But you've got a chance right now to say, 'Hell no!'" McVeigh responds by saying, "We can't do that." He "can't do that" because he doesn't want to lie. We see the same thing in his first answer, "The only way we can really answer that...." The

115

word "really" means truly or genuinely. McVeigh is saying the only way we can answer that question truthfully is by saying "we are going to plead not guilty." If he said, "No. I didn't do it" that would be a lie. Since he doesn't want to tell us the truth, and he doesn't want to lie, he chooses not to answer the question.

Notice that McVeigh uses the pronoun "we" instead of "I." Is it possible he is referring to a co-conspirator? Since his attorney is present during this interview, and since he is speaking in legal jargon, more than likely the "we" refers to McVeigh and his attorney Stephen Jones. Still the question was asked of him and not of McVeigh and his attorney.

Nine months after his *Newsweek* interview, McVeigh allowed *TIME* correspondent Patrick E. Cole to interview him. The interview was published in the April 15, 1996 issue of *TIME*. Let's look at some excerpts from this interview.

TIME: "You have been painted as a kid from a working class family who somewhere along the line became disenchanted with the government and became involved in the bombing. Are you the killer people think you are?"

McVeigh: "If it means that I was angered at Waco and I enjoy guns as a hobby, I do go to gun shows, and I follow the beliefs of the Founding Fathers. If it means that I was involved in the bombing, then that means about a billion other Americans were involved as well. I don't think it is right to take someone's beliefs and convict them because of those beliefs."[4]

As I previously mentioned this is a poorly worded question. In his answer, McVeigh refers to the question saying, "If it means that I was angered at Waco and I enjoy guns as a hobby...." He then goes on and tells us he does go to gun shows. He believes in the right to bear arms. He mentions that he was angered by the Waco Tragedy, but he chooses not to expound on it. We can assume that Waco did bother him and it is a sensitive issue with him.

McVeigh never answers the interviewer's question. He doesn't tell us, "I didn't do it" or "I am not the killer people think I am."

Therefore, we cannot assume he didn't do it since he doesn't tell us that. By not answering the question, he is hiding something from us.

> TIME: "Have you ever built a bomb?"
> McVeigh: "I've never had my hand on one. I used to watch other people do it. I won't go into that. There were plastic soda bottles. They would put vinegar and baking soda in and screw the cap on, and it would burst."[5]

McVeigh gives what appears to be a good answer, "I've never had my hand on one." However, the question requires a "yes" or "no" answer. McVeigh never says "yes" or "no." He doesn't answer the question. Therefore, he is withholding some information.

> TIME: "Why do you want to take the stand at your upcoming trial?"
> McVeigh: "So that the jurors know me and not what they've read."[6]

Here McVeigh does answer the question. He wants the jurors to "know me." But what does he want the jurors to know about him? Does he want them to know he is innocent? We don't know because he doesn't tell us. If you were accused of this crime of which you did not commit, how would you answer this question? You would take the stand to tell the jurors that you didn't do it. You would want them to know you are innocent. McVeigh doesn't tell us that when answering this question.

> TIME: "Why don't you come out and maintain your innocence?"
> McVeigh: "I have, and I've said I'm not guilty."[7]

Even a year after the bombing, McVeigh had remained so quiet as to his innocence this question had to be asked. He still hasn't told us, "I didn't do it" or "I did not blow up that building." Instead he says, "I'm not guilty." The word "guilt" can be used in two different ways. It can be the state of having done something wrong, or it can be the feeling of remorse for believing that one has done something wrong. If McVeigh is referring to the latter sense of the word, then he can honestly say he is not guilty. Since he so strongly believes in what he did, he is guilty of nothing.

When in court at his arraignment hearing, McVeigh stated he was not guilty when answering the question, "How do you plea?" The far majority of the time defendants will plead "not guilty" at the arraignment hearing. Only once in my career as a law enforcement officer have I heard a defendant plead "guilty" at his first appearance before a judge. When it happened, it took everyone by surprise. Even the magistrate continued with the hearing in routine fashion as if the defendant had pled "not guilty" until he realized the defendant had said "guilty." The point is most people plead "not guilty." Their attorney advises them to do so. This gives them a chance to set a trial date and look at the evidence. If the evidence is overwhelming against them, then later we usually see a change of plea.

When McVeigh said he was "not guilty" he wasn't saying "I didn't do it." He was only answering the question "How do you plea?" In his mind he is thinking, "I am going to plead not guilty." He was never asked, "Are you guilty?" or "Did you commit this crime?" If later a defendant decides to change his plea to "guilty" the court will hold a change of plea hearing. At this time a judge will ask a series of questions, some of which are to ensure the defendant is making this plea under his own free will, and that he has not been promised anything. The judge will also ask him "Are you now pleading guilty because you did in fact commit this crime?" This is a straight forward question which requires a "yes" or "no" answer. At the arraignment hearing though, a defendant is only asked, "How do you plea?" This type of question is just a formality which invites everyone to say "not guilty."

Nearly two years after the bombing, Timothy McVeigh was brought to trial. He was charged in federal court with the deaths of eight federal agents killed in the blast. On June 2, 1997, the jury reached its verdict of guilty. The verdict was hardly a shock. Based on the physical evidence and eyewitness testimony, most people had expected the jury to find him guilty. Through Statement Analysis we can also see that McVeigh was guilty of this crime. He avoided answering many questions which means there were things he wasn't telling us. More importantly he never said, "I didn't do it."

Chapter 19

The Nicole Brown Simpson And Ronald Goldman Murders

June 12, 1994 was a beautiful sunny Sunday in Los Angeles, CA. The temperature was comfortably in the mid 70s with a gorgeous blue sky. Former NFL football player O.J. Simpson began this day at 6:00 a.m. teeing off at the Riviera Country Club with some of his golfing buddies. The Country Club was not far from Simpson's home in Brentwood, CA. After their round of golf, the foursome would have lunch and play gin rummy in the clubhouse.

Nicole Brown Simpson was the 35-year-old ex-wife of O.J. Simpson. She lived in a four-bedroom condominium on South Bundy Drive in Brentwood, with her two children Sydney, age 8, and Justin, age 6. She and Simpson were divorced in 1992. During the past year they made an attempt to get back together. However, by May 1994, it was apparent their relationship would not evolve beyond friendship. Nicole spent her morning shopping for her children at Star Toys in Brentwood.

Ronald Goldman, 25, was a waiter at Mezzaluna, an Italian restaurant, located in Brentwood. Nicole frequently ate at Mezzaluna and she became acquainted with Goldman who had been working there for four months. Goldman began his day working out at the Gym which was located near the restaurant. He would later join his friends at the Starbucks coffee shop. In the afternoon, he played in a softball game.

The three of them started out the day by taking advantage of the beautiful weather and doing what they enjoyed. As evening approached they attended to their business and scheduled events. By late evening, all three of their paths would cross resulting in a deadly encounter.

At 4:30 p.m., Nicole Simpson, her mother Juditha Brown, and some friends attended a dance recital at the Paul Revere Middle School in Brentwood. O.J. Simpson arrived late and didn't sit with Nicole and the others. They were there to watch Sydney perform a dance routine. After the recital, Nicole and Simpson spoke briefly outside in the school parking lot. At around 6:30 p.m., Nicole took her children, mother and father, sister Denise and four friends to Mezzaluna. Ron Goldman happened to be working that night.

Nicole's party left the restaurant at 8:30 p.m. She then took her children to Ben and Jerry's ice cream shop located across the street from Mezzaluna. Unknown to Juditha Brown, she accidently dropped her eyeglasses near the Mezzaluna valet parking stand. Nicole and her children returned to their condominium at 9:00 p.m. Shortly thereafter, Juditha Brown called Mezzaluna to see if anyone had found her eyeglasses. Her glasses were located and placed in an envelope. Nicole then called the restaurant and asked to speak with Ron Goldman. At 9:45 p.m., Goldman left the restaurant with the envelope containing Juditha Brown's eyeglasses. He made a quick stop home and then proceeded to Nicole's residence on South Bundy Drive which is only three blocks from the restaurant.

At 10:30 p.m., screenwriter Steven Schwab was walking his dog when he noticed another dog walking down the street. The dog was not wearing any tags and it's paws were covered in blood. Not knowing whom the dog belonged to, Schwab's neighbor, Sukru Boztepe, took the dog in for the night. However, the dog was so agitated, Boztepe and his wife decided to search for it's owner. At 12:00 a.m., the dog led them to 875 South Bundy Drive. There they saw a body lying on the ground with lots of blood in the area. The police were immediately called.

The first officer on the scene arrived at 12:09 a.m. He found two bodies sprawled on the walkway leading into the condominium. They were the bodies of Nicole Brown Simpson and Ronald Goldman. Both victims had slash wounds on their neck as well as puncture wounds on their bodies. Their hands had several cuts indicating they tried to defend themselves from the attacker's knife. On the ground near Ronald Goldman's body was the envelope containing Juditha Brown's eyeglasses. The door to Nicole's condominium was opened. The police searched the house and found her children upstairs asleep. They were taken into police custody.

After the police identified Nicole Brown Simpson as one of the victims, officers responded to O.J. Simpson's residence at 360 North Rockingham Avenue. It was now about 5:00 a.m. They got no answer using the intercom or telephoning the residence. O.J. Simpson's white Bronco was parked on the street. They noticed blood on the Bronco's door. Believing that Simpson might be in danger, detective Mark Furman climbed over the wall surrounding the residence. As the officers entered the Simpson complex they found additional blood in the driveway leading up to the front door. The police awakened Simpson's daughter Arnelle and friend Kato Kaelin who was staying in the guest house. Simpson was not at home. At 11:45 p.m., he flew to Chicago to play in a golf tournament the next day. Kaelin told the detectives he heard some noises outside of his room. The police searched the area and found a right-handed bloody glove. The glove appeared to match the left-handed glove left at the murder scene. At 5:45 a.m., Simpson was located in Chicago and told of Nicole's death. He was asked to return to Los Angeles. When Simpson arrived at his residence in Brentwood, he was momentarily handcuffed. The handcuffs were removed and he voluntarily went to the police station for questioning. Four days later Simpson was charged with the murders of Nicole Brown Simpson and Ronald Goldman. As the Los Angeles police conducted their investigation the evidence seemed to point to one person as the perpetrator of this crime, O.J. Simpson. The victim's blood and Simpson's blood were found at the murder scene and at Simpson's residence. There were the bloody gloves found at both residences. Simpson stated he was at home preparing for his trip to Chicago at the time of the murders. However, there were no witnesses to verify he was at his residence. The limo driver who took Simpson to the airport that night stated that when he arrived at Simpson's residence at 10:40 p.m., no one answered when he rang the buzzer at the gated entrance. At 10:52 p.m., the limo driver saw a person fitting Simpson's description enter the house through the front door. Shortly thereafter, Simpson answered the intercom claiming he had overslept. In addition, there was the 911 call Nicole had made years previous when Simpson was abusive. Things did not look good for Simpson. The Los Angeles Police and the District Attorney's Office felt they had their man.

On January 24, 1995, O.J. Simpson went on trial for the double homicide. Simpson's legal counsel was known as the "Dream Team" because of the high profile attorneys such as Robert Shapiro, F. Lee Bailey and Johnnie Cochran which represented him. The trial lasted for 37 weeks. It was a lengthy trial because of the large amount of evidence, and because both sides scrutinized the DNA evidence. On October 3, 1995, after four hours of deliberation, the jury came back with it's verdict. "Not guilty."

The verdict set off a national debate as to whether or not Simpson got away with murder. Many people felt he was guilty, and that the state did a lousy job in prosecuting him. Others believed the defense's argument that the blood evidence was tainted, and that the police may have planted some evidence. Since the trial, Simpson has given many interviews, written a book and even made a videotape claiming he is innocent. Yet the controversy over his guilt or innocence still remains.

The physical evidence was not enough to convict Simpson of these murders. The defense was able to create a doubt in the jurors minds. Putting aside the physical evidence, let's take a look at Simpson's own words. If he didn't commit this crime, then we expect him to tell us that. He shouldn't say anything that is contrary to him being innocent. Listen and then judge for yourself.

On June 13, 1994, the day after the murders, O.J. Simpson was interviewed at the Los Angeles Police Headquarters by detectives Philip Vannatter and Thomas Lange. Simpson had a bandage on the knuckle of his middle finger on his left hand. The detectives questioned him about this injury.

Vannatter: "How did you get the injury on your hand?"
Simpson: "I don't know. The first time, when I was in Chicago and all, but at the house I was just running around."
Vannatter: "How did you do it in Chicago?"
Simpson: "I broke a glass. One of you guys had just called me, and I was in the bathroom, and I just kind of went bonkers for a little bit."
Lange: "Is that how you cut it?"
Simpson: "Mmm, it was cut before, but I think I just opened it again, I'm not sure."

Lange: "Do you recall bleeding at all in your truck, in the Bronco?"

Simpson: "I recall bleeding at my house and then I went to the Bronco. The last thing I did before I left, when I was rushing, was went and got my phone out of the Bronco."

Lange: "Mmm hmm. Where's the phone now?"

Simpson: "In my bag."

Lange: "You have it.......?"

Simpson: "In that black bag."

Lange: "You brought a bag with you here?"

Simpson: "Yeah, it's ....."

Lange: "So do you recall bleeding at all?"

Simpson: "Yeah, I mean, I knew I was bleeding, but it was no big deal. I bleed all the time. I play golf and stuff, so there's always something, nick and stuff here and there."

Lange: "So did you do anything? When did you put the Band-Aid on it?"

Simpson: "Actually, I asked the girl this morning for it."

Lange: "And she got it?"

Simpson: "Yeah, cause last night with Kato, when I was leaving, he was saying something to me, and I was rushing to get my phone, and I put a little thing on it, and it stopped."[1]

At this point during the interview, detective Vannatter questions Simpson about the Bronco and who has access to it. He also asked Simpson about the type of clothing he was wearing on the night of the murders. He then gets back to the blood issue.

Vannatter: "O.J., we've got sort of a problem."

Simpson: "Mmm hmm."

Vannatter: "We've got some blood on and in your car, we've got some blood at your house, and sort of a problem."

Simpson: "Well, take my blood test."

Lange: "Well, we'd like to do that. We've got, of course, the cut on your finger that you aren't real clear on. Do you recall having the cut on your finger the last time you were at Nicole's house?"

Simpson:	"A week ago?"
Lange:	"Yeah."
Simpson:	"No. It was last night."
Lange:	"Ok, so last night you cut it."
Vannatter:	"Somewhere after the recital?"
Simpson:	"Somewhere when I was rushing to get out of my house."
Vannatter:	"Ok, after the recital."
Simpson:	"Yeah."[2]

Simpson then proceeds to tell the detectives why he has "a bunch of guns, guns all over the place"[3] because of an apparent attempted car jacking he experienced the previous month. The detectives then asked Simpson if anyone was threatening Nicole. They also inquire about Simpson's relationship with Nicole and Simpson's willingness to take a polygraph. Simpson says he will talk to his attorney about that.

Lange:	"Understand, the reason we're talking to you is because you're the ex-husband."
Simpson:	"I know, I'm the number one target, and now you tell me I've got blood all over the place."
Lange:	"Well, there's blood at your house in the driveway, and we've got a search warrant, and we're going to go get the blood. We found some in your house. Is that your blood that's there?"
Simpson:	"If it's dripped, it's what I dripped running around trying to leave."
Lange:	"Last night?"
Simpson:	"Yeah, and I wasn't aware that it was.....I was aware that I.....You know, I was trying to get out of the house. I didn't even pay any attention to it, I saw it when I was in the kitchen, and I grabbed a napkin or something, and that was it. I didn't think about it after that."
Vannatter:	"That was last night after you got home from the recital, when you were rushing?"
Simpson:	"That was last night when I was.....I don't know what I was. I was in the car getting my junk out of the car. I was in the house throwing hangers and stuff in my suitcase. I was doing my little crazy

what I do.....I mean, I do it everywhere. Anybody who has ever picked me up says that O.J. Simpson's a whirlwind, he's running, he's grabbing things, and that's what I was doing."[4]

Detective Lang then questions Simpson about the last time he saw Nicole. Detective Vannatter tries to locate the photographer to take a picture of the cut on Simpson's hand. The interview then ends when Simpson is taken out of the room to be photographed.

Simpson tells the detectives he cut his hand on the night of the murders some time after the recital while he was at home preparing to go to Chicago. He does not remember how he received the cut. "I don't know." "Somewhere when I was rushing to get out of my house." He wants us to believe he obtained the cut while he was "throwing hangers and stuff in my suitcase" or while he was "getting my junk out of the car." He remembers bleeding, "I knew I was bleeding, but it was no big deal. I bleed all the time." The bottom line is he never tells the detectives specifically when or how he cut his hand. He only alludes to possibilities. Now use your common sense. He is bleeding enough to drip blood in his car, on his driveway and in his house. Yet he doesn't remember how he obtained the cut. He doesn't remember feeling a little pain on his knuckle as he was grabbing some hangers. He doesn't remember that scratching sensation on his hand as he was removing stuff from his car. Possible but not probable.

When detective Vannatter asked Simpson how he injured his hand, Simpson responded, "I don't know. The first time, when I was in Chicago and all, but at the house I was just running around." Simpson tells the detectives the "first time" he cut his hand was "when I was in Chicago..." Based on his answer, he was then asked "How did you do it in Chicago?" After he tells them about the broken glass, he is then asked "Is that how you cut it?" Simpson then changes his story. "Mmm, it was cut before, but I think I just opened it again, I'm not sure." Here Simpson is being deceptive. He would like for everyone to think he cut his hand in Chicago well after the murders. However, he knows he cut his hand before he left for Chicago. He knows he was dripping blood at his house, "I recall bleeding at my house..." So he hesitates before answering the question, "Mmm." He is thinking about how he will answer the question. Then he tells us he did cut his hand while he was in California.

Towards the middle of the interview, detective Vannatter tells Simpson, "O.J., we've got sort of a problem." This is an interviewing mistake made by the detective. By telling Simpson there is a problem, he is alerting Simpson. In essence he is telling Simpson that what we are about to discuss is something very serious. This causes Simpson to raise his guard and concentrate as to how he will answer the questions. Simpson is told they have found blood in his car and at his house. Simpson volunteers to take a blood test.

> Lange: "Well, we'd like to do that. We've got, of course, the cut on your finger that you aren't real clear on. Do you recall having the cut on your finger the last time you were at Nicole's house?"
> Simpson: "A week ago?"
> Lange: "Yeah."
> Simpson: "No. It was last night."[5]

The question asked by detective Lang is a good question. Simpson has not explained how he received the cut on his hand. Suspicions are he may have cut himself while committing these murders. If that is the case, then he would have a cut on his finger the last time he was at Nicole's house. However, the detectives let Simpson get away with not answering the question. Simpson qualifies the question by asking, "A week ago?" Lang tells him "Yeah." Simpson is then able to honestly answer the question with a "No." Detective Lange should have responded by saying, "The last time you were at Nicole's house." This would have forced Simpson to answer his original question.

We also see that Simpson answered the question with a question. This tells us that the question concerning the cut on his finger is a sensitive question. The question asked of Simpson is a straight forward question. "Do you recall having the cut on your finger the last time you were at Nicole's house?" It doesn't matter if it was two days ago, a week ago or a month ago. The detective just wanted to know the last time he was at her house did he have a cut on his finger. So why does Simpson answer the question with a question? Some would say he is asking for clarification. What needs to be clarified? "Do you recall having the cut on your finger the last time you were at Nicole's house?" Simpson knows the answer to that question is "yes" because he sustained the injury while committing the murders. He doesn't want to admit to that and he doesn't want to lie. So he leads the detectives away from the night of the murder by referencing the next to the last time he was at Nicole's house.

Near the end of the interview we find the following exchanges:

Lange: "Well, there's blood at your house in the driveway, and we've got a search warrant, and we're going to go get the blood. We found some in your house. Is that your blood that's there?"
Simpson: "If it's dripped, it's what I dripped running around trying to leave."[6]

The question is "Is that your blood that's there?" Simpson doesn't answer the question. Instead he gives an explanation. This indicates there is something he doesn't want the detectives to know. He has already told them he cut his finger and was bleeding. So why not tell them "It is probably my blood from the cut on my finger." If he did commit these murders and had Nicole's and Ron's blood on him, this would still be a truthful answer, "....it's what I dripped running around trying to leave."

Vannatter: "That was last night after you got home from the recital, when you were rushing?"
Simpson: "That was last night when I was....I don't know what I was. I was in the car getting my junk out of the car. I was in the house throwing hangers and stuff in my suitcase. I was doing my little crazy what I do....I mean, I do it everywhere. Anybody who has ever picked me up says that OJ. Simpson's a whirlwind, he's running, he's grabbing things, and that's what I was doing."[7]

Simpson's first two sentences are very interesting. "That was last night when I was....I don't know what I was." It sounds like these two sentences are part of his over all answer that he unknowingly cut his finger while rushing around the house preparing for his trip to Chicago. If that is true, then why didn't he say "That was last night when I was rushing."? All he had to do was confirm what they were asking. Instead he says, "That was last night when I was....." Let's finish the sentence for him. "That was last night when I was *rushing around*." or "That was last night when I was *killing Nicole*." He does it again, "I don't know what I was." Let's finish the sentence for him. "I don't know what I was *doing*." This could be in reference to rushing around or to killing Nicole and Ron. If he did not commit these murders and had nothing to do with these murders, then Simpson should be giving straight forward answers. However, because he is speaking in incomplete sentences, it shows us he is hesitating and thinking. He knows what the truth is but he doesn't want to tell it. Therefore, he stumbles when answering the question.

There is one other interesting question and answer.

Vannatter: "Is Nicole seeing anybody else that you ...."
Simpson: "I have no idea. I really have absolutely no idea. I don't ask her. I don't know. Her and her girlfriends, they go out, you know, they've got some things going on right now with her girlfriends, so I'm assuming something's happening because one of the girlfriends is having a big problem with her husband because she's always saying she's with Nicole until three or four in the morning. She's not. You know, Nicole tells me she leaves her at 1:30 or 2 or 2:30, and the girl doesn't get home until 5, and she only lives a few blocks away."[8]

Simpson doesn't allow Vannatter to finish his question. The detective was probably going to ask, "Is Nicole seeing anybody else that you *know of*?" By cutting off the detective, this shows us Simpson was eager to answer this question. Why was he eager to answer the question? Because Simpson knew this could be used against him as a possible motive for the murders. If Nicole was seeing someone else and Simpson became jealous, this could be a crime of passion. Therefore, he quickly gives an answer not allowing the question to be completely asked. His answer was "I have no idea. I really have absolutely no idea. I don't ask her. I don't know." Four times Simpson tells the detectives he doesn't know if Nicole is seeing anybody. Why four times? Because he wants his answer to be convincing. I am sure some of Nicole's friends were asked this question. Those that didn't know if she was seeing someone probably answered, "I don't know," or "I have no idea." Simpson's repetitive answer tells us this is a very sensitive question for him.

In chapter five, we saw that Simpson confessed to this murder when he spoke with Detective Tom Lange on the cell phone during the slow speed Bronco chase. Simpson told Detective Lange that he was worthy of death when he said, "I'm the only one that deserves it."[9] During his conversation with the detective, Simpson also stated, "All I did was love Nicole. That's all I did was love her."[10] Simpson tells us twice that he did something. That something is loving Nicole. Love can be expressed in many ways such as sending a card and flowers. However, it can also be expressed in what may be viewed as a not so loving way. In a parent/child relationship, discipline is done out of love, not out of anger. Although at the time the child may disagree. Simpson states he loved Nicole but he doesn't tell us what he did to express that love.

Keep in mind the context in which Simpson makes this statement. Simpson is considering committing suicide. Lang tells him to throw the gun out the window and no one will get hurt. Simpson says he is the only one that deserves it. Lang tells him he doesn't deserve it and not to do this. Simpson then says, "All I did was love Nicole. That's all I did was love her." What is the link between Simpson contemplating suicide and what he did to love Nicole? If he killed Nicole out of love or jealousy, then we can see why he wouldn't want to live when he realized what he had done.

The Bronco chase ended safely at Simpson's home. Simpson was then taken into custody. On the same day, a letter Simpson had written just prior to the Bronco chase was found. It read:

"To whom it may concern:
First, everyone understand I~~had~~ nothing to do with Nicole's murder. I loved her, always have and always will. If we had a problem, it's because I loved her so much. Recently, we came to the understanding that for now we were not right for each other, at least for now. Despite our love we were different and

that's why we mutually agreed to go our separate ways. It was tough splitting for a second time, but we both knew it was for the best. Inside I had no doubt that in the future, we would be close friends or more. Unlike what has been in the press, Nicole and I had a great relationship for most of our lives together. Like all long-term relationships, we had a few downs and ups. I took the heat New Year's 1989 because that's what I was suppose to do. I did not plead no contest for any other reason but to protect our privacy and was advised it would end the press hype. I don't want to belabor knocking the press, but I can't believe what is being said. Most of it is totally made up. I know you have a job to do, but as a last wish, please, please, please, leave my children in peace. Their lives will be tough enough. I want to send my love and thanks to all my friends. I'm sorry I can't name every one of you, especially A.C. man, thanks for being in my life. The support and friendship I received from so many: Wayne Hughes, Lewis Markes, Frank Olson, Mark Packer, Bender, Bobby Kardashian. I wish we had spent more time together in recent years. My golfing buddies, Hoss, Alan Austin, Mike, Craig, Bender, Wyler, Sandy, Jay, Donnie, thanks for the fun. All my teammates over the years, Regie, you were the soul of my pro career. Ahmad, I never stopped being proud of you. Marcus, you've got a great lady in Catherine, don't mess it up. Bobby Chandler, thanks for always being there. Skip and Kathy, I love you guys, without you I never would have made it through thus far. Marguerite, thanks for the early years. We had some fun. Paula, what can I say? You are special. I'm sorry we're not going to have our chance. God brought you to me I now see. As I leave you'll be in my thoughts. I think of my life and feel I've done most of the right things. What ever the outcome, people will look back and point. I can't take that. I can't subject my children to that. This way they can move on and go on with their lives. Please, if I've done anything worthwhile in my life. Let my kids live in peace from you (press). I've had a good life. I'm proud of how I lived. My mama taught me to do unto other. I treated people the way I wanted to be treated. I've always tried to be up and helpful so why is this happening? I'm sorry for the Goldman family. I know how much it hurts. Nicole and I had a good life together. All this press talk about a rocky relationship was no more than what every long-term relationship experiences. All her friends will confirm that I have been totally loving and understanding of what she's been going through. At times I have felt like a battered husband or boyfriend but I loved her, make that clear to everyone. And I would take whatever it took to make it work. Don't feel sorry for me. I've had a great life, great friends. Please think of the real O.J. and not this lost person. Thanks for making my life special. I hope I helped yours. Peace and love, O.J."[11]

As I have already mentioned in chapter twelve, the most obviously thing in Simpson letter was the fact that he crossed out the words "I had." Simpson could not bring himself to say he had nothing to do with Nicole's murder.

The next thing we see in Simpson's letter is his statement, "Unlike what has been in the press, Nicole and I had a great relationship for most of our lives together. Like all long-term relationships, we had a few downs and ups." Remember that order is important. Most people would say "ups and downs" because we like to think we have more ups in our lives than we do downs. Simpson tries to deny they had a rocky relationship by stating "Unlike what has been in the press........Nicole and I had a great relationship." However, his words betray him when states they had a few "downs and ups." This tells us they had a lot more downs than they did ups. This is what the 911 calls and the pictures of Nicole's bruised face would indicate.

Simpson goes on to say, "I don't want to belabor knocking the press, but I can't believe what is being said. Most of it is totally made up." The key word here is "most." Simpson tells us that some of what the press has reported is true. He doesn't tell us what they have made up and what is true. We see the same thing when he states, "I think of my life and feel I've done most of the right things." Simpson clearly tells us he has done things in his life that were not right, but he does not share with us what they were.

Simpson then states, "I'm sorry for the Goldman family. I know how much it hurts." Simpson was a suspect in the death of Nicole Brown Simpson and Ronald Goldman. Simpson only attempted to deny killing Nicole, but he makes no denial in the death of Ron Goldman. He only feels sorry for them. We cannot believe he did not kill Ron Goldman if he does not deny it.

Towards the end of his letter Simpson makes another interesting statement: "At times I have felt like a battered husband or boyfriend but I loved her, make that clear to everyone. And I would take whatever it took to make it work." Simpson tells us he "would take whatever it took to make it work." He is not referring to things he may possibly do, but he is referring to things he has done "to make it work." Does this include killing Nicole so she could not be with another man? Remember in his conversation with detective Tom Lange during the Bronco chase Simpson stated, "All I did was love Nicole. That's all I did was love her." Faye Resnick was a good friend of Nicole Simpson. In her book, *Nicole Brown Simpson, The Private Diary of a Life Interrupted*, Resnick writes that after the murders she met with O.J. Simpson. When she asked him what happened, Simpson responded, "Girl....you out of all of them know that I loved her too much."[12]

One of the last things Simpson tells us is to "Please think of the real O.J. and not this lost person." The phrase "the real O.J." indicates there is another O.J. he doesn't want people to remember. Simpson refers to this other O.J. as a lost person. Is this lost O.J. capable of committing murder?

In 1995, Simpson wrote a book entitled *I Want To Tell You*. The book contains letters that people had written to Simpson while he was in jail. Simpson responds to some of these letters. Most of the book is Simpson sharing his thoughts about his predicament. Simpson starts out with a dedication. "This book is dedicated to all the people who brought love into my life. And a special thanks to Burt, who was the inspiration for this book."[13] Put yourself in Simpson's shoes. Who would you dedicate this book to? You would think he would dedicate it to the memory of Nicole or to his kids. Technically, they are included in the group of "people who brought love into my life." However, you would think he would make a direct reference to them. I do not know who Burt is. It may be a nickname for Nicole, but this seems unlikely since he is thanking Burt. Apparently Burt is still alive.

Simpson begins chapter one with the following statement:

"I have been accused of the crime of murder, a double murder. The State of California charged me on June 17, 1994, with the deaths of my former wife Nicole Brown Simpson and Ronald

Goldman, and arrested me later that same day. Since the day of my arrest I have had to defend myself not only in court but in the eyes of the public and the news media. In this book, I am speaking publicly for the first time since my arrest for two reasons. First and foremost, I want to respond to the more than 300,000 people who wrote to me....The second reason is financial."[14]

If you were arrested and charged with two murders that you did not commit, what would be your reasons for writing a book? Thanking people for their support and raising money for a defense fund are very good reasons. However, the number one reason why I would be writing a book is to let people know I DIDN'T DO IT. For Simpson, that is not the reason for writing this book.

"I want to state unequivocally that I did not commit these horrible crimes. I loved Nicole, I could never do such a thing. I don't think I even know anyone who's capable of doing such things. I can't think of anybody I've ever known who could do something this terrible. I have tried all of my life to be a good citizen."[15]

This sounds like a good denial. However, there are several problems with his statement. Basically, Simpson is telling us he is innocent because he would never do this. Everybody is capable of doing things they thought they would never do. Simpson then gives us a lot of fluff. He tells us he doesn't know of anyone "who could do something this terrible." What does that have to do with his guilt or innocence? Then he tells us he has "tried" to be a good citizen all of his life. This means he hasn't been a good citizen throughout his life. He makes this statement in close proximity to his denial. It is possible that his crime of murder falls into the time when he wasn't a good citizen.

The biggest problem with this denial has to do with what immediately preceded Simpson's statement. In keeping with the book's format, Simpson printed two letters from two individuals. The first writer stated, "Please say you didn't kill that woman like that."[16] The second writer called Simpson a coward and stated, "Beating up on women and killing two unarmed people in your selfish rage."[17] Both people used the word "kill" in their letter to Simpson. In responding to their letters, Simpson has the perfect opportunity to say, "I did not kill Nicole and Ronald Goldman," but he chooses not do so. In fact he never once says in his book, "I did not kill Nicole." He shies away from using the word "kill." This is probably because the word "kill" basically has one meaning, "to put an end to."[18] Whether you are killing a person, killing a car engine, killing a light or killing time, it all means the same thing. If Simpson used the word "kill," he wouldn't be able to play the word game or use his own interpretation. Therefore, he makes statements like the following:

> "I had nothing to do with his death."[19]
> "The prosecution is trying to use DNA to convict me, but I'm innocent."[20]
> "I did not commit these murders."[21]
> "Now I sit in my jail cell unjustly accused of something I did not do."[22]

All of these statements only sound like Simpson is saying he didn't kill anyone. Simpson has his own interpretation of what these statements mean. For example, if you killed someone in what you believed was self defense, then you can honestly state you did not commit a murder. If Simpson did not kill his ex-wife and Ronald Goldman, he would specifically state that.

> "I can't even keep pictures of my family in my cell. It's not because I'm not allowed to. I am. I just can't have a picture of my younger kids, Sydney and Justin, because it is so — it's all so debilitating for me when I see a picture of them. I can't control my emotions. I cry. I pray for my kids every morning, every night. I can't have a picture of their mother either. If you cry every day in here, you'll never survive."[23]

Simpson tells us that when he sees a picture of his younger kids, it becomes "so debilitating" for him. "I can't control my emotions. I cry." He says the same thing about having a picture of Nicole in his cell. This doesn't makes sense if you are an innocent person. You would want to have pictures of your kids with you. They would be your motivation for surviving while incarcerated. Your goal would be that once you get out of jail you will be with your children again. However, if you murdered your children's mother, then it would be hard to look at a picture of them. This is exactly what Simpson tells us earlier in his book. "I could never kill anyone, especially Nicole. How could I deprive my kids of a mother. How could I look them in the eyes every day. I couldn't do that."[24] Simpson can have pictures of his two children from a previous marriage in his cell, but he cannot look at pictures of Nicole's kids because that would essentially be looking "them in the eyes every day."

> "My whole life has been one of 'I paid the price.' I mean there is one thing you can say about O.J.: O.J. wasn't given anything. I worked hard for everything I got. I paid the price for everything, and I owned up to everything, even when I thought I was getting the short end of the stick, whether it was my personal life or my football career. But I ask myself over and over: If I'm innocent, why should I pay any price?"[25]

Focus on the last sentence in this statement. "But I ask myself over and over: If I'm innocent, why should I pay any price?" Even though he is asking himself a question, Simpson could have declared his innocence here. If Simpson was innocent, he would have said, "But I ask myself over and over: *I'm innocent*, why should I pay any price?" Instead, he says, "If I'm innocent." This means he may be or may not be innocent. An innocent person would declare even to himself that he is not guilty.

Simpson wrote this book to raise money for his defense fund, and to respond to some of the letters he had received. What is missing in his book is a clear denial. Simpson does not tell us, "I did not kill Nicole or Ronald Goldman." What Simpson did talk about is his guilt concerning these murders.

On January 24, 1996, Simpson was interviewed by Ed Gordon on the Black Entertainment Television network. This was his first full televison interview since his acquittal on the murder charges. Three times during the interview Simpson stated he did not commit the murders. The first time was at the beginning of the interview.

> Gordon: "Let's go over that. Did you, indeed, commit those murders?"
>
> Simpson: "<u>No, I did not commit those murders. I couldn't kill anyone</u>. And I don't know of anyone that was

involved. Anything that I might say along those lines would be pure speculation."²⁶

The next two times Simpson denied committing these murders was at the very end of the interview.

Gordon: "I've got about two minutes left, Mr. Simpson. As best you can, tell those who look at this interview, look at you, look at your story with a skeptical eye, with a jaundiced eye, something that you feel might help them along in bringing them back to at least allowing you, as you say, as someone who's been through this system, the grace that you should have, in your words, because you were found innocent."

Simpson: "Well, I - this country's been a great country for 200 years because we have laws in this country, and like them or not, people have abided by those laws. There've been decisions made - Mike Tyson, a decision I didn't necessarily agree with, but he was convicted, he served his time. Many people in America say he's a racist - I mean, a - a rapist. I was accused of a crime. I was, I feel, vindicated in the court of law. I shouldn't be called anything but O.J. Simpson at this time. I didn't kill anybody; I could not kill anybody. Nicole Brown Simpson was the mother of my kids. She was a great mother. It hurts me today to know that my kids will not know her as a mother. I certainly would not have left my kids there to see that side - that - that horrible, gruesome scene that was outside her house. I love my kids. I loved Nicole. I could not have killed anyone, and I did not kill anyone. I'm an American, and I just want to be treated like an American. I want people to treat me the way I treated all of you. And for the last 20 years, I've met thousands - hundreds of thousands of people, and I treated you - what my mother always taught me, 'Do unto others' - I treated you like I wanted to be treated, and that's the only thing I'm asking now. If you don't like

	me, leave me alone. I'm not bothering you. Let me raise my family and give me an opportunity to earn a living and support my family and friends...."
Gordon:	"All right."
Simpson:	"....as best I can."[27]

Every time Simpson tells us he did not commit these murders he also tells us he is not capable of committing this crime. "I didn't kill anybody; I could not kill anybody." He is qualifying his denial. Simpson's thinking is that since it is impossible for him to commit murder, he could not have killed these two people. He is trying to convince us he didn't do it. This is not as strong of a denial as simply saying "I did not kill anyone."

Two years after the BET interview, Simpson would be interviewed by Chris Myers on ESPN's *UpClose* program.

Myers:	"Are you capable of killing somebody?"
Simpson:	"You know I would say, actually I would say no, even though I'm sure if someone was presenting some imminent danger to my kids or something I'm sure everybody would be capable."[28]

Simpson answers the question with a "no" but then he makes an exception talking about if his kids were in danger. Therefore, he is not telling us he is not capable of killing someone. Simpson doesn't want to say "I am capable of killing someone." So he says, "I'm sure everybody would be capable" of killing somebody under certain circumstances. Everybody includes Simpson.

Myers:	"Would you for Nicole?"
Simpson:	"If I thought someone was going to hurt her. You protect the people you love....But I think that most people to protect their home and their family would do that. I caught a guy in my house one night, and I have asked myself this question: My kids weren't there, but here's a guy in my house....You wonder, if my kids were there and I would have walked into my daughter's room and this guy would have come upstairs and was in my

daughter's room, I don't know what I would have been capable of doing."[29]

Here Simpson tells us he is capable of killing someone if he had to defend Nicole, "If I thought someone was going to hurt her." Simpson may even kill in order to protect his kids, "I don't know what I would have been capable of doing."

When we look back at Simpson's interview on the BET program, three times he stated he did not kill anyone. These denials were linked to his claim he couldn't kill anyone. Two years later in the ESPN interview, we see he is capable of killing. Simpson lied in the BET interview when he said, "I couldn't kill anyone." "I could not kill anybody." "I could not have killed anyone."[30] Therefore, we cannot believe him when he says he did not commit these murders.

Simpson made one other interesting statement in the BET interview. In an effort to prove his innocence he stated, "I certainly would not have left my kids there to see that side - that - that horrible, gruesome scene that was outside her house."[31] Simpson starts out saying he did not want his kids, "to see that side." It is possible he was about to say he didn't want his kids "to see that side *of me*." Knowing this would be a damning statement, he then changed from "side" to "outside."

Simpson's football and movie career had made him a worldwide celebrity. Because his criminal trial had been televised, the whole world watched as the drama unfolded. After the trial, there was still a high interest in Simpson. On May 13, 1997, Simpson participated in a television interview which took place in Great Britain. The interview was conducted by Richard Madeley and Judy Finnigan on Granada TV. Let's examine some excerpts from this interview.

> Finnigan: "Now, let's talk about some of the other reasons, the evidential reasons, why some people find it hard to get their heads around the fact that you are innocent. What about this business of the blood, your blood, which was found not only at the murder scene site but also in the grounds and garden of your own house?"

Simpson: "Well, I don't find it unusual if something was found around my own home. I am very suspect as to whose blood that was. I think a lot of people, the press overlooked that fact that when Mazzola, who collected the blood, after they lied and said Fung had collected it, when she collected the blood at the Bundy scene where the murders were taken, she testified she processed that blood and she put her initials on each one of the bindles. They laid that blood out for to dry, which normally takes two to three hours to dry, they laid it out for roughly eight or nine hours. Later on when those blood drops went to the various labs - Cellmark and the Justice Department - to be tested, Mazzola's initials were no longer on the bindles. Now, the prosecution then brought her back and tried to convince her that maybe she didn't put her initial on the bindle, when she had testified twice under oath -"

Madeley: "Are you saying that ...."

Simpson: "So what I am saying is that I don't believe that those were the same blood drops that were sent to Cellmark and the Justice Department."

Madeley: "Are you saying that the police planted them?"

Simpson: "I don't know who did what. I don't know what they did. I am making no accusation ...."

Finnigan: "Well, isn't that the obvious implication ...."

Simpson: "All I know is that nobody has explained that to us, and nobody explained why those bindles have wet transfers. Barry Scheck did an excellent job on that."

Finnigan: "But the implication is, if you're right and the LAPD Department were wrong, it's either a gigantic cock-up or it's frankly, it's a frame up, somebody's framed you, and if so, why don't you sue?"

Simpson: "You know, once again, I've got to get through this, a whole lot of people are going to be sued when I have finished with this. You know, I have a, especially against some of the tabloids. I mean when you look at this case, the only people we

	know who lied, on the stand, under oath, we know for a fact Vannatter lied. Judge Ito said he had a 'reckless disregard for the truth.' We know for a fact Fund lied, he was caught right on the stand lying."
Madeley:	"But if you're so ...."
Simpson:	"We know Furhman lied."
Madeley:	"Yes, indeed, and Furhman was shown to be a liar, but ...."
Simpson:	"But the only liars were these people who were a part of this first day on the scene and the collection of the evidence. Those are the people we know lied on the stand. My question is, why?"[32]

Simpson is suggesting that the blood evidence was planted to make him look like the killer. The interviewers even brought this to his attention. "Well, isn't that the obvious implication?" This was part of his defense strategy which helped him win an acquittal. By showing that the LAPD may have mishandled the blood evidence, this created a reasonable doubt in the minds of the jurors. The problem is Simpson only suggests this. He does not say, "Yes, I believe I was set up." Why doesn't he tell us he was framed? What would your response be? You know you did not commit these murders. You were not wearing any gloves that night. You know you were not at Nicole's house on the night of the murders. There is no way you could have left your blood at Nicole's residence. The only way your blood could show up there is if someone planted it. Therefore, you would most certainly tell everyone that you were framed. There is no other explanation in your mind. Simpson will not say that. He doesn't tell us he will sue the LAPD. All he said was "a whole lot of people are going to be sued." Years after his acquittal, I haven't seen where he has sued anyone. Simpson only alludes to being framed because he knows he committed these murders.

Finnigan:	"Do you regard yourself as a violent man?"
Simpson:	"The press wrote time and time again that I was a violent person. That is the only incident of anything physical that happened between Nicole and I. They investigated me - I was the most

> thoroughly investigated person ever. They spoke to every person I have ever been involved with and not one person has ever said that they ever saw me become violent or physical. One person ...."

Madeley: "Briefly."
Simpson: "....I have been in some relationships."[33]

Simpson does not answer the question. Therefore, he is withholding information. He only alludes to the possibility he is not a violent man. He blames the press for the rumors he may be violent. He says his friends have never seen him become violent. What Simpson himself does not tell us is that he is not a violent man. Therefore, we cannot believe Simpson is not violent since he did not tell us that.

After his acquittal in the criminal trial, the families of Nicole Brown Simpson and Ronald Goldman filed a civil suit against O.J. Simpson. The odds of proving Simpson guilty in a civil trial were slightly greater than that of a criminal trial. In a civil case, the jury only needs to find one guilty by a preponderance of the evidence. In a criminal case, they must reach that same decision beyond a reasonable doubt. On October 23, 1996, the jury began to hear the civil case. Evidence not available at the criminal trial was introduced at this trail. Photos of Simpson wearing Bruno Magli shoes, the same kind of shoe prints found at the murder scene, were entered into evidence. Unlike his criminal trial, this time Simpson took the stand in an effort to defend himself.

Let's take a look at some excerpts from Simpson's testimony during the trial. The plaintiffs attorney was Daniel Petrocelli. On November 22, 1996, he questions Simpson about his involvement in the murders.

Petrocelli: "And the reason why you didn't get in the Bronco is because you used that Bronco to go to Nicole's condominium that evening, after you came back from McDonald's, true?"
Simpson: "That's not true."
Petrocelli: "You had gloves; you had a hat; you were wearing a dark sweat outfit, and you had a knife.

	And you went to Nicole Brown's condominium at 875 South Bundy, did you not, sir?"
Simpson:	"That's absolutely not true."
Petrocelli:	"And you confronted Nicole Brown Simpson and you killed her, didn't you?"
Simpson:	"That is absolutely not true."
Petrocelli:	"And you killed Ronald Goldman, sir, did you or did you not?"
Simpson:	"That's absolutely not true."[34]

Petrocelli could have done a better job here by asking straight forward questions like, "Did you kill Nicole Brown Simpson?" In the first question he states that Simpson drove to Nicole's in his Bronco after returning from McDonald's. Petrocelli then asks if this is true. Simpson does answer the question by saying, "That's not true." However, the next three questions Simpson does not answer the question. He is asked, "did you not, sir?" "didn't you?" and "did you or did you not?" All three times Simpson answers saying, "That's absolutely not true." Unless you are asked if something is true, saying that something is not true is not answering the question. It is only verifying a statement. For example, if the statement is, "You took the cookie," a good response would be, "That is not true." You are verifying the validity of the statement. However, if it is in the form of a question, "You took the cookie, didn't you?" the only proper answers are "yes" or "no." Saying "That is not true" is not answering the question but verifying the question. Questions cannot be verified as to truth for they are seekers of truth. His refusal to answer the question is easier seen in the question concerning Ronald Goldman's death. Here Simpson is asked both the positive and the negative, "Did you or did you not?" He should have answered, "I did not" but instead he said, "That's absolutely not true." What is not true? It is not true that he did not kill Ronald Goldman? Simpson does not tell us he did not kill Nicole Brown Simpson or Ronald Goldman.

On February 4, 1997, the jury reached it's unanimous verdict. They found Simpson liable for the killings of Nicole Brown Simpson and Ronald Goldman. The jury awarded the Goldman family $8.5 million in compensatory damages. The Brown family did not seek the same type of damages. Because the jury found that Simpson had acted with malice and oppression, they would also have to decide how much in punitive damages should be awarded. On February 10, 1997, the jury agreed upon $25 million in punitive damages splitting it between the estates of Nicole Brown Simpson and Ronald Goldman. The total monetary award was $33.5 million.

On January 15, 1998, Simpson appeared for a live interview on ESPN's *UpClose* program. The question-and-answer format was hosted by Chris Myers. I have already mentioned Simpson's answer to the questions "Are you capable of killing someone?" and "Would you kill for Nicole?" Chris Myers further probed this area asking Simpson the following questions:

Myers: "But love could cause you to go into rage to kill?"
Simpson: "I don't think so. I don't believe so at all."[35]

Simpson waivers on his answer. He doesn't answer the question with a firm "No." All he tells us is he doesn't "think" or "believe" he would do such a thing. Since he doesn't tell us he wouldn't do it, he leaves open the possibility he could go into a rage and kill.

Myers: "Are you capable of going into a rage and not remembering exactly what you did?"
Simpson: "I don't believe so, no."[36]

Simpson answers the question with a "no." However, by adding the phrase "I don't believe so" he is not committing to his "no" answer. Since he only believes he would not go into a rage that he wouldn't remember, we cannot assume this would not happen to him.

Myers: "Have you ever done that?"
Simpson: "No. I mean I have been in a rage, and when it was over you kind of regret some of the things you might have said, but I don't feel that I've ever in my life done something that, when it was over, I wasn't aware of what I did."[37]

Again Simpson answers the question with a "no." However, as soon as he said "I mean" he invalidates the "no" answer. "No" no longer means "no" because he is about to tell us what "no" means. He then tells us he doesn't "feel" he could have done something and not remember it. Feeling is not the same as saying "I have never done that." Simpson leaves open the possibility he could go into a rage and do something he later would not remember.

In the February 1998 issue of *Esquire* magazine, Simpson is quoted in an article as saying, "Let's say I committed this crime, even if I did do this, it would have to have been because I loved her very much, right?"[38] Later on in another interview, Simpson would explain this comment by saying this was only a hypothetical question. However, many people including myself believe this is a form of admission. Sometimes people will tell the truth by joking about it. No one takes them seriously because it is only a joke. This allows them to get it off their chest without suffering any consequences. The same thing applies here. Simpson doesn't want us to believe he was admitting to this crime because he was only speaking hypothetically.

Simpson further explained what he meant by this hypothetical question.

> "And we get into an evidence thing. And I say, 'Well what was the motive of this crime?'.....Then someone said, 'Well love, obsessive love.' And I say, 'OK, let's see, if I killed her, you say it's because of love, because I loved her right? Why would I have to kill a person who is begging me to move back in with me, who has written me letters that you all saw publicly, "I'll do anything for you." "I'll move anywhere with you." "I'll go anywhere, I just want to wake up and go to sleep with you." It makes no sense.'"[39]

Simpson tries to bring a little rationality into the possible motive he killed Nicole out of obsessive love for her. He tells us this doesn't make any sense. Most people would probably agree with that analysis. Why would you kill someone whom you love? However, we must remember that Simpson in his "hypothetical" question in *Esquire* magazine stated, "....if I did do this, it would have to have been because I loved her very much...."

Having been acquitted in his criminal trial, O.J. Simpson is a free man. Despite the verdict, many people believe he did commit these murders. Their beliefs are legitimate. In his letter and book, Simpson never says, "I did not kill Nicole" or "I did not kill Ronald Goldman." During his various interviews, there were questions he did not answer which tells us he is withholding some information. Simpson told us that in protecting his family, he would be capable of killing. He also told us it is possible for him to go "bonkers" and do something he doesn't remember. The most convincing evidence though that he did commit these murders is his own confessions. In reference to these murders, he told us he was the only person who deserved to die. He made reference to his guiltiness in these killings. The theme Simpson has portrayed throughout the years since these murders is his obsessive love for Nicole. We can with certainty conclude, that O.J. Simpson did kill Nicole Brown Simpson and Ronald Goldman. The motive behind the killings is as Simpson hypothetically stated, "because I loved her very much."

Chapter 20

Sexual Molestation Allegations Against Michael Jackson

Known as the "King of Pop," Michael Jackson has lived his entire life in front of an audience. At the age of five, he began singing with his brothers performing on stage before millions of people. Years later, Jackson would continue his rise to fame with a solo career that has made him one of the biggest selling artists of all time. Over the years, Jackson has been surrounded by controversies including his eccentric behavior and the gradual lightening of his skin. In 1993, Jackson found himself in another controversy which had serious implications. A 13-year-old boy accused Jackson of sexual molestation.

Jackson had befriended the boy in 1992. Soon the boy became a regular guest at Jackson's Neverland ranch in Santa Ynez, California. Jackson gave the boy gifts and paid for several vacation trips around the world. In 1993, the boy started to spend the night at Jackson's residence. This was not unusual as Jackson would often have children sleep over at his Neverland ranch. According to the allegations, Jackson had kissed and fondled the boy while they were alone in bed. Allegedly, this repeatedly took place during a four-month period.

At the suggestion of the boy's father, a civil lawsuit was filed in 1993. Jackson denied the accusations. He continued to tour and make public appearances. The boy's father talked to the Jackson camp about a financial settlement while the police continued their investigation. On January 25, 1994, Michael Jackson settled the civil lawsuit paying an undisclosed amount to his accuser. Many believe that he paid between 15 and 20 million dollars. After receiving the settlement, the boy refused to testify in any criminal matters. Therefore, the prosecution was not able to pursue a criminal case.

Jackson's attorneys insisted that the settlement was not an admission of guilt. However, many believed an innocent person would not pay his accuser a large sum of money. Jackson is very well known for his generosity and work with children. It was usual for him to have children staying at his Neverland ranch. Others questioned why a 35-year-old man would invite children over to his house for a sleep over. The controversy continued. Did Michael Jackson sexually molest a 12-year-old boy, or were his motives and actions completely innocent? Only Jackson and the boy know for sure. Because of his age and primarily the settlement, the boy isn't talking. However, Jackson did release a statement and granted an interview concerning the allegations. Let's look at Jackson's statement to see what he is telling us.

On December 22, 1993, Jackson gave the following videotaped statement from his Neverland ranch via a satellite hook up:

"I am doing well and I am strong. As you may already know, after my tour ended I remained out of the country undergoing treatment for a dependancy on pain medication. This medicine was initially prescribed to soothe the excruciating pain that I was suffering after recent reconstructive surgery on my scalp. There have been many disgusting statements made recently concerning allegations of improper conduct on my part. These statements about me are totally false. As I have maintained from the very beginning, I am hoping for a speedy end to this horrifying experience to which I have been subjected. I shall not in this statement respond to all the false allegations being made against me since my lawyers have advised me that this is not the proper forum in which to do that. I will say I am particularly upset by the handling of this matter by the incredible, terrible mass media. At every opportunity, the media has dissected and manipulated these allegations to reach their own conclusion. I ask all of you to wait to hear the truth before you label or condemn me. Don't treat me like a criminal because I am innocent. I have been forced to submit to a dehumanizing and humiliating examination by the Santa Barbara County Sheriff's department and the Los Angeles Police Department earlier this week. They served a search warrant on me which allowed them to view and photograph my body, including my penis, my buttocks, my lower torso, thighs and any other areas that they wanted. They were supposedly looking for any discoloration, spotting or other evidence of a skin color disorder called vitiligo which I have previously spoken about. The warrant also directed me to cooperate in any examination of my body by their physician to determine the condition of my skin, including whether I have vitiligo or any other skin disorder. The warrant further stated that I had no right to refuse the examination or photographs and if I failed to cooperate with them they would introduce that refusal at any trial as an indication of my guilt. It was the most humiliating ordeal of my life, one that no person should ever have to suffer. And even after experiencing the indignity of this search, the parties involved were still not satisfied and wanted to take even more pictures. It was a nightmare, a horrifying nightmare. But if this is what I have to endure to prove my innocence, my complete innocence, so be it. Throughout my life, I have only tried to help thousands upon thousands of children to live happy lives. It brings tears to my eyes when I see any child who suffers. I am not guilty of these allegations. But if I am guilty of anything it is of giving all that I have to give to help children all over the world. It is of loving children of all ages and races, it is of gaining sheer joy from seeing children with their innocent and smiling faces. It is of enjoying through them the childhood that I missed myself. If I am guilty of anything, it is of believing what God said about children, 'Suffer little children to come unto me and forbid them not, for such is the kingdom of heaven.' In no way do I think that I am God, but I do try to be Godlike in my heart. I am totally innocent of any wrongdoing and I know these terrible allegations will all be proven false. Again, to my friends and fans, thank you very much for all of your support. Together we will see this through to the very end. I love you very much and may God bless you all. I love you. Goodbye."

The very first thing we notice is that Jackson never said, "I didn't do it." He never said, "I did not molest this boy." That is something we would expect an innocent person to say. If it was me, I would tell the world point blank that I did not do it. Let's examine the denials Jackson does make.

"There have been many disgusting statements made recently concerning allegations of improper conduct on my part. These statements about me are totally false." All Jackson is telling us is that recently made allegations are false. We know how the press can be and how rumors get started. I am sure there were some allegations concerning Jackson that were not true. However, Jackson is not referring to every allegation made. He is only talking about "disgusting statements made recently." He is only denying those statements which he considered disgusting and which were recently made. The boy's allegations were made public several months before Jackson gave this statement. It appears Jackson is not referring to the accuser's allegations since they were not recently made.

"I ask all of you to wait to hear the truth before you label or condemn me. Don't treat me like a criminal because I am innocent." This sounds like a good denial. Jackson is telling us not to make any rash judgements, but wait until all the evidence is presented. Think about it though. Why should we wait? An innocent person would not want you to wait. He would want you to believe right now that he did not commit this crime. If Jackson would come out and say "I didn't do it," I might believe him and label him as innocent, but he hasn't said that. Furthermore, the truth never did come out because Jackson chose to settle this case. We are still waiting to hear the truth.

Jackson does state, "I am innocent." This is a truthful statement. In the eyes of the court, Jackson is innocent until proven guilty. He compares his innocence with that of a criminal. The word criminal can mean someone who has legally been convicted of a crime. Since Jackson has not been convicted he is indeed innocent. However, that does not mean he didn't do it.

Jackson talked about how his strip-search was "dehumanizing and humiliating." There is no doubt such an experience would be humiliating. Jackson further stated, "It was the most humiliating ordeal of my life." Now that is an interesting statement. Apparently for Jackson, being labeled a child molester is not as humiliating as being strip-searched. One month after giving this statement, Jackson settled the lawsuit. Did he settle it because he was humiliated by this examination? In his statement, Jackson refers to his strip-search by saying, "But if this is what I have to endure to prove my innocence, my complete innocence, so be it." Now we know he did not settle because of humiliation.

"I am totally innocent of any wrongdoing and I know these terrible allegations will all be proven false." Again we have him claiming he is innocent which is technically true. He is "innocent of any wrongdoing." Jackson may have done things which he does not consider to be wrong. This would also allow him to say he is innocent. A better statement would have been, "I am innocent of molesting this boy." In hindsight, we can see these allegations were not proven false, as Jackson claimed they would be, because he settled the case.

No one was asking Jackson any questions. He gave this statement on his own free will. He could talk about and say anything. What he didn't tell us directly is that he did not molest this boy.

On June 14, 1995, Michael Jackson and his wife Lisa Marie Presley were interviewed by Diane Sawyer on *Prime Time Live*. The interview started discussing their recent marriage. Sawyer then turned her questions to the child molestation allegations. Listed below are excerpts from the interview.

Sawyer: [Addressing Michael] "Well because I know that you've wanted to express similar sentiments for a long time, I want to ask a few things about the charges. But first I want to establish for the viewers here, there are no ground rules. You have said to me you are not afraid of any questions. So, I wanted that understood by everybody before we proceed. I think I want to begin by making sure that the terms are clear. You have said you would never harm a child. I want to be as specific as I can. Did you ever, as this young boy said you did, did you ever sexually engage, fondle, have sexual contact with this child, or any other child?"

Jackson: "Never, ever. I could never harm a child, or anyone. It's not in my heart, it's not who I am. And it's not what I'm....I'm not even interested in that."[1]

Sawyer, like many journalists, makes the mistake of asking a compound question. Jackson says, "Never, ever" but which question is he answering? Is he telling us he has never fondled this child? Or, is he telling us he has never fondled any other child? Maybe he is referring to having sexual contact. Some might say he is answering all of the questions. However, we really don't know.

Based on the rest of his answer, "I could never harm a child" it appears Jackson is answering, "Never, ever harm a child." He was never asked if he harmed a child. He was specifically asked about sexual contact with the boy or any other children. Jackson did not answer the question. Not answering the question means there is something he does not want to tell us.

> Sawyer: "And what do you think should be done to someone who does that?"
>
> Jackson: "To someone who does that? What I think should be done? Gee....I think they need help....in some kind of way....you know."[2]

Here we have Jackson answering the question with two questions. He wasn't looking for clarification because he does not wait for Sawyer to answer his questions. Jackson is stalling for time to think about how he should answer this question. This tells us this is a sensitive question for Jackson.

Michael Jackson loves children. In his December 22, 1993 statement, Jackson said, "It brings tears to my eyes when I see any child who suffers." You would think Jackson like most people would be outraged with someone who molested a child. You would think he would want some type of punishment for the person who would do such a terrible thing. His response, "Gee....I think they need help," does not show that. We have to wonder why he is showing sympathy towards a child molester.

> Sawyer: "Why did you settle the ...."
>
> Jackson: "Why am I still here then?" [A reference to the previous question about markings on Jackson's body.]
>
> Presley: "You're not going to ask me about them, are you? [laughing] Sorry. About the markings?"
>
> Sawyer: "You volunteered."
>
> Presley: "No, I'm just....the point is, is that when that finally got concluded that there was no match-up, then, it was printed this big [showing a tiny area], as opposed to how big it was, what the match-up was supposed to be."
>
> Jackson: "Because it isn't so."
>
> Sawyer: "Why did you settle the case then?"

Jackson: "The whole thing is a lie."

Sawyer: "Why did you settle the case? And, it looks to everyone as if you paid a huge amount of money....."

Jackson: "That's .... that's, most of that's folklore. I talked to my lawyers, and I said, 'Can you guarantee me, that justice will prevail?' And they said, 'Michael, we cannot guarantee you that a judge, or a jury will do anything.' And with that I was catatonic. I was outraged!"

Sawyer: "How much money...."

Jackson: "Totally outrageous. So, I said ... I have to do something to get out from under this nightmare. All these lies and all these people coming forth to get paid and all these tabloid shows, just lies, lies, lies, lies. So what I did, we got together again with my advisors and they advised me. It was hands down unanimous decision - resolve the case. This could be something that could go on for seven years!"

Sawyer: "How much money was ...."

Jackson: "We said, let's get it behind us."

Sawyer: "Can you say how much?"

Jackson: "It's not what the tabloids have printed. It's not all this crazy outlandish money, no it's not at all. I mean, the terms of the agreement are very confidential."[3]

Three times Sawyer had to ask Jackson why he settled the case because Jackson wouldn't answer the question. This means Jackson is withholding information. Jackson finally does give an answer. He states his attorneys could not guarantee what a judge or jury would do. This caused Jackson to become outraged. He still hasn't told us why he settled the case.

Jackson goes on to say he is "totally outraged." He needs "to get out from under this nightmare." Jackson meets with his advisors again who believe he should "resolve the case." Jackson's answer is he settled the case because his advisors told him to do so. A good follow-up question would have been, "Why did your advisors tell you to settle the case?" There is the possibility Jackson's advisors knew there was some serious evidence against him. Going to trial may have revealed other personal information about Jackson, and it may have led to his conviction. Perhaps this is why they urged him to settle the case. It is interesting Jackson complains about people lying and "coming forth to get paid...." Yet in the end, he paid someone who he wants us to believe was lying.

When it comes to how much money Jackson paid his accuser, Sawyer again has to ask him three times. The press had reported that Jackson paid a large amount of money. Jackson responds by saying, "That's .... that's, most of that's folklore" and "It's not what the tabloids have printed. It's not all this crazy outlandish money, no, it's not at all." Jackson doesn't tell us it is all folklore, he says that "most" of it is folklore. This qualified statement shows us that some of it is true. The exact dollar amount Jackson paid was to remain confidential. The tabloids were guessing and probably did print the incorrect dollar amount. This allows Jackson to say, "It's not what the tabloids have printed." Only Jackson knows what dollar amount constitutes "crazy and outlandish." What you consider to be crazy may not be crazy for him. After all the guy is a multi-millionaire.

Sawyer: "Any other settlements .... in process now or previously with children making these kinds of claims? We have heard .... that there is one, not, not a case that the prosecutors would bring to court."
Jackson: "No."
Sawyer: "....but, but once again, you're talking about shelling out ...."
Jackson: "No. That's not true. No. It's not true. I think, I've heard everything is fine and there are no others."[4]

Jackson tells us there are no other cases against him, past or present, like this one. However, he then qualifies his answer by saying, "I think." Therefore, he is not certain everything is fine and there are no other cases against him. We cannot not believe there are no other cases pending since Jackson did not tell us ("I think") there were no other potential cases.

Sawyer: "What is a thirty-six-year-old man doing, sleeping .... with a twelve-year-old boy? Or a series of them?"

Jackson: "Right. OK, when you say 'boys,' it's not just boys, and I've never invited just boys to come in my room. C'mon, that's just ridiculous. And that's a ridiculous question. But since people want to hear it .... y'know, the answer, I'll be happy to answer it. I have never invited anyone into my bed, ever. Children love me, I love them. They follow me, they want to be with me. But .... anybody can come in my bed, a child can come in my bed if they want."[5]

Sawyer asks a reasonable question. It is odd that a 36-year-old man allows young children, who are not his own, to sleep in his bed. Jackson doesn't view this as being strange. He responds to Sawyer's questions by stating, "that's a ridiculous question." There are many reasons why parents allow their children to be in their beds; to read a book, after experiencing a nightmare or when they are ill. These same parents would not allow neighborhood kids to get into bed with them to read a book. This would be unacceptable behavior. Jackson further states "I have never invited anyone into my bed, ever." He doesn't have to because they follow him into bed. If he invites a kid into his room who is spending the night and Jackson gets into bed, where do you think the kid is going to sleep?

As the interview continued, Sawyer moved away from questions dealing with the accusations. She then asked questions about their marriage and where they planned to live. Although they were no longer talking about the child molestation charges, Jackson was still being evasive in his answers.

Sawyer: "We also heard a report that maybe you were planning to adopt children."
Jackson: "Oh, I would love to adopt children. I think that's something I've always wanted to do. But children of all races: Arab children, Jewish children, black children all races."
Sawyer: "But, Lisa's children?"
Jackson: "I love Lisa's children. It's been a mission ...."
Sawyer: "But are you going to adopt ...."
Jackson: "Pardon?"
Sawyer: "To adopt them, though?"

Jackson:	"Oh, I love her children, they're sweet."
Sawyer:	"But to adopt? No?"
Jackson:	"Of course."[6]

Four times Sawyer asked Jackson if he was going to adopt his wife's children. Jackson never answers the question. The second time he was asked the question, Jackson answered the question with the question, "Pardon?" The question needed no clarification. He simply does not want to answer the question. Sawyer's fourth question was a compound question "But to adopt? No?" We do not know to which question Jackson's answer "of course" applies to. Is he saying of course he will adopt, or is he saying of course no he will not adopt? Because he refused to answer the question, we can be certain that at this point in his life, Jackson does not want to adopt Lisa's kids.

Sawyer:	"But .... but, do you wish you were .... the color you were, again?"
Jackson:	"Do I wish I was the color?"
Sawyer:	"Black color."
Jackson:	"You have to ask nature that. I loved .... I love black, I love black."
Sawyer:	"But do you wish you were that way?"
Jackson:	"I envy her [pointing to Lisa Marie], 'cause she can tan and I can't."[7]

Three times Jackson is asked if he would like to be black again. All three times he doesn't answer the question. Again we have him answering a question with a question, "Do I wish I was the color?" He is being asked a personal question that only he can answer. He avoids answering it by saying, "You have to ask nature that." Nature doesn't know what Jackson wants or feels. Even though Jackson's skin has lightened over the years, he still claims to be a black person. We see here though, he also considers himself to be a white person. "I loved .... I love black, I love black." Jackson begins talking in the past tense, "I loved." It appears he was about to say, "I loved *being* black." A statement like this would be an admittance that he is no longer black. He realizes what he is about to say so he changes the tense, "I love black, I love black." His desire to be white is further confirmed when he tells us he envies his wife because she can tan and he cannot.

One month after this interview, Jackson settled the lawsuit by paying his accuser an undisclosed amount of money. It could be said and has been said, that Jackson just wanted to end this ordeal. We do not know how much he paid, but we are fairly certain it was in the millions. Most people would agree that a person would not be willing to give an accuser 10 million dollars if that person had done nothing wrong. Ten million dollars is a lot of money even to Michael Jackson. With that much money, he could have hired an aggressive legal team to defend him.

It is a common sense conclusion that Michael Jackson settled this suit because there was some damaging information he did not want to be made public. This is further backed by the fact he did not answer many of the questions asked of him. He told us he could not harm a child, but he never told us he could not and did not molest a child. Jackson also refused to tell us specifically why he settled the case. He told us to wait until we hear the truth before condemning him. We have yet to hear the truth.

Chapter 21

The Assassination Of Dr. Martin Luther King, Jr.

Dr. Martin Luther King, Jr. was a civil rights leader in the 1950's and 60's. On April 4, 1968, Dr. King was in Memphis, Tennessee to help lead a strike by the city's sanitation workers. While in Memphis, Dr. King stayed on the second floor of the Motel Lorraine which was black owned. His decision to stay there was influenced by the fact he had been criticized for staying at a white owned Holiday Inn on a previous visit to Memphis. On the same day, a man checked into a boarding house across from the Motel Lorraine. Near his room was a common bathroom which had a clear view of Dr. King's second story room.

At around 6:00 p.m., Dr. King's chauffeur, Solomon Jones, arrived at the motel to take Dr. King to dinner. Jesse Jackson, Andrew Young and James Orange were waiting at the limousine for Dr. King. At 6:01 p.m., Dr. King left his motel room. He leaned over the railing and asked, "Do I really need a coat?"[1] Before his question could be answered, a single shot rang out from a high-powered rifle. Dr. King fell back and onto the floor of the balcony. He was rushed by ambulance to the St. Joseph's hospital. At 7:11 p.m., Dr. Martin Luther King, Jr. at the age of 39 was pronounced dead.

Witnesses believed the shot came from the boarding house across the street. Other witness stated that a young white man came running out of the boarding house immediately after the shooting. Several minutes after the shooting, the police found a bundle in the doorway of the Canipe Amusement Company located next door to the boarding house. The bundle contained a Remington 30.06 rifle fitted with a scope. Within two weeks, the only fingerprints on the rifle were identified as belonging to James Earl Ray.

James Earl Ray was born on March 10, 1928 in Alton, Illinois. While growing up, Ray had several run-ins with the law and spent time in jail. On October 19, 1959, Ray and an ex-con named James Owens were arrested in St. Louis for robbing several grocery stores. Ray was found guilty and sentenced to 20 years in a maximum security prison in Jefferson City, Missouri. With help from some fellow inmates, Ray escaped from prison on April 23, 1967 by concealing himself in a breadbox that contained a false bottom. Once on the run, Ray jumped aboard a train and headed for St. Louis. He would crisscross the country traveling to Canada, Mexico, Indianapolis and California before arriving in Memphis on April 4, 1968.

After Dr. King's assassination, Ray made his way to Canada. On May 6, 1968, he flew to London only to fly to Portugal on the next day. On May 17, he flew back to London contemplating how he would get out of England. On June 8, Ray attempted to fly to Belgium. Upon presenting his passport at Heathrow airport, he was detained for questioning in the murder of Dr. King. On July 19, Ray was extradited back to the United States. The evidence against Ray appeared to be damaging. He was in Memphis on the day Dr. King was shot, and his finger prints were on the rifle left near the scene of the crime. Six days before the shooting, Ray had purchased a rifle fitted with a scope. Witnesses placed Ray in the boarding house where the sniper allegedly was situated. On March 10, 1969, Ray pled guilty to the murder of Dr. Martin Luther King, Jr. He was immediately sentenced to 99 years in prison. Three days later, Ray would fire his attorney and write a letter to the presiding judge requesting a change of plea, and that he be allowed to have a trial. The request was denied.

Over the years, Ray renewed his request for a trial. He always maintained that a man named Raoul for whom Ray was running guns was responsible for Dr. King's murder. Ray claimed he was an unknowing participant in a conspiracy to kill Dr. King. Each time, his requests for a new trial were denied. In 1981, while in a prison law library, Ray was stabbed 22 times by some black inmates. He survived the attack but may have contracted hepatitis from a blood transfusion. In late 1996, Ray was in poor health suffering from cirrhosis of the liver. He was in need of a liver transplant. More than a dozen times he was admitted to the hospital. On April 23, 1998, at the age of 70, James Earl Ray died from liver failure.

There have been many theories about who killed Dr. King. Many feel Ray was not the lone gunman, but he was a fall guy in a large conspiracy. These beliefs are fueled by the fact that some witnesses stated the single shot came from the bushes across from the motel and not from the boarding house. The shooter appeared to exit the boarding house immediately after the shooting. Some questioned how Ray could have bundled up the rifle and his belongings so quickly, and why would he leave them on the sidewalk where they would obviously be found? The credibility of certain witnesses was in question. Perhaps most importantly was the fact that Ray maintained his innocence throughout the years. There was no deathbed confession. To determine Ray's guilt or innocence, let's examine some of the statements he has given over the years. Let's see what James Earl Ray had to say about Dr. King's assassination.

The first document we will look at is a transcript of the guilty plea entered by Ray on March 10, 1969 before Judge W. Preston Battle. Before the judge accepted the guilty plea, he questioned Ray to ensure he understood his rights, had not been promised anything, and was not being coerced into pleading guilty.

Court: "Have your lawyers explained all your rights to you and do you understand them?"
Ray: "Yes, Sir."
Court: "Do you know that you have a right to a trial by jury on the charge of murder in the first degree against you, the punishment for murder in the first degree ranging from death by electrocution to any time over twenty years? The burden of proof is on the State of Tennessee to prove you guilty beyond a reasonable doubt and to a moral certainty, and the decision of the jury must be unanimous both as to guilt and to punishment. In the event of a jury against you, you would have the right to file a motion for a new trial addressed to the trial judge. In the event of an adverse ruling against

	you on your motion for a new trial, you would have the right to successive appeals to the Tennessee Court of Criminal Appeals and the Supreme Court of Tennessee and to file a petition for review by the Supreme Court of the United States. Do you understand that you have all of those rights?"
Ray:	"Yes, sir."
Court:	"You are entering a plea of guilty to murder in the first degree, as charged in the indictment, and are compromising and settling your case on an agreed punishment of 99 years in the State Penitentiary. Is this what you want to do?"
Ray:	"Yes. I have been — That's — yes. "
Court:	"Is that what you want to do?"
Ray:	"That's right."[2]

When the judge asked Ray if he wanted to plead guilty and accept a 99-year prison sentence, Ray answered "Yes." He then began to make an additional comment, "I have been — That's — yes." It is impossible to determine what Ray was thinking about saying. Maybe he was going to say, "Yes. I have been *coerced into pleading guilty.*" Then again he might have been thinking, "Yes. I have been *wanting to confess this crime for a while.*" Because of these comments, the judge wanted to make sure Ray wanted to plead guilty. So he asked him again if that is what he wanted to do. Ray answered "That's right."

Court:	"Do you understand that you are waiving, which means giving up, a formal trial by your plea of guilty, although the laws of this State require the prosecution to present certain evidence to a jury in all cases of pleas of guilty to murder in the first degree? By your plea of guilty, you are also waiving your right to: One, your motion for a new trial; Two, successive appeals to the Supreme Court, to the Tennessee Court of Criminal Appeals, and the Supreme Court of Tennessee; and, Three, a petition to review it by the Supreme Court of the United States."[3]

The judge also asked Ray if he was "abandoning and waiving"[4] ten other motions and petitions that Ray had filed. These included things such as a motion to remove lights and cameras from the jail and a motion to permit photographs.

Court: "You are waiving and giving up all these rights?"
Ray: "Yes, sir."[5]

Over the years Ray tried several times to withdraw his guilty plea and take his case to trial. His requests were always denied not because there is a government coverup, but because in his plea agreement he gave up his right to a trial and appeals.

Court: "Has anything besides your sentence of 99 years in the penitentiary been promised to you to get you to plead guilty?"
Ray: "No, no one has used pressure."[6]

Ray answers the question but he adds to his answer by saying that he wasn't pressured into pleading guilty. The judge did not ask Ray if was being pressured. Ray voluntarily gave this information. Years later, Ray would change his story about being pressured into pleading guilty. In his book, *Who Killed Martin Luther King Jr.?*, Ray makes the following statements concerning his attorney, Percy Foreman, and his plea agreement:

> "As February was ending, Foreman had no assurances that I'd plead guilty, so he resorted to terror tactics usually attributed to dictators. He said if I didn't plead guilty, my brother might be arrested for conspiracy to kill Dr. King. And, he added, my failure to cop a plea could bring federal authorities after my 77-year-old father."[7]

> "Finally, Foreman said, if I insisted on a trial, he couldn't swear that he'd do his utmost to defend me."[8]

> "I was succumbing to the grind — the cage, the glare, the stale air, Foreman's incessant demands that I plead guilty. In late February, I tentatively agreed to enter a plea of guilty."[9]

"The next day Foreman phoned Huie from Houston, musing about whether I was still a client, then returned to Memphis and visited me in jail. He was upset, again implying that if I forced him to try the King case before a jury he wouldn't put forth his best effort, and again raising the specter of my brother and father going to jail."[10]

At his plea agreement, Ray voluntarily stated "no one has used pressure"[11] to get him to plead guilty. If he was being pressured, why would he volunteer to make such a statement? When asked if anything had been promised to him, he could have answered with a simple "no." After being sentenced and escaping the death penalty, Ray then changes his story. Let's go back to the transcript of his guilty plea.

Court: "Are you pleading guilty to murder in the first degree in this case because you killed Dr. Martin Luther King under such circumstances that would make you legally guilty of murder in the first degree under the law as explained to you by your lawyers?"

Ray: "Yes, legally guilty, uh-huh."[12]

The judge finally asked Ray if he was pleading guilty because he did indeed kill Dr. King. Ray answers with a "Yes." Ray then goes onto say he was "legally guilty." The reason he says this is because he is using the same language the judge is using.

The Attorney General, Phil Canale, addressed the court stating, "we have no proof other than Dr. Martin Luther King, Jr. was killed by James Earl Ray and James Earl Ray alone, not in concert with anyone else."[13] Ray's attorney Percy Foreman also spoke to the court agreeing with the government's assertion there was no conspiracy to kill Dr. King. Ray objected to his attorney endorsing the government's case. Ray told the court he did not accept these theories. The judge wanted to make sure Ray was not changing his mind about his guilty plea. Therefore, he asked him the following questions:

Court: "You still — your answers to these questions that I asked you would still be the same?"

Ray:	"Yes, sir. The one thing is I just didn't want to add anything onto them. That was all."
Court:	"There is nothing in these answers to these questions I asked you, in other words, you change none of those?"
Ray:	"No, sir. No, sir."
Court:	"In other words, you are pleading guilty and taking 99 years, and I think the main question here that I want to ask you is this: Are you pleading guilty to murder in the first degree in this case because you killed Dr. Martin Luther King under such circumstance that would make you legally guilty of murder in the first degree under the law as explained to you by your lawyers?"
Ray:	"Yes, sir, make me guilty on that."
Court:	"Your answers are still yes?"
Ray:	"Yes, sir."[14]

The judge asked Ray three times if his previous answers were still the same. All three times Ray stated he did not want to change any of his answers. The judge again asked him if he was guilty of killing Dr. King. Ray answered, "Yes, sir, make me guilty on that." It should be noted that Ray did not say, "I am guilty." Instead he said, "Make me guilty on that." Ray is not denying his involvement. He is simply using the same language the judge used.

There is no doubt the government and Ray's attorneys preferred that Ray plead guilty rather than have a public trial. Therefore, there was probably some pressure on Ray to plead guilty. However, the decision whether or not to stand trial would have to be made by Ray. Ray told the judge several times he was guilty of committing this crime, and that he wanted to plead guilty and receive a prison sentence rather than face a death penalty.

In September 1976, the U.S. House of Representatives voted to form a Select Committee to investigate the murders of President Kennedy and Dr. King. The committee was originally chaired by Texas Representative Henry Gonzalez. In 1977, Gonzalez resigned and Ohio Representative Louis Stokes replaced him as chairman. That same year, the Select Committee held a public hearing on Dr. King's assassination. The star witness was James Earl Ray. The committee was attempting to track Ray's movements. They believed Ray may have been stalking Dr. King. They wanted to know of Ray's whereabouts on April 1, 1968. Dr. King had been in Atlanta then, and they suspected Ray was also in Atlanta on that date. Chairman Louis Stokes questioned Ray.

    Stokes: "You didn't return to Atlanta?"
    Ray: "I know I didn't return to Atlanta. And if I did, I'll just take responsibility for the King case here on TV."[15]

Ray answers the question by saying he did not return to Atlanta. He then makes a very bold statement to prove his innocence. He states that if he did return to Atlanta, then he will "take responsibility for the King case." Taking responsibility for the King case equals "I did it." What happened next is chairman Stokes produced a large blowup of a laundry receipt from the Piedmont Laundry in Atlanta. The receipt showed that Ray had dropped off laundry there on April 1. This proved Ray was in Atlanta on the day in question.

    Ray: "This is some type of forged document because I know I did not take the laundry in on April 1."[16]

If Ray had never returned to Atlanta, he would have responded by saying something like, "I did not drop off laundry there because I did not return to Atlanta." Ray only denies taking the laundry in on April 1. In his answer, he alludes that he dropped off some laundry in Atlanta on another date. Years later, he would confirm his Atlanta visit in his book *Who Killed Martin Luther King Jr.?* "I did leave laundry at the Piedmont, but that was on or before March 29 — I'd left Atlanta that day to begin my trip to Memphis. And on April 1 I spent the night in a motel in Corinth, Mississippi — 240 miles from Atlanta. But I couldn't document my Mississippi motel stay, or explain the April 1 Piedmont receipt."[17] So we see that Ray did return to Atlanta. He claims it was in March. The evidence says it was in April. What is most important though is what Ray had stated earlier, "I know I didn't return to Atlanta. And if I did, I'll just take responsibility for the King case here on TV."[18]

The U.S. House Select Committee on Assassinations concluded that Ray did kill Dr. King. They also found that a racist group in St. Louis had offered a $50,000 bounty if Dr. King was killed. This probably influenced Ray's decision to murder Dr. King.

In 1992, Marlowe & Company published a book written by James Earl Ray entitled *Who Killed Martin Luther King Jr.? The True Story by The Alleged Assassin.* The book is Ray's opportunity to tell us what happened. He sticks to his story that a man named Raoul for whom he was running guns was responsible for Dr. King's assassination. Ray insists he was coerced into pleading guilty. He tells of a plot by the government to frame him for the assassination. He talks about the fact he has never received a trial, and his eight requests for a trial have been denied. What Ray does not tell us are the words, "I didn't do it." Not once do these words appear in his book. If I didn't commit this crime, I would be telling you in every chapter that I didn't do it. Ray claimed he was innocent, but in our society everyone is legally innocent until proven guilty. The closest Ray came to a denial can be found on page 120 in his book where he writes how his attorney Percy Foreman was not interested in actively defending him.

> "As far as Foreman's investigative technique went, the two main questions in the case were: 'Was there a conspiracy to kill Dr. King?' and 'Did James Earl Ray fire the weapon?' He never asked me either question. I would have answered that I did not shoot Dr. King but that I was unwittingly part of a conspiracy since I was hired to purchase a weapon of the type allegedly used in the killing and did bring it to Memphis."[19]

Ray makes a strong denial when he says "I did not shoot Dr. King." However, we must remember this is a hypothetical answer to a hypothetical question. He is not stating for the record he did not shoot Dr. King. He is telling us if he was asked, he would state he did not shoot Dr. King. There is a difference between the two. We do not know for sure if he would have answered it that way because he was never asked that question by his attorney. Although he says he would have answered it that way, people often change their minds. There is an old saying, "Would have, could have, should have." If Ray was innocent, he would have told us "I didn't do it." He could have told us "I didn't do it." He should have told us "I didn't do it." However, he never makes that denial.

We find one other denial in his book. In the epilogue to *Who Killed Martin Luther King Jr.?* Ray writes:

> "I do admit that I did some very stupid things back then, but I did not fire the shot that killed Martin Luther King Jr."[20]

This denial is similar to his previous denial in that he does not tell us he did not kill Dr. King. He only states he "did not fire the shot that killed Martin Luther King Jr." This leaves the possibility Ray fired a shot but missed Dr. King. Perhaps someone else fired the fatal shot. However, witnesses only reported hearing one shot.

In the years prior to his death, Ray received some unusual support in his request for a trial. The family of Dr. Martin Luther King, Jr. believes Ray was framed for the killing. They wanted Ray to stand trial so questions concerning a possible conspiracy would be answered. On March 27, 1997, Dexter King, the son of the slain civil rights leader, met with Ray in a state prison hospital in Nashville, Tennessee.

King: "I just want to ask you for the record, did you kill my father?"[21]

Unfortunately, I have not obtained a copy of the transcripts of this interview. I have seen in print several different answers to this question. I thought a quote was supposed to be a quote! They differ slightly in how they are worded which can be important when analyzing a statement. Here are two versions of his answer that I have seen.

Ray: "No. I didn't. No. No. But sometimes you have to make your own evaluation and maybe come to the conclusion. I think that could be done today, but not 30 years ago...."[22]

Ray: "No. No. I didn't. But I could say that sometime, these questions are difficult to answer. You have to make perfect examination. And of course some facts missed. Dr. Pepper have written things like that. Maybe it could come in conclusion, but I think it could be done — I think it could be done

30 years ago, because something with — to do with actual facts."²³

In the first version of his answer, Ray denies killing Dr. King. However, he then says, "But sometimes you have to make your own evaluation and maybe come to the conclusion." Assuming he made this statement, Ray is saying, "I didn't do it, but you better decide for yourself." This is not a very strong denial. An innocent person would say he didn't do it, and he doesn't care what you think. Ray is not saying everyone is entitled to his own opinion. He is saying that to find the truth, "You have to make your own evaluation." Others have made their own evaluation and concluded that Ray is guilty of murder. Ray does not tell us if we do our own evaluation, we will find he is telling the truth. He only states, "maybe come to the conclusion."

Other sources quote Ray as saying, "No. No. I didn't, no. Sometimes these questions are difficult to answer."²⁴ It appears Ray did make the statement "These questions are difficult to answer." Remember, the question was, "Did you kill my father?" What is so difficult about answering that question? An innocent person would find this question very easy to answer.

In the interview with Dexter King, Ray also stated, "I had nothing to do with shooting your father."²⁵ As we saw with the O.J. Simpson case, saying "I had nothing to do with" is different from saying "I didn't do it." Even if Ray wasn't the triggerman as he claims, he still had something to do with Dr. King's murder. He purchased and brought a rifle to Memphis which was allegedly used in the killing. Ray himself claimed he was "unwittingly part of a conspiracy."²⁶ Well, if you were part of a conspiracy then I would say you had something to do with it.

On April 12, 1997, Larry King interviewed Ray from a prison hospital on his *Larry King Live* show broadcasted on CNN. Here are some excerpts from the interview.

King: "First, as to your health, James, what's the current status?"

Ray: "Well, I'm under treatment here at Nashville prison hospital. It is special — it's referred to as 'special needs.' And I really don't know about —

	you know, I have a liver a problem. I don't know what the status is on that."
King:	"Is it cancer of the liver?"
Ray:	"No."
King:	"It is not cancer of liver?"
Ray:	"No."
King:	"So, you are not under any deathwatch, so to speak, as has been reported in the papers?"
Ray:	"No."[27]

Later during the interview, Ray's attorney William Pepper would comment, "He is terminally ill. He's a little shy about that. He has cirrhosis of liver, not cancer."[28] We have to believe Ray knew he had cirrhosis of the liver. He had been in the hospital several times. Even his attorney knew about his condition. Ray withholds this information from King when he is asked about his status.

Ray did answer the cancer questions truthfully. However, he apparently lies when he says he is not under a deathwatch. Ray was suffering from and dying from cirrhosis of the liver. I would say that qualifies as being on a deathwatch. Time is running out. Without a liver transplant, he will die. This is exactly what happened a year after this interview. Ray's attorney explains his client's answer by saying, "He is a little shy about that." What if Ray is shy when he talks about Dr. King's assassination? Will he lie about that also?

King:	"What is — why — first let's go back a little to refresh the audience. Why did you confess if you didn't do it?"
Ray:	"That's kind of complicated. The — well, first, the attorney got me involved in various contracts."
King:	"Percy Foreman?"
Ray:	"Yes, the last one said that if I would enter a guilty plea, he would give my brother $500 to get another attorney. And also, every one involved in the case, at that time, wanted to play." [He may have said "plea" but the transcript reads "play."]
King:	"Yes, but if you didn't do it, why plead to something as horrible as that if you didn't do it?"

Ray: "Well, I mean, I made a mistake there. What I should have done. I — you know, you don't have too many options. The judge took the position that he wanted to plead because he was concerned if I went to trial I would be found not guilty, or get a hung jury. But, of course, the option I had was to create some type of scene with Percy Foreman in the jail. And, of course, you don't do those things in jail, you know, get into some type of physical confrontation with your attorney."[29]

When asked why he confessed to the murder, Ray responded, "That's kind of complicated." What is so complicated about it? Why didn't he say he was pressured into pleading guilty which is what he claimed in his book? King then repeats the question looking for a more definite answer. Ray says he made a mistake. He then begins to say what he should have done, but he never does tell us. He says, "What I should have done. I — you know, you don't have too many options." Ray claimed the judge felt Ray may have been found not guilty if the case went to trial. This would be even more reason not to plead guilty. Ray then talks about a "physical confrontation" with his attorney if he were to insist on a trial. If a person wanted to plead not guilty and take his case to trial, why would that turn into a physical confrontation with his attorney? Ray's answer doesn't make much sense.

King: "So, you agreed to take a life sentence?"
Ray: "Well, no. There was no agreement. It was just an agreement that (inaudible) he'd give me sufficient funds, I could hire another attorney, and the new attorney would reopen the case."
King: "I see. So the late Percy Foreman was, in a sense, lying to you?"
Ray: "Well, he lied to everybody, the judge, the prosecutor. He was after the ....."[30]

Ray says he did not agree to a life sentence. Technically this is true because he was not sentenced to life in prison. He was given a 99 year sentence which basically is a life sentence. For him to say he did not agree contradicts his plea agreement in which Ray affirmed the court's question of "compromising and settling your case on an agreed punishment of 99 years in the State Penitentiary."³¹ When Larry King asked Ray if his attorney lied to him, Ray did not answer the question. He did not say, "Yes, he lied to me." He told us his attorney lied to the judge and to the prosecutor, but he did not specifically say he had lied to him.

King:	"Are you swearing that you never fired a gun that day?"
Ray:	"Yes. I have referred to as indirectly when I write a book, or things like that, but usually you don't run around a penitentiary telling people you are innocent of this, innocent of that. Usually you refer to it as indirectly."
King:	"I don't understand."
Ray:	"Try to put evidence out that, you know, what you might want to hear."³²

Ray answers "yes" to this question, but then he makes an interesting comment. He says he refers to his innocence "indirectly." This is puzzling because most innocent people would boldly declare they didn't do it. Ray says in prison they do not talk like that. So, maybe they don't. However, you would think in his book he would directly proclaim his innocence. As we saw earlier, he only alluded to not killing Dr. King.

Larry King doesn't understand what Ray means by "indirectly." Ray further explains stating you release "what you might want to hear." Of course, Ray wants to hear he is innocent. So, he puts out indirect information that he is innocent.

King:	"All right, when you heard of the shooting where were you?"
Ray:	"Um, probably about — uh — 4 or 5 blocks from the — from the rooming house where I was staying at."
King:	"All right. Did you think that you would be implicated?"
Ray:	"No. The way I heard it. When — I left this area. I've been through this 100 times. I left this area, and I was coming back, to park the car in the same position where was, so this Raoul could use it. Well, at the time the — I had a flat tire, and of

course the FBI knows that, they've got all these records."[33]

In this exchange, Ray reveals the identity of Raoul. When talking about Raoul, he refers to him as, "this Raoul." When a person uses the adjective "this" before a name, they are distancing themselves from that person. They are referring to someone whom they do not know. Ray claims he did not know much about Raoul including his last name. Even so, this is someone whom he has known for the eight to nine months prior to the killing of Dr. King. Ray claims Raoul was his employer giving him money to run guns. Some of Ray's movements were directed by Raoul. On the day Dr. King was killed, Ray was in Memphis meeting with Raoul. In his book, Ray refers to Raoul as a "traveling companion."[34] Since Raoul was not a total stranger, Ray should have said, "I was coming back to park the car in the same position where it was, so Raoul could use it." Since he knows Raoul, he should have called him Raoul and not "this Raoul." If Ray made up the story about Raoul, then there would be no relationship with Raoul. There would be no communicating with Raoul. There would be no personal contact with Raoul. Therefore, when referring to Raoul, it would make sense to call him "this Raoul" because he never existed. If Raoul existed, Ray would not have called him "this Raoul." It could be argued Ray was distancing himself from Raoul. If that was the case, then he should consistently distance himself from Raoul which he didn't do. James Earl Ray slipped up and the truth came out. Raoul never existed.

King: "I understand what you are saying. Do you think, James, that you were set up?"

Ray: "Well, I think I was taken advantage of. I was the — some people use a different word. They use 'dupe' and all that stuff. But I just use some type of — refer to it, as a prison language, as a fool or something like that. Run around saying well, I'm this or that."[35]

A lot of Ray's supporters claim he was a patsy set up to take the fall. Ray tells us he was not set up. All he tells us was that he was "taken advantage of."

King:	"Well with all the years you have spent there and all this time, for something you didn't commit, you must be going a little crazy. I mean, if you really didn't do this, to serve all this time for a horrendous crime that is going to go down through the ages, you must — aren't you a little upset, angry, crazed?"
Ray:	"Well, I'm not happy about it. But I asked for it, more or less. I escaped from a Missouri prison, I came down here, and of course I was committing minor offenses down here."
King:	"But you didn't kill anybody, you're saying."
Ray:	"No. They didn't do that. But you do these things, foolish things, I was driving a car without a license, things like that, where if you get arrested, for — you just got to take the consequences for it. But in the meantime, we did everything we could to get a trial in the case. It is difficult, to — once the system gets you in prison, it is difficult to get a trial, you know, and try to ...."
King:	"All right, you hold it right there, James, we are going to take a break...."[36]

Ray tells us he is "not happy about" being in prison. He doesn't tell us he is upset, angry or crazed as King expected he would be. I think most innocent people who have been wrongfully imprisoned would be very angry. Ray says he "asked for it, more or less" because he was "committing minor offenses." He then tells us one of those minor offenses was driving a car without a license. Is there anyone who believes that a person caught driving a car without a license should get 99 years in prison? Apparently Ray thinks so because he says, "You just got to take the consequences for it." Ray is accepting his sentence of 99 years, and it is not because he committed some minor offenses. It is because he killed Dr. Martin Luther King.

It should also be noted that when King stated, "But you didn't kill anybody, you're saying." Ray responded, "No. They didn't do that. But you do these things, foolish things, I was driving a car without a license...." Ray is trying to say he did not kill Dr. King but he did do some "foolish things." The problem is he used the pronoun "they." We can only wonder who he was referring to when he said "They didn't do that."

Later in the interview, Jesse Jackson, a former associate of Dr. King, was asked to participate in the interview. Jackson commented on how the U.S. House Select Committee on Assassinations concluded that Ray was stalking Dr. King and that he was the triggerman. Jackson further stated he believed Ray was not telling the whole truth.

King: "James, how do you react to what Jesse just said?"
Ray: "Well, I think Reverend Jackson has always taken that position, so I, you know, he has a right to take whatever position he wants."[37]

Everything Ray said in his response is true. Jackson, of course, is entitled to his own opinion. If you were convicted of this crime which you did not commit, how would you respond to Jackson's comments? You may say that Jackson can believe whatever he wants, but you would also say you didn't do it. Ray does not do that. He does not proclaim his innocence.

King: "James, is there something you are not telling us?"
Ray: "I don't what — don't know what it would be. I have, over the years, I have had a book published trying to get my, you know, our version on the ...."[38]

At this point it appears Ray's attorney, William Pepper, cut Ray off by interjecting that Jesse Jackson did the foreword for Ray's book. Ray does not answer King's question. Therefore, he is withholding some information. He does not tell us he is not hiding something. Ray states he published a book "trying to get my, you know, our version." Notice the change in pronouns from "my" to "our version." Apparently, in his book Ray is not telling us his version of how Dr. King was killed. He is telling us a version influenced by his attorney and perhaps by others.

The last part of the interview consisted of Dexter King, Jesse Jackson and William Pepper discussing Ray's guilt or innocence and the need for a trial. Larry King then concluded the interview without ever asking Ray the most important question, "Did you kill Dr. Martin Luther King, Jr.?"

James Earl Ray died on April 23, 1998, taking with him the complete truth about what happened in Memphis on April 4, 1968. Throughout the years, Ray maintained his innocence claiming he was unknowingly part of a conspiracy which involved a man named Raoul. Although Ray never confessed to this murder, we can see he is a terrible liar. Ray would always insinuate he did not kill Dr. King, but he would stop short of saying, "I didn't do it." He would avoid answering certain questions which means there is something he is not telling us which is what many people have always suspected. Ray's own words indicate that Raoul may never have existed. There is no doubt James Earl Ray was not the innocent person he wanted us to believe. There is every indication he did kill Dr. Martin Luther King, Jr.

Chapter 22

The Lindbergh Kidnapping And The Trial Of Bruno Richard Hauptmann

Charles A. Lindbergh was an aviation hero. On May 20 - 21, 1925 as a 25-year-old major in the National Guard Reserves, Lindbergh made his historic non-stop flight from New York to Paris in his plane the Spirit of St. Louis. Upon returning to the United States, Lindbergh's popularity grew because of his accomplishment. He received many offers for product endorsements. He wrote a book and appeared on the cover of *TIME* magazine becoming its first "Man of the Year." President Coolidge commissioned him as a Colonel in the Officers Reserve Corps.

On May 27, 1929, Colonel Lindbergh married Anne Spencer Morrow. Anne came from a wealthy and prominent family. She was the daughter of Dwight W. Morrow the U.S. Ambassador to Mexico. About one year later, Anne gave birth to a son, Charles A. Lindbergh, Jr. By the winter of 1931, the Lindberghs were building a house in Hopewell, New Jersey. In the spring of 1932, the house was nearly completed and suitable for living despite being unfinished. Because the residence was still under construction, the Lindberghs usually spent the weekends at the Hopewell estate, and lived at the Morrow home in Englewood during the week. On Tuesday, March 1, 1932, the Lindberghs decided to break from their routine and stay at their home in Hopewell. Residing at the house with the Colonel and his wife was their 20-month-old son Charles A. Lindbergh, Jr. In addition, the Lindberghs had a hired staff which consisted of a butler, Oliver Whateley, a cook, Elsie Whateley, and a nursemaid, Betty Gow.

At around 6:00 p.m. on that Tuesday, Betty Gow fed Charles Jr. and put him to bed. Because the baby had contracted a cold, she gave him some medicine and then watched as he rested. By 8:00 p.m., the baby was soundly sleeping. At approximately 8:30 p.m., Colonel Lindbergh arrived home. He inquired about the baby and then ate dinner with his wife. At around 9:10 p.m., Colonel Lindbergh heard a cracking noise outside. He asked his wife about the noise, but he did not investigate the matter. Just before 10:00 p.m., Betty Gow went into the baby's room to check on the infant. As her eyes adjusted to the darkness of the room, she discovered the baby was missing from his crib.

The police were immediately called to the Lindbergh residence. A ransom note was found on the window sill in the baby's room. The note read:

"Dear Sir!
   Have 50000 $ redy 25000$ in 20 $ bills 15000 $ in 10 $ and 10000 $ in 5 $ bills. After 2-4 days we will inform you were to deliver the money.
   We warn you for making anyding public or for notify the police the child is in gute care. Indication for all letters are signature and three holds."[1]

At the bottom of the note was the "signature" which was two interlinked circles with three punched out holes. The police searched the grounds and found a crudely made ladder. It appeared the kidnappers had used the ladder to reach the baby's bedroom on the second floor of the home. A search the following morning in the daylight hours yielded no further clues to the kidnappers' identity. All the police had was a ladder with no distinguishable fingerprints and a poorly written ransom note. During March, 1932, the Lindberghs would receive several more notes from the kidnappers. On April 2, 1932, the Lindberghs using a mediator, Dr. John Condon, paid $50,000 to a man who identified himself as "John" in the St. Raymond's Cemetery located in the Bronx, NY. The man gave Dr. Condon a written note indicating the baby was safely aboard a boat named Nelly. The note also contained directions to the boat. A search by the police and the Coast Guard found no boat named Nelly. On May 12, 1932, the decomposed body of Charles Lindbergh, Jr. was found in a shallow grave about five miles from the Lindbergh home. The cause of death appeared to be from a skull fracture. It was believed the baby died on the night he was taken.

Three days after discovering the corpse, a bill from the ransom money surfaced in New York City. Throughout the summer and on through the next year, ransom money continued to surface in the New York City area. This pattern continued into 1934. On September 18, 1934, a bank in New York received two ten-dollar gold certificates. One of the bills was from the ransom money and had a license plate number written on it. It was determined the bill had been deposited by a gas station not too far from the bank. The police interviewed the gas station manager who remembered receiving the bill. The bill had caught his attention because in 1933, President Roosevelt ordered that all gold certificates be turned into a bank. The manager also knew the Lindbergh ransom money consisted of gold certificates. The manager stated that on September 15, 1934, a man had purchased gas for his car. As the man drove off, he wrote the car's license plate number on the bill. The police checked with the Department of Motor Vehicles and found that the license plate was registered to Bruno Richard Hauptmann who lived in the Bronx at 1279 East 222nd Street.

Hauptmann was born in Germany in 1899. His father died while Hauptmann was a teenager. This left the teen with little supervision which would allow him to get into trouble. In 1919, Hauptmann was convicted of several burglaries including armed robbery. In 1923, he escaped from jail and fled Germany as a stowaway aboard an American ship. As an illegal immigrant, Hauptmann worked several odd jobs including carpentry work to support himself. In 1925, he married German-born, Anna Schoeffler who was working as a waitress. As the Depression set in, the Hauptmanns seemed to be doing quite well. Hauptmann was very conservative with his money and began dealing in the stock market.

The police now had a prime suspect in Bruno Richard Hauptmann. They believed that an arrest was imminent. On the morning of September 19, 1934, the police had Hauptmann's house under surveillance. At 8:55 a.m., Hauptmann left his residence and drove away in his car. He was quickly pulled over and searched. Some of the Lindbergh ransom money was found in his possession. On September 20, 1934, while Hauptmann was being questioned, the police searched his garage. More of the ransom money, $14,600, was found hidden in his garage. Later, the police would find Dr. John Condon's telephone number and address written on a piece of wood in Hauptmann's closet.

Hauptmann had an explanation for the money. He said a friend and business partner, Isador Fisch, had recently returned to Germany. Shortly before he left, Fisch gave Hauptmann a small box to keep for him until he returned to the United States. In March 1934, Fisch died while in Germany. Hauptmann had forgotten that Fisch had given him the box. In August 1934, rain had leaked into a closet where Hauptmann had stored the box. While cleaning the closet he found the box and opened it. To his surprise, he discovered it contained money. He stated he did not know it came from the Lindbergh kidnapping. Because Fisch owed Hauptmann some money, Hauptmann took part of the money and spent it.

The investigators felt Hauptmann's story of discovering the money had some problems. Hauptmann claimed he did not count the money upon finding it. Furthermore, he did not advise his wife of his discovery. In his letters to Fisch's family in Germany after Isador's death, Hauptmann stated he had some of Fisch's belongings, but he failed to mention the box of money. There were other problems. On the day Dr. Condon delivered the ransom money, Hauptmann quit his job. Hauptmann's handwriting closely resembled the writing in the ransom notes. Perhaps most damning though was the wooden makeshift ladder used by the kidnappers. The police discovered that a board had been sawed away from Hauptmann's attic. The police matched a board in the kidnapper's ladder with the missing board in Hauptmann's attic.

Hauptmann was arrested in New York on the charge of extortion. Since the kidnapping and murder took place in New Jersey, Hauptmann would have to be extradited from New York to New Jersey to face the more serious charges. On October 15, 1934, the extradition hearing began in the Bronx County Courthouse. The evidence was great enough that on October 16, Hauptmann was remanded to New Jersey officials. Hauptmann's murder trial began on January 2, 1935. The prosecution took sixteen days to present their case. The defense then called their witnesses with the first one being Bruno Richard Hauptmann. After the defense rested, several rebuttal witnesses were called. On February 13, 1935, the thirty-second day of the trial, the case went to the jury. After 11 hours of deliberation, the jury reached a verdict of guilty of murder in the first degree.

Hauptmann and his attorneys would spend the next year appealing the conviction. They petitioned the Court of Errors, the U.S. Supreme Court, and the governor of New Jersey to no avail. On April 3, 1936, at 8:41 p.m., Hauptmann was led into the death chamber at the Trenton State Prison in Trenton, New Jersey. Prison guards strapped him into an electric chair. For three minutes, two thousand volts of electricity passed through his body. At 8:47 p.m., Bruno Richard Hauptmann was pronounced dead.

Over time Hauptmann's guilt has been questioned. Many theories as to who killed the Lindbergh baby have evolved. Some have even claimed that a member of the Lindbergh family killed the child, and that Colonel Lindbergh faked the kidnapping to protect the family member. The reason this case has not died is because of Hauptmann himself. From the time of his arrest, to the day he was executed, Hauptmann proclaimed his innocence. However, if we listen to what Hauptmann had to say about his involvement in this crime, we find that he wasn't so innocent.

Hauptmann was arrested on September 19, 1934, by a New York City Police Department task force. He was taken to the NYPD's Second Precinct on Greenwich Street to be questioned. With several law enforcement authorities present, Hauptmann was questioned by Inspector John Lyons of the NYPD. Hauptmann stated he did not know the gold certificates he was spending came from the Lindbergh ransom. Lyons asked Hauptmann where he got the gold certificates.

Lyons:	"Can you tell us where you got this money from?"
Hauptmann:	"Sometimes I took some out of the bank - I was asking for gold certificates and gold - then I took out gold coins."
Lyons:	"What bank?"
Hauptmann:	"The Central Savings Bank, 73rd Street and Broadway."
Lyons:	"And they gave you gold certificates whenever you requested? That was the latter part of March?"
Hauptmann:	"I got all the gold from there about March."[2]

Hauptmann also stated that the $20 gold certificate on his person at the time of his arrest was the last of the gold certificates he had collected. On the next day, the police would discover more of the ransom money hidden in Hauptmann's garage. Hauptmann then admitted he lied to Inspector Lyons about where he had gotten the money and how much he had in his possession.

On the first day he was interrogated, Hauptmann told another lie. He was asked if he had ever been arrested. Hauptmann responded, "No." He was then asked if he was ever arrested in Germany. Again, Hauptmann replied, "No."[3] The police would later discover that Hauptmann had a criminal history in Germany.

The investigators continued to question Hauptmann throughout the evening of September 19, 1934. Hauptmann stated that he did not know how he came into possession of the Lindbergh ransom. Deputy Chief Inspector Vincent Sweeney of the NYPD also interviewed Hauptmann. Let's look at a remark Sweeney made to Hauptmann.

Sweeney: "Now you are the man who delivered that note. There's lots of explanations for that. Our belief is that you are trying to help somebody out and cover somebody. You are not going to get anywhere doing that. Now is your time to help out."

Hauptmann: "I'm sorry I can't do anything on it."[4]

Hauptmann is accused of three things by Inspector Sweeney: delivering the note, helping and covering for someone. He also tells him now is the time to help. Think about how you would respond to these allegations. You would probably respond to them specifically. "I did not deliver that note." "I am not covering for someone." You may say, "I do not know anything." Hauptmann says that he "can't do anything." This is a truthful statement. If he tells them the complete truth, he will be in trouble. It is not that he doesn't know anything. He just "can't do anything."

The Hauptmann interrogation continued the next morning, September 20, 1934. While Inspector Lyons was questioning Hauptmann, the police found $14,600 of the ransom money hidden in Hauptmann's garage. Later in the afternoon, Hauptmann was questioned about this money which he claimed Isador Fisch had left with him in a box. Mr. J. Edgar Hoover asked the following questions:

Hoover:	"How often did you count it?"
Hauptmann:	"Only one time."
Hoover:	"When did you first learn money was in that box?"
Hauptmann:	"About three weeks ago when the rain came in."
Hoover:	"Did you ever open it before then?"
Hauptmann:	"No."
Hoover:	"You didn't know what was in the box?"
Hauptmann:	"I didn't open it yet; if the rain didn't come through ...."[5]

Hauptmann didn't answer Hoover's last question, "You didn't know what was in the box?" Hauptmann only tells us that he "didn't open it yet." Is it possible to not have opened a box and yet know what is in it? Of course it is. Since he didn't answer the question, there is something Hauptmann doesn't want us to know. Ransom money had been surfacing in the New York area for the past two years. Hauptmann said he only started spending the money during the last three weeks. Hoover's final question to Hauptmann:

Hoover:	"Why did you lie last night about this money, to the officers, you didn't tell them?"
Hauptmann:	"I figured it would put me in a more difficult spot to explain and now I have to explain anyway."[6]

Hauptmann tells J. Edgar Hoover the reason he lied is because telling the truth would place him "in a more difficult spot." Hauptmann is telling us that at the time of his arrest, he was in a difficult spot. Telling the truth would put him in a "more difficult spot." We have to ask ourselves why would telling the truth put him in such a bind? If Isador Fisch left him this money, then tell that to the police. If it is the truth, then speak out. We know that Fisch had died and could not corroborate Hauptmann's claim. However, an honest person would tell the truth. Inspector Vincent Sweeney then began asking questions.

Sweeney:	"Listen, you heard yesterday that was Lindbergh money, didn't you?"
Hauptmann:	"Yes."
Sweeney:	"Why didn't you, like a decent man, father of a boy and husband of a good woman, tell the story you are now telling?"
Hauptmann:	"The money was too hard to tell my wife, she gets too excited."
Sweeney:	"When you heard it was the Lindbergh money, why didn't you say that money was given to me by so and so under these circumstances; why didn't you?"
Hauptmann:	"I lose on this fellow seven thousand dollars."
Sweeney:	"Why didn't you tell us that story this morning and yesterday?"
Hauptmann:	"Because it really didn't belong to me and I was afraid you take the money away this $40,000."
Sweeney:	"You want us to believe that? You knew it was blood money."
Hauptmann:	"I was afraid to tell you about it yesterday. I figured on how can I explain where I got them $40,000."[7]

It appears that Hauptmann did not answer the Inspector's second question. At least it wasn't the answer they were looking for. The investigators wanted to know why he didn't tell them the truth about the money at the time of his arrest. Hauptmann answers saying he didn't want to tell his wife about the money when he found it. Sweeney then rephrases the question several times. Hauptmann's response is that the police would have confiscated the money, and he would lose the money owed to him by Fisch.

Sweeney:	"Didn't it ever suggest itself to you to tell the truth?"
Hauptmann:	(No answer)
Sweeney:	"If you were an innocent man or an honest man, as soon as you heard it's Lindbergh money, you would come out and tell the truth. Instead of that for twenty-four hours you have sat there and lied."

Hauptmann: (No response)[8]

Sweeney ends this portion of the interview not with a question but with a statement. Hauptmann does not respond to Sweeney's observation. Since it is not a question, he is not obligated to say anything. However, the Inspector insinuates that Hauptmann is not innocent, "If you were innocent..." We would expect an innocent person to respond to this comment with a denial. If he did not commit this crime, Hauptmann should have admitted he lied, that he was dishonest, and that he didn't commit this kidnapping.

Later in the interview, Inspector Sweeney questions Hauptmann about when he discovered the money. Earlier Hauptmann told the police Fisch had given him a small box which Hauptmann placed on the upper shelf in a closet. Rain water had leaked into the closet and onto the box. While Hauptmann was cleaning up the water he rediscovered the box. When he opened it he found it contained money.

Sweeney: "Then you never disturbed this package until three weeks ago?"

Hauptmann: "It was in the closet. I was looking the rain was coming down. The rain was coming down. I looked at the package, I didn't tell you yesterday because it sounds funny."[9]

Hauptmann's answer may be truthful. Maybe he did have the box stored in the closet. Maybe rain did leak into the closet and he removed the box. However, he never answers the question as to when he first "disturbed this package." This time the reason Hauptmann didn't tell the authorities about the money is "because it sounds funny." Even if it sounds a little strange, if it is the truth most people would tell it.

The interview continued on into the evening. Later a line-up was conducted. Several people identified Hauptmann as the man who handed them a gold certificate from the ransom money. On September 24, 1934, a Bronx grand jury indicted Hauptmann for extorting $50,000 from the Lindberghs. The next month, Hauptmann would be extradited to New Jersey to face murder charges. In January of 1935, he would go on trial for murder.

At his trial, Hauptmann testified in his own defense. His lawyer was Edward J. Reilly. He questioned Hauptmann on his life in the United States which included his work history and his marriage to Anna. He then inquired about Hauptmann's business dealing with Isador Fisch and the money Fisch allegedly left with Hauptmann. Reilly then turned his questioning to the night of the kidnapping.

Reilly:	"I am pointing now to State's Exhibit 1, which shows the estate of Colonel Lindbergh as of March 1, 1932. Hauptmann, were you ever in Hopewell in your life?"
Hauptmann:	"I never was."
Reilly:	"On the night of March 1, 1932, were you on the grounds of Colonel Lindbergh at Hopewell, New Jersey?"
Hauptmann:	"I was not."
Reilly:	"On the night of March 1, 1932, did you enter the nursery of Colonel Lindbergh ——"
Hauptmann:	"I did not."
Reilly:	"——and take from that nursery Charles Lindbergh, Jr.?"
Hauptmann:	"I did not."
Reilly:	"On the night of March 1, 1932, did you leave on the window seat of Colonel Lindbergh's nursery a note?"
Hauptmann:	"Well, I wasn't there at all."[10]

Hauptmann starts out giving straightforward answers. He even answered one question before it was completely asked of him. However, when he was asked if he left a note on the ledge of the nursery window, his answer "Well, I wasn't there at all" doesn't answer the question. His previous answers of "I did not" would have been an acceptable answer to this question. We must remember that Hauptmann is being questioned by his own attorney. These questions are not designed to trip him up. They should be easy to answer. Since Hauptmann did not answer the question, there is something he doesn't want to tell us. Later he would be asked this same question about the note but worded differently.

Reilly:	"Did you leave it in the Lindbergh nursery?"
Hauptmann:	"I did not."[11]

This time he answers the question. It may be he can say he did not leave the note in the nursery, but he did not say that he did not leave it on the window sill which is where it was found.

Reilly continued his questioning, accounting for Hauptmann's whereabouts on the night of the kidnapping. Hauptmann claimed that on that night he picked up his wife at the restaurant where she worked and the two of them spent the evening together at home.

Reilly:	"What time did you and your wife leave there?" [from the restaurant]
Hauptmann:	"Came home before nine o'clock; it was after nine o'clock. I can't remember the exact time."
Reilly:	"Well, it would be fair to say it was in the neighborhood of nine o'clock; is that right?"
Hauptmann:	"Yes, that is about right."
Reilly:	"Did you stay there?"
Hauptmann:	"Took the car in the garage, went right away to bed."[12]

Hauptmann does not answer the question, "Did you stay there?" He tells us he "Took the car in the garage, went right away to bed." However, he could have gotten out of bed, taken the car out of the garage and driven to the Lindbergh estate. We should also note that Hauptmann doesn't tell us who came home before 9:00 or who put the car in the garage. He doesn't use the pronouns "We or I." A good answer would have been "We came home before 9:00." Or, "I took the car in the garage." Some might say the subject is understood. However, if Hauptmann doesn't tell us that he did something, then we cannot assume that he did it.

Reilly:	"You have seen this ladder here in court, haven't you?"
Hauptmann:	"Yes."
Reilly:	"Did you build the ladder?"
Hauptmann:	"I am a carpenter." (Laughter.)
Reilly:	"Did you build the ladder?"
Hauptmann:	"Certainly not."[13]

Hauptmann wants us to believe that because he is a carpenter he would not build such a poorly constructed ladder of the type used in the kidnapping. However, Hauptmann did not answer his attorney's question. When his attorney asked him the same question a second time, Hauptmann gave a less than straightforward answer of "Certainly not." This answer is a weak denial because it still implies this is something he wouldn't do. People sometimes do things they wouldn't do. The best possible answer for an innocent person would be "No."

Reilly: "I am calling your attention now to the young lady, Miss Alexander, who says sometime in March 1932, she was standing in a railroad station, in upper part of the Bronx — I think she described it as the Pelham New York Central railroad station — that Dr. Condon was in front of you, he was very much excited, he was talking to a telegrapher, and you were standing at one side of the room looking at him. Were you ever in that station?"

Hauptmann: "I never was in this railroad station. I just happened — I know the railroad station, but I never was in there, had nothing to do in any railroad station."[14]

Hauptmann states "I was never in this railroad station." That is a very good denial. However, he then begins to tell us something else "I just happened" but he doesn't finish his sentence. He may have been thinking "I just happened *to walk in the station*" or "I just happened *to walk by the station*." It sounds like Hauptmann is qualifying his denial which mean we cannot believe he was never in this railroad station.

The state's chief prosecutor was David Wilentz, the attorney general of New Jersey. Wilentz cross-examined Hauptmann.

Wilentz: "You have had an opportunity in this Court today, and you still have an opportunity this minute to tell the whole truth. Have you told the whole truth?"

Hauptmann: "I told the truth already."

Wilentz:	"All right. So that you stand now on the story that you have given today?"	
Hauptmann:	"I do."	
Wilentz:	"You stand on the story that you gave in the Bronx, in the courthouse?"	
Hauptmann:	"To a certain extent."	
Wilentz:	"Well, I am talking about the story that you swore to before a court in the Bronx. Do you stand on that?"	
Hauptmann:	"To a certain extent, yes."	
Wilentz:	"You say you told the truth today?"	
Hauptmann:	"I told the truth to District Attorney Foley about my treatment in the Bronx; that is correct."	
Wilentz:	"About this case, not about the treatment; about the Lindbergh case, the murder: did you tell him the truth about that?"	
Hauptmann:	"To a certain extent."[15]	

When asked if he told the truth, Hauptmann replies with the vague answer "I told the truth already." He is not necessarily saying he told the whole truth that day. We do not know when he told the truth and what he told the truth about. We cannot believe Hauptmann was telling the complete truth about the Lindbergh kidnapping because he stated he was being truthful "to a certain extent." Hauptmann changed the subject by saying he was truthful when he complained about how he was treated in the Bronx. Wilentz recognized that Hauptmann did not answer the question so he asked him again if he was telling the truth about the murder. Hauptmann gave the same "to a certain extent" response. For some reason, Wilentz did not pursue questioning Hauptmann about what it was he was untruthful about.

Wilentz then questions Hauptmann about his handwriting. He presented the defendant with a notebook that belonged to Hauptmann. In the notebook, the word "boat" was spelled "boad" just as it was in the ransom note.

Wilentz:	"Now, let's get to this word that you use."
Hauptmann:	"Yes."
Wilentz:	"That is your word then, isn't it?"
Hauptmann:	"I can't remember if I ever put it in."

Wilentz:	"Well now, this isn't a joke. You know either it is your handwriting, or it isn't. Is it your handwriting?"
Hauptmann:	"It looks like my handwriting."
Wilentz:	"Now, tell me how do you spell 'boat.'"
Hauptmann:	"B-o-a-t."
Wilentz:	"Yes. Why did you spell it b-o-a-d?"
Hauptmann:	"You wouldn't mind to tell me how old that book is?"
Wilentz:	"I don't know how old it is. You know; I don't know."
Hauptmann:	"Let me see it."
Wilentz:	"Well, why did you spell 'boat' b-o-a-d?"
Hauptmann:	"This book is probably eight years old."
Wilentz:	"All right. Why did you spell b-o-a-d?"
Hauptmann:	"Well, after you make improvement in your writing."
Wilentz:	"All right. So that at one time you used to spell 'boat' b-o-a-d?"
Hauptmann:	"Probably eight or ten years ago, and I am not quite sure if I put it in."
Wilentz:	"At one time you used to spell 'boat' b-o-a-d, didn't you? Isn't that right?"
Hauptmann:	"No, I don't think so."
Wilentz:	"Eight years ago, six years ago, ten years ago, whenever it was, you used to spell 'boat' b-o-a-d; isn't that right?"
Hauptmann:	"I don't know."
Wilentz:	"You spelled it in there, didn't you?"
Hauptmann:	"I—"
Wilentz:	"You tell the truth now. Didn't you spell it in here?"
Hauptmann:	"Now listen. I can't remember I put in there."[16]

Hauptmann knows this notebook is crucial evidence linking him to the ransom note. Therefore, he does not want to admit he wrote the word "boad" in his notebook. He answers the question, "Why did you spell it b-o-a-d?" with a question, "You wouldn't mind to tell me how old that book is?" Hauptmann is stalling for time so he can think about how he will answer this question. He alludes that the notebook may be eight or ten years old, and that he may have spelled "boat" b-o-a-d years ago.

When Wilentz tries to get Hauptmann to admit he used to spell "boat" b-o-a-d, Hauptmann states, "No, I don't think so." By saying "I don't think so" Hauptmann is not committing to his answer of "no." Therefore, we cannot believe his denial that he never spelled the word boat as it was written in the ransom note b-o-a-d.

Wilentz then inquires about Hauptmann's relationship with Isador Fisch.

Wilentz: "He was your best friend wasn't he?"
Hauptmann: "Well, I don't say best friend, but —"
Wilentz: "You don't say so?"
Hauptmann: "He was very good friend."
Wilentz: "Did he help you kidnap this Lindbergh child and murder it?"
Hauptmann: "I never saw —"
Wilentz: "You never saw?"
Hauptmann: "— Mr. Lindbergh's child."
Wilentz: "But Fisch didn't help you, did he?"[17]

At this point Hauptmann's attorney objected stating that his client was not being afforded the opportunity to finish his answer. Wilentz agreed and moved onto a new line of questioning. Therefore, Hauptmann did not have to answer this last question asked of him.

When asked if Fisch helped him in the kidnapping and murdering of the child, Hauptmann didn't answer the question. He stated, "I never saw — Mr. Lindbergh's child." One could participate in a kidnapping and a murder without ever seeing the victim. By not answering the question, Hauptmann is hiding something. We see a good example of him withholding information by not answering the question in the next line of questioning. The police had discovered five holes drilled into a board in Hauptmann's garage. Hidden in the holes was part of the ransom money. There was also a sixth hole which was larger than the other holes. Wilentz wanted to know what Hauptmann kept in that larger hole.

Wilentz:. "What did you drill the other hole for?"

Hauptmann:	"To put something in."
Wilentz:	"What did you put in?"
Hauptmann:	"It wasn't money."
Wilentz:	"Answer the question."
Hauptmann:	"I put something in there."
Wilentz:.	"Answer the question."
Hauptmann:	"I put a small pistol in it."[18]

    Hauptmann does answer the first question when he replies, "To put something in." When asked what he put in the hole, Hauptmann avoids answering the question by saying, "It wasn't money." Wilentz recognizes that Hauptmann did not answer the question so he tells him to answer the question. Hauptmann responds, "I put something in there" which still does not answer the question. Wilentz does a good job in that he is persistent. He tells Hauptmann a second time to answer the question. Recognizing he cannot avoid answering the question, Hauptmann finally comes clean, "I put a small pistol in it." Now we know what it was that Hauptmann was trying to hide.

    Later in the cross-examination, Wilentz would question Hauptmann concerning the address and telephone number of Dr. Condon which was discovered written on a board in Hauptmann's closet.

Wilentz:	"Do you know what this is, Mr. Defendant? [Showing a board to the witness] You do, don't you?"
Hauptmann:	"A piece of board, yes."
Wilentz:	"From your house?"
Hauptmann:	"I really don't know if it is from my house. That is a piece of trimming and a piece of trimming from every house looks the same."
Wilentz:	"That is from your closet, isn't it?"
Hauptmann:	"I am not quite sure."
Wilentz:	"You are not quite sure?"
Hauptmann:	"No."
Wilentz:	"That is your handwriting on it, isn't it?"
Hauptmann:	"No."
Wilentz:	"What?"
Hauptmann:	"No sir."
Wilentz:	"That is not your handwriting?"

Hauptmann:	(Shaking his head.)	
Wilentz:	"You take a look at that. You have seen it many times before. I will take the paper off for you so it will be easier. Take your time about it, now. First, tell me are the numbers your handwriting?"	
Hauptmann:	"The numbers look familiar upwards. I can't remember for putting it on."	
Wilentz:	"Just keep looking at those numbers and tell me whether or not they are in your handwriting."	
Hauptmann:	"I can't remember putting them numbers on."[19]	

Three times Hauptmann tells us the handwriting on the board does not belong to him. Wilentz asked him again, "First, tell me are the numbers your handwriting?" Hauptmann replies, "The numbers look familiar upwards. I can't remember for putting it on." Instead of denying for a fourth time that this is not his handwriting, Hauptmann now begins to change his denial by saying that "the numbers look familiar." He then tells us twice he cannot remember writing those numbers. Telling us he cannot remember is not telling us he did not do it. Therefore, we cannot believe that Hauptmann did not write Dr. Condon's address and telephone number in his closet. Hauptmann's testimony concluded with a few redirect questions by his attorney Mr. Reilly, and then several more questions by Mr. Wilentz during recross-examination.

There has been a letter circulating on the internet that purportedly was written by Bruno Hauptmann shortly before his execution. I have not verified the authenticity of this document. If Hauptmann is the author of this letter, he must have had help in writing it. Because German was his first language, Hauptmann spoke broken English and would misspell words. The letter contains no misspellings or broken English. It is possible the letter was ghost written by Hauptmann's wife or another writer. I believe the letter was written by Hauptmann with the aid of an editor. I will discuss my reasons for believing this later. Therefore, I will refer to the writer as Hauptmann. Despite who wrote the letter, we can still analyze it to see what the writer is telling us. We expect the writer, whether it was Hauptmann or someone else, to say "I didn't do it" or "I did not kill the Lindbergh baby."

The letter is somewhat lengthy comprising of six type-written pages. Therefore, we will examine some excerpts from the letter. Hauptmann begins saying, "I am writing this literally within the shadow of the electric chair."[20] He goes on to say he will be executed on April 3. "On that night I shall be led out on a walk from which I shall never return."[21] In the second paragraph, we find the following denial:

> "I shall say with a voice that is the same as voice of other men that a tragedy is being enacted, that a life is being wantonly taken, that I am innocent of the crime of which I have been convicted, as innocent as any one in the world; and then if the decision of the court is carried out, I shall be strapped into the chair, and in a few fleeting seconds this body that is mortal will be no longer living and breathing but just a mass of clay."[22]

We know a person can truthfully claim he is innocent because everyone is innocent until proven guilty. Therefore, stating that one is innocent is not a denial of having committed the crime. However, in this case Hauptmann has been found guilty, and yet he still claims he is innocent. "I am innocent of the crime of which I have been convicted." This does give a little more credibility to his denial. Though he does proclaim his innocence there is one problem. Hauptmann defines his innocence by saying he is "as innocent as any one in the world." If Hauptmann is innocent, then there is someone else out there "in the world" who committed this crime. Therefore, Hauptmann cannot say he is "as innocent as any one in the world." Is he as innocent as the killer? What he should have said is, "I am as innocent as everyone else in the world with the exception of the killer." If the world is innocent as Hauptmann is telling us, then there can only be one killer, Bruno Richard Hauptmann. The letter goes on to say:

> "I am as innocent of the crime of killing the Lindbergh baby or even the slightest participation in that or any crime like it, as any one who reads this."[23]

This denial is very similar to his previous denial. Hauptmann compares his innocence to "any one who reads this." What if the killer reads his letter? We would then have a problem with his statement. Hauptmann is saying that anyone who reads his letter is innocent. Therefore, Hauptmann himself must be guilty.

> "I had no thought that I ever would be more than an honest, diligent, upright citizen, a faithful husband and, if it should please God, a loving father."[24]

Hauptmann is saying that it never occurred to him he would be more than honest, diligent, upright, faithful and loving. He doesn't tell us what it was that made him "more than" these five characteristics. We like to think that when people talk this way they are referring to additional qualities. They are even more honest than what they had thought. However, this would be interpreting what a person is saying. Remember, we do not interpret. When Hauptmann says he never thought he "would be more than honest," the "more" could be referring to doing things that are dishonest such as killing the Lindbergh baby.

> "Is there anyone that can't see that I could not be guilty of this crime?"[25]

First we must recognize this is not a denial. Hauptmann is simply asking a question which alludes to him being innocent. He wants to know if there is anyone who cannot see that he could not be guilty. Well, there were at least twelve people who couldn't see his innocence, the members of the jury.

Hauptmann then reviews the testimony at the trial. He divides the testimony into four parts: the witnesses, the ransom money, the handwriting experts, and the wood experts. He starts examining the witnesses' testimony. He points out what he believes to be inconsistencies which prove that some witnesses have been discredited.

> "Very clearly, no reputable eyewitness has ever placed me within the State of New Jersey, at, before, or after the kidnapping."[26]

While this may be a good statement, again it is not a denial. He is only saying that no one can place him in New Jersey around the time of the kidnapping. A good denial would have been for Hauptmann to say, "Very clearly, no reputable eyewitness has ever placed me within the State of New Jersey, at, before, or after the kidnapping *because I wasn't there.*"

Hauptmann then looks at Dr. Condon's testimony. He talks about how he and Dr. Condon frequented some of the same places. Although they did not know each other, Hauptmann believed they probably had seen each other. Therefore, he felt the doctor should have easily recognized him at the cemetery if Hauptmann was the person who received the ransom money.

> "But Dr. Condon in January, 1935, had not the slightest hesitation in going on the witness stand and positively identifying me as the man he had talked to in Woodland Cemetery and the man he paid the ransom money to at St. Raymond's. Was he telling the truth?"[27]

Again, this is not a denial. He is only asking us a question. Based on his analysis, Hauptmann wants us to answer the question with a "No." Why doesn't Hauptmann answer the question for us? He should have said, "Was he telling the truth? *He was not because I was not at the cemetery. I did not kidnap this baby.*"

As to the construction of the ladder used in the kidnaping, Hauptmann states:

> "I am a carpenter. I am considered a good carpenter...It is impossible that any carpenter, any man skilled in that trade could have built the kidnap ladder."[28]

Because of his carpentry skills, Hauptmann tells us "it is impossible" he would build such a poorly constructed ladder. Even though Hauptmann finds this ladder to be of poor workmanship, it is not impossible for him to construct a ladder of this quality.

Hauptmann then mentions he built a garage at his house, and he was continually going to the lumbar yard. He wants us to reason why he would use wood out of his attic to build the ladder when he could obtain wood from the lumber yard.

"Is it possible that I or any man planning the use of a ladder in such a crime, would climb up a trap door into the attic and use a piece of board from the floor for such a ladder? I say it is beyond possibility."[29]

Hauptmann is right in that it doesn't make sense he would use a board out of his attic to build a ladder. He is wrong though when he says "it is beyond possibility." While it doesn't make sense, it is possible. Most criminals are not smart. That is why they get caught. Remember, only one board from the attic was used. It is possible Hauptmann bought or gathered the wood needed, and then found he was one board short. Instead of purchasing one board just before the kidnapping was to take place, he improvised by using a board out of his attic.

Hauptmann then goes on to talk about his life in Germany and his life in the United States. He then gives us his final denial.

"I knew nothing about the Lindbergh baby. I knew nothing about the ransom money. I knew nothing about that crime or any crimes in connection with it, and I confidently expected that within a day or two I would be returned to my home, my wife, and my baby."[30]

"I knew nothing about" is not the same as saying "I didn't do it." This is a constant theme throughout this letter. Hauptmann never said, "I did not kill the Lindbergh baby" or "I did not kidnap the Lindbergh baby." Hauptmann only tells us he is innocent, and that he is not capable of committing such a crime. We cannot believe he did not commit this crime if he doesn't tell us that he didn't do it.

I said earlier that I believed Hauptmann to be the author of this letter with the aid of an editor. If someone else wrote this who believed that Hauptmann did not commit this crime, they would have told us that in the letter. Speaking for Hauptmann they would have said, "I did not kill the Lindbergh baby." Since they want to prove his innocence, it would be easy for them to say that. The evidence indicates that Hauptmann did commit this crime. Since he is guilty, it is hard for him to deny the crime. Therefore, he makes several denials but never says "I did not do it."

Over sixty years ago, Bruno Richard Hauptmann was executed for the murder of Charles Lindbergh, Jr. There are those who feel that an innocent man was put to death. Many books have been written, and many theories have been proffered as to who really killed the Lindbergh baby. When we listen to Hauptmann's own words, we find he is deceptive in his answers and explanations. We know he lied and at times did not answer certain questions. Perhaps the most convicting evidence that he committed this crime is the fact that Hauptmann never tells us, "I did not kill the Lindbergh baby."

Chapter 23

President Clinton And Monica Lewinsky Scandal

In January 1998, it was alleged that President William Jefferson Clinton had an affair with a 24-year-old White House intern named Monica Lewinsky. Lewinsky had confided to her friend and co-worker, Linda Tripp, that she had a sexual encounter with the President. She further stated that the President asked her to lie about the affair. Unknown to Lewinsky, Tripp was secretly recording her telephone conversations with the young intern. Tripp then turned the taped conversations over to independent counsel Kenneth Starr. Starr was investigating the President's involvement in a failed corporation known as Whitewater. After receiving the tapes, Starr then expanded his investigation to include the alleged Presidential affair and cover-up.

When the scandal broke, the President was preparing for the upcoming Paula Jones trial which involved alleged improper sexual requests. Lewinsky, in a sworn affidavit relating to the Jones case, stated she did not have an affair with the President. After Tripp had revealed the tapes, Lewinsky was scheduled to be deposed by lawyers in the Paula Jones case. It was reported she planned to invoke her Fifth Amendment right against self-incrimination. She was not going to testify.

The White House was careful in commenting about the alleged affair. They would not discuss anything in great detail. They would always assert that because this was an ongoing investigation, they were limited in what they could say. In the months that followed, President Clinton denied several times to having a sexual relationship with Monica Lewinsky. Starr continued with his investigation throughout the summer of 1998. Many Clinton associates were subpoenaed to testify before the grand jury.

Lewinsky's lawyers were meeting with Starr in an effort to obtain immunity for their client. After an agreement was reached, Monica Lewinsky testified before the grand jury in August, 1998. Portions of Lewinsky's testimony were leaked to the press. It was reported that she admitted to having a sexual relationship with the President. Starr now focused his attention on having the President testify before the grand jury. On August 17, 1998, President Clinton testified before the grand jury via closed circuit televison from the Map Room in the White House. The press was speculating as to what the President would say to the members of the grand jury. Some felt he would change his story. Others believed he would stick to his denials. Later that evening, the President addressed the nation and admitted he had an inappropriate relationship with Miss Lewinsky. Upon hearing this admission, many of the Presidential aides as well as many Americans were stunned. For seven months, their leader had denied any wrong doing and they had believed him. They now felt betrayed.

The President's admission on August 17 should have surprised no one. Throughout 1998, the President and others were telling us that something inappropriate did indeed occur. The problem was most people were not listening. Let's go back to January 1998 and look at some of the statements that were given prior to the President's admission in August 1998.

January 21, 1998

On January 21, 1998, President Clinton first commented on the alleged affair in an interview conducted by Jim Lehrer on PBS's News Hour.

Lehrer: "You had no sexual relationship with this young woman?"
President: "There is not a sexual relationship - that is accurate."[1]

The President's statement "There is not a sexual relationship" is probably a truthful statement. However, realize he did not say, "I did not have a sexual relationship with her." He gives this statement in the present tense which indicates at the time of the interview, he was not having a sexual relationship with Lewinsky.

I am sure when this became a public scandal the affair ended. When the President states, "that is accurate" he is not verifying Mr. Lehrer's question. The President is making it known that his statement, "there is not a sexual relationship" is accurate. A better statement for the American people would have been, "There has never been a sexual relationship."

The President denies a "sexual relationship." We have to ask ourselves what is a relationship? Most people view a relationship as an ongoing long-term commitment between two people. Miss Lewinsky described her rendevous with the President as infrequent. Infrequent meetings do not necessarily qualify as a relationship. The President could have said, "I did not have sex with Monica Lewinsky." However, he does not want to lie so he tells us they did not have a sexual relationship. The other reason he uses the term "sexual relationship" is because that is what Jim Lehrer called it. The President adopted the interviewer's language. On January 27, 1998, Lewinsky's former high school drama teacher, Andy Bleiler, admitted to having an affair with Monica Lewinsky. The affair lasted for five years. Everyone who commented on the situation referred to it as a "relationship" because that is exactly what is was. It was a long running affair.

Mr. Bleiler, in his disclosure of his affair with Lewinsky, stated she told him she was frustrated because the President would not have regular sex but only oral sex. We again can see how the President can make the statement he did not have a sexual relationship with Lewinsky. A relationship is a two-way street. There is give and take and commitment by both partners. When one person only performs a sexual act, and the other person's participation is to only receive it, that is not necessarily a relationship. That is a one-way street. The point is, if two people have sex we can say they had a sexual relationship. However, most people are not going to describe infrequent meetings, that are one-sided, as a relationship. Therefore, the President can honestly deny he had a relationship with Lewinsky.

One other point needs to be addressed about this statement. A reporter confronted Mark McCurry, the spokesman for the President, about the term "sexual relationships." The reporter said the dictionary defined sexual relationships as having sexual intercourse. The reporter wanted to know if the President was telling us he did not have sexual intercourse with Monica Lewinsky. McCurry would not specifically comment on it and basically said the President has said what he said. Lewinsky allegedly made the comment that she and the President did not have "regular sex" but only oral sex. If that is true, then we can see how the President's statement of not having a "sexual relationship" is true. Since they did not have sexual intercourse, there was no relationship. The question that needed to be asked of the President was, "Did you have oral sex with Monica Lewinsky?" Lehrer continued his interview of the President.

> Lehrer: "You had no conversations with this young woman, Monica Lewinsky, about her testimony, possible testimony before in giving a deposition?"
> President: "I did not urge anyone to say anything that was untrue. I did not urge anyone to say anything that was untrue. That's my statement to you. And beyond that, I think it's very important that we let the investigation take its course. But I want you to know that that is my clear position. I didn't ask anyone to go in there and say something that's not true."[2]

Jim Lehrer wants to know if the President had a conversation with Monica Lewinsky about her testimony in giving a deposition in the Paula Jones case. The President does not answer the question. Therefore, he is withholding information. He does not tell us, "I did not have a conversation with her prior to her testimony." All he tells us is he "did not urge anyone to say anything that was untrue."

On the same day, the President was also interviewed by the National Public Radio. They too asked a question concerning his conversations with Monica Lewinsky.

> N.P.R.: "But you're not able to say whether you had any conversations with her about her testimony, any conversations at all?"
> President: "I think, given the state of this investigation, it would be inappropriate for me to say more. I've said everything I think I need to say now. I'm going to be cooperative and we'll work through it."[3]

Again the President refuses to answer the question. If he had no conversations with Lewinsky about her testimony, he would tell us that. He claims it would be inappropriate for him to comment any further on this issue. Would it be inappropriate for him to tell us he did not have any conversations with her? He also says, "we'll work through it." If he had no conversations with her, then what does he have to work through? Based on his answers, we can assume the President did talk to Lewinsky about her testimony prior to her giving a deposition in the Paula Jones case.

Lehrer continued his interview by asking the President about the allegations he asked his friend, Vernon Jordan, to tell Monica Lewinsky to lie in her deposition. The President denied the allegation. In his denial he made the statement "I didn't ask anybody not to tell the truth. There is no improper relationship. The allegations that I have read are not true."[4]

President Clinton tells us that the allegations he has read are false. Keep in mind this is not a denial of the allegations. He did not tell us, "I did not do this." The President's statement is probably a truthful statement. When people allege something, the allegations can sometimes start to grow and get distorted. More than likely there is something in the allegations he read that is not true. We would also want to know what allegations he read. It is possible he read different (false) allegations than what we were reading in the press.

Lehrer: "Would you acknowledge, though, Mr. President, that this is a very serious business, this charge against you that's been made?"
President: "And I will cooperate in the inquiry of it."[5]

Once again the President does not answer the question and Jim Lehrer allows him to get away with it. Apparently the President does not want to acknowledge this is a very serious charge that has been made against him.

On the same day Lehrer interviewed the President, Sam Donaldson on ABC's *Prime Time Live* interviewed George Stephanopoulos a former White House employee. Donaldson questioned Stephanopoulos about the alleged affair.

Donaldson: "George, do you believe it?"

George: "I, I, I sure hope it's not true Sam. I don't know whether to be sad or angry or both you know. Either the President is the victim of one of the gravest injustices that, that any President has ever faced or he's done something unforgivable that could cripple his presidency."[6]

Stephanopoulos does not answer the question. He only hopes it is not true. If he felt it wasn't true, he would have told us that. A part of George Stephanopoulos believes the allegations to be true.

January 22, 1998

On January 22, President Clinton met with Chairman Yasser Arafat at the White House. During a photo opportunity a reporter asked the President the following question:

Question: "Forgive us for raising this while you're dealing with important issues in the Middle East, but could you clarify for us, sir, exactly what your relationship was with Ms. Lewinsky, and whether the two of you talked by phone, including any messages you may have left?"

President: "Let me say, first of all , I want to reiterate what I said yesterday. The allegations are false and I would never ask anybody to do anything other than tell the truth. Let's get to the big issues there, about the nature of the relationships and whether I suggested anybody not tell the truth. Those, that is false."[7]

The President told us he "would never ask anybody to do anything other than tell the truth." This sounds like a good denial, but it is not a denial. He did not say, "I did not tell anybody to do anything other than tell the truth." He simply said this is something he wouldn't do. Nine times out of ten he may not do it, but perhaps this time he did.

The President goes on to say he wants to "get to the big issues." He then tells us what those issues are, "the nature of the relationship and whether I suggested anybody not tell the truth." He then begins to address these issues when he refers to them as "those." However, he then changes his language and focuses on only one issue when he says, "that is false." "That is false" refers to whether he suggested someone not tell the truth. Even though he said he wanted to "get to the big issues" President Clinton doesn't clarify for us the nature of the relationship he had with Monica Lewinsky.

January 26, 1998

The next time the President commented on these allegations was on January 26. At the end of an after-school event held at the White House, the President shook his finger at the TV camera and said, "I want to say one thing to the American people. I want you to listen to me. I'm going to say this again. I did not have sexual relations with that woman, Miss Lewinsky. I never told anybody to lie, not a single time - never. These allegations are false and I need to go back to work for the American people."[8] The President did not go into detail and he did not answer any questions concerning the allegations.

The press had picked up on the fact that in his January 21 statement, the President used the present tense in describing his relationship with Lewinsky, "There is not a sexual relationship." No doubt his damage control team was made aware of this as well as questions concerning the definition of the word "relationship." This time the President issued a much stronger denial. The first thing he did was to use the past tense in his statement. "I did not have...." He is letting us know that he is denying the allegations which supposedly occurred many months ago. The second thing he did was, he denied having "sexual relations" with Miss Lewinsky. In his previous statement he called it a "sexual relationship." He could have called it the same thing, "I did not have a sexual relationship with that woman, Miss Lewinsky." However, this time he chose to slightly change his language. To fully understand what the President is telling us, we have to know how he defines the word "relations" or more specifically "sexual relations." The word "relations" does refer to intercourse. As previously mentioned, if the President only engaged in oral sex then he could truthfully say he, "did not have sexual relations with that woman."

You may be thinking I am getting picky. That all of this is just a matter of semantics as to what words the President uses. Keep in mind this is the same man who, when he first ran for President, led the American people to believe he did not have an affair with Gennifer Flowers. She claimed they had a twelve-year relationship. In 1992, on the CBS news program *60 Minutes*, candidate Clinton stated he had caused some pain in his marriage. However, he denied to CBS news correspondent Steve Kroft of having an affair with Gennifer Flowers.

> Kroft: "I'm assuming from your answer that you're categorically denying that you ever had an affair with Gennifer Flowers."
>
> Clinton: "I've said that before and so has she."[9]

This is not a very strong denial. Clinton is simply agreeing with Kroft. We saw the reason for his weak denial in 1998, during his deposition in the Paula Jones case. At that time, President Clinton admitted to having sexual relations one time with Gennifer Flowers in 1977.

Still skeptical? When candidate Clinton was on the campaign trail he was asked, "Have you ever smoked marijuana?" That is a question that requires a "yes" or "no" answer. Clinton replied, "I have never broken the laws of my country."[10] We can see he did not answer the question which means he is hiding something. A good interviewer would have immediately posed the question to him again to get an answer to that question. Based on his answer, it was fairly obvious what Clinton's strategy was in avoiding telling us he had smoked marijuana. However, it took reporters several months until they finally listened to what the President had said. Then in reference to smoking marijuana he was asked if he had broken the laws of another country. That is when candidate Clinton admitted that while in England he experimented a time or two but didn't inhale. The truth finally came out. In this case the right question was asked, "Have you ever smoked marijuana." The President gave an answer which only appeared to be a denial. The President like all of us chooses his words and answers carefully. Therefore, we should examine them carefully.

January 27, 1998

The first lady Hillary Rodham Clinton was interviewed by Matt Lauer on NBC's *Today* show. The following are excerpts from that interview:

Lauer: "There has been one question on the minds of the people in this country, Mrs. Clinton, lately, and that is what is the exact nature of the relationship between your husband and Monica Lewinsky. Has he described that relationship in detail to you?"

H. Clinton: "Well, we've talked at great length, and I think as this matter unfolds, the entire country will have more information. But we're right in the middle of a rather vigorous feeding frenzy right now. And people are saying all kinds of things, and putting out rumor and innuendo. And I have learned over the last many years, being involved in politics, and especially since my husband first started running for president, that the best thing to do in these cases is just be patient, take a deep breath and the truth will come out. But there's nothing we can do to fight this firestorm of allegations that are out there."

Lauer: "But he has described to the American people what this relationship was not, in his words."

H. Clinton: "Right."

Lauer: "Has he described to you what it was?"

H. Clinton: "Yes. And we'll find that out as time goes by, Matt. But I think the important thing now is to stand as firmly as I can and say that, you know, the president has denied these allegations on all counts, unequivocally. And been married for 22 years. And the one thing I always kid him about...."[11]

In the first excerpt, Matt Lauer asked a rather lousy question. He never asked Mrs. Clinton what was the nature of the relationship between the president and Monica Lewinsky. He only stated that this question is on the minds of the American people. Since the question was never really asked, Mrs. Clinton doesn't have to answer it, which is what she chose to do. She knows that everyone is interested in what kind of relationship existed. However, she chooses not to tell us.

The only question Lauer did ask in this first excerpt was, "Has he described that relationship in detail to you?" Mrs. Clinton responded with a lengthy statement consisting of 111 words. She used only six words in an attempt to answer the question, "Well, we've talked at great length." The majority of her statement is an attempt to distract us from the issue at hand. If we assume the President and Mrs. Clinton talked at great length about the nature of his relationship with Monica Lewinsky, then we know Mrs. Clinton has some details. So why doesn't she answer Lauer's question with "Yes, the president has described that relationship in detail with me. "If she answered his question with a "yes" the next logical question would be, "What are the details?" Mrs. Clinton doesn't want to share those details with us.

Lauer recognizes the first lady did not answer his question. He mentions that the president has told us what the relationship was not. Then he basically repeats the question concerning the relationship, "Has he described to you what it was?" Mrs. Clinton answers the question with a "Yes" and then quickly lets Lauer know she will not reveal those details by stating, "And we'll find that out as time goes by, Matt."

If there is no improprieties, why does Mrs. Clinton and the President refuse to tell us about the relationship? Remember the President said he wanted to get to the big issues about the nature of the relationship, but then he never addressed it. When people have something to hide, they don't want to talk about it.

February 17, 1998

As the weeks passed by, special prosecutor Kenneth Starr subpoenaed Clinton confidants to testify before the grand jury. White House insiders were beginning to feel the strain of the scandal. One of the next damaging statements came from press secretary Mike McCurry. In an interview published in the *Chicago Tribune*, McCurry told reporter Roger Simon:

> "Maybe there'll be a simple, innocent explanation. I don't think so, because I think we would have offered that up already....We are not in a position to provide a full and complete account, so the art is to make sure everything we say is truthful and credible. I think it's going to end up being a very complicated story, as most human relationships are. And I don't think it's going to be entirely easy to explain maybe."[12]

McCurry had always stated he did not know details of the relationship between President Clinton and Monica Lewinsky. Therefore, the statements he gave to the *Chicago Tribune* were his opinions of the situation. Since he is a close friend to the president, he has more insight into what probably happened than the man on the street. McCurry tells us he does not believe there will be a "simple, innocent explanation." In other words, he believes the president is guilty of something involving Monica Lewinsky. He further tells us he believes it will not be "easy to explain maybe." If there were no improprieties between Clinton and Lewinsky, then it should be easy to explain their relationship. However, since the President has refused to explain his relationship with Lewinsky, the public as well as his close friends can presume that something of a sexual nature did happen. McCurry also confirms the President is very cautious as to how he answers questions. This is because the President wants "to make sure everything we say is truthful and credible."

McCurry's statements set off a storm of speculation in Washington. Was he paving the way for the president to admit to certain things? Was he protecting himself from a sinking ship? The press was inquiring so McCurry addressed his comments at his daily press briefing. He told reporters "I said what I said. I just shouldn't have said it." He said that he was being "stupid, not clever." It was a "lapse in my sanity" and that "I was proving that only fools answer hypothetical questions." He reasserted he does not know details of Clinton's relationship with Lewinsky. "There is nothing about the article that indicates anything other than I speculated about matters that I don't know anything about."[13]

McCurry never said his comments to the *Chicago Tribune* were incorrect or not how he really felt. All he said was "I shouldn't have said it." McCurry is upset with himself because he betrayed his boss. He let the public know he believes the president is guilty of some type of improper relationship with Monica Lewinsky.

March 13, 1998

The rumors were President Clinton had admitted, in his Paula Jones deposition given on January 17, 1998, to having an affair with Gennifer Flowers. The press was reporting this almost as a fact that the President admitted to sleeping with her. All of this seemed to contradict what the President told the American people during his *60 Minutes* interview in 1992. The President addressed these rumors saying he told the truth during the *60 Minutes* interview and during his deposition.

On March 13, the President's deposition was made public. When we read the deposition we find the President didn't exactly admit to having an affair with Gennifer Flowers. Prior to the deposition, both parties agreed to a definition for the term "sexual relations." They agreed to the following:

> "For the purpose of this deposition, a person engages in 'sexual relations' when the person knowingly engages or causes:
> (1) contact with the genitalia, anus, groin, breast, inner thigh, or buttocks of any person with an intent to arouse or gratify the sexual desire of any person;
> (2) contact between any part of the person's body or an object and the genitals or anus of another person; or
> (3) contact between the genitals or anus of the person and any part of another person's body.
> 'Contact' means intentional touching either directly or through clothing."[14]

With those terms established, the deposition began with President Clinton being asked the following question:

> Question: "Did you ever have sexual relations with Gennifer Flowers?"

Arkansas Trooper Danny Ferguson's attorney objects to the question on the basis that a proper predicate has not been laid. He gives a somewhat lengthy objection which the President's attorney Bob Bennett joins in. The judge overrules the objection. Mr. Bennett tells the President, "You may answer the question."

> President: "The answer to your question, if sexual relations are defined as —."
> Bennett: "No, Mr. President."
> President: "What?"
> Bennett: "Go ahead."

President:	"That's right, that was upheld by the Court. The answer to your question, if the definition is section one there in the first piece of paper you gave me, is yes."
Question:	"On how many occasions?"
President:	"Once."
Question:	"In what year?"
President:	"1977."[15]

The president does admit to having sexual relations with Gennifer Flowers but only "if the definition is section one there in the first piece of paper you gave me." Section one defines sexual relations as "contact with the genitalia, anus, groin, breast, inner thigh, or buttocks of any person with an intent to arouse or gratify the sexual desire of any person." According to the agreement reached by both parties, contact means "intentional touching, either directly or through clothing." Based on this definition, if a fully clothed man placed his hip against a fully clothed woman's buttocks with the intent to arouse her sexual desires, this would be considered a sexual relation. I don't think that is what most people would deem as a sexual relation. Basically, we haven't learned anything from this deposition. The President did not admit he had sexual intercourse with Gennifer Flowers. The definition of "sexual relations" for this deposition was so broad it was easy for the President to answer the question with a "yes." If he purposely bumped into her, that could be considered a sexual relation. We now see how he can make the claim that he told the truth in both the *60 Minutes* interview and in his Paula Jones deposition.

One other interesting note. Gennifer Flowers has stated that she and Bill Clinton had sex hundreds of times. Yet, the President has only admitted to one encounter with her. Some people have questioned why he would admit to only one time if indeed they did meet many times. The answer is simple. This is his way of telling the truth without telling the complete truth. He is under oath so he admits to the affair. In his mind, he has told the truth, and that is all that needs to be said. To the President, how many times is inconsequential.

March 15, 1998

On March 15, CBS's *60 Minutes* broadcasted an interview with Kathleen Willey. Mrs. Willey was a friend of President Clinton and worked at the White House in the Correspondence Office and then in the Social Office as a volunteer. Mrs. Willey stated that in 1993, her family finances were in shambles. On November 29 of that year, she went to see President Clinton to ask for a paying job at the White House. While alone with the President in a study adjacent to the Oval Office, Mrs. Willey stated the President gave her a big, long-lasting hug and "kissed me on my mouth and pulled me closer to him." She further alleged that "he touched my breast with his hand" and that he placed one of her hands on his aroused genitals. She further said that the President whispered into her ear, "I wanted to do this ever since I laid eyes on you."[16] She then claimed she pushed the President away.

President Clinton, in a sworn deposition, has denied making a sexual advance towards Mrs. Willey. The President has stated he recalls meeting with Willey in the Oval Office. He remembers she was distraught and that he gave her a hug. The President said he may have given her a comforting kiss her on the forehead, but there was nothing sexual about the encounter. *60 Minutes* asked Mrs. Willey, "If the President said that under oath is he lying?" "Yes" she replied. She was asked again, "He is lying?" "Yes."[17]

March 16, 1998

Kathleen Willey's interview on *60 Minutes* caused a stir. The very next day the headlines in one newspaper read, "White House Denies Latest Claim Against Clinton."[18] Let's examine the quotes in the article to see just what is being denied.

> White House spokeswoman Ann Lewis:
> "What I saw last night was someone who talked about being angry, feeling that she had been taken advantage of. And yet in 1996, when she was no longer associated with the president or the White House, she came to see me and said, 'I really want to work in this campaign.'.......There was such a contradiction between what I saw and heard last night and the person I met with in 1996."[19]

Lewis denied she was spreading a rebuttal message for the White House. "No, this is my personal message. Watching last night, I thought, gee if I hadn't had my personal experience, (with Mrs. Willey) how would I feel about it?"[20]

The White House issued a statement stating the President "has no idea why she said what she did or whether she now believes that's what happened."[21]

Robert Bennett, President Clinton's lawyer:
"There is substantial material of what she has said which is under seal, which has not been released, which seriously undercuts her story."[22]

Jack Quinn, a former White House counselor:
"I think in fairness it's important....to note that there have been at least five versions of this encounter."[23]

As you read the article and the various quotes, you do not find any denials. All they did was question the credibility of Kathleen Willey. If someone accuses you of doing something you did not do, you would of course deny it. You would tell the world "I didn't do it." Kathleen Willey went on national televison and basically called President Clinton a liar; yet, the president hasn't directly responded to these allegations. When we look at the White House's response, we do not see them saying, "The president didn't do that." We do not see the President or the White House stating that Mrs. Willey is lying. The reason for this is because there is some truth in her allegations.

March 17, 1998

On March 17, a newspaper headline read, "President Tries to Discredit Allegations."[24] The White House released some 20 letters that Kathleen Willey had written to the president from 1993 to 1997. They were attempting to discredit her allegations by showing she remained friends with the president after the alleged incident. White House spokesman Mike McCurry explained the strategy:

"I think that there was an effort to put factual material out so that Americans could place this story in context. Obviously we hope that context is more favorable to the President. But it is not done with any sense of animosity towards Ms. Willey."[25]

McCurry says, "I think" which tells us he is not certain of the White House's strategy for releasing the letters. A better statement would have been, "This is an effort to put factual material out." More importantly though, we still do not have a denial from the President or the White House concerning Kathleen Willey's allegations. This time the press got it right in their headline when they used the word "tries." The President is attempting to discredit the allegations, but he has yet to do so.

March 18, 1998

On March 18, newspapers were reporting that Kathleen Willey had been seeking a book deal about her life, her alleged encounter with the President, her husband's suicide and her views of the political life in Washington. Willey's attorney, Daniel Gecker, was unable to find a publisher. What we did not see reported was a denial of Willey's allegations from the President or the White House. By March 19, it was clear the White House was not going to be issuing any firm denials of Willey's allegations. The press was now focusing on the upcoming Paula Jones trial and the testimony of Arkansas Trooper Danny Ferguson.

One other interesting note. On the *60 Minutes* interview with Kathleen Willey, correspondent Bill Bradley reported, "When the story first emerged last summer, the President's lawyer Bob Bennett said that President Clinton had no specific recollection of ever meeting Willey in the Oval Office. But in a sworn deposition two months ago, the President contradicted his own lawyer saying he remembers very well an Oval Office meeting with Kathleen Willey. Still President Clinton denied emphatically any sexual encounter."[26]

August 17, 1998

After Willey's interview on *60 Minutes*, the White House was quiet when it came to commenting on the Lewinsky scandal. President Clinton was no longer publically discussing the subject. Kenneth Starr pressed on with the investigation which led up to the August 17, 1998 appearance of the President before the grand jury.

In an effort to save his presidency, the President addressed the nation with the following speech:

"Good evening.

This afternoon in this room from this chair, I testified before the Office of Independent Counsel and the grand jury. I answered their questions truthfully. Including questions about my private life. Questions no American citizen would ever want to answer. Still I must take complete responsibility for all my actions both public and private. And that is why I am speaking to you tonight.

As you know, in a deposition in January I was asked questions about my relationship with Monica Lewinsky. While my answers were legally accurate, I did not volunteer information. Indeed, I did have a relationship with Miss Lewinsky that was not appropriate. In fact, it was wrong. It constituted a critical lapse in judgement, and a personal failure on my part. For which I am solely and completely responsible. But I told the grand jury today and I say to you now, that at no time did I ask anyone to lie, to hide or destroy evidence or to take any other unlawful action.

I know that my public comments and my silence about this matter gave a false impression. I misled people including even my wife. I deeply regret that. I can only tell you I was motivated by many factors. First by a desire to protect myself from the embarrassment of my own conduct. I was also very concerned about protecting my family. The fact that these questions were being asked in a politically inspired lawsuit which has since been dismissed was a consideration too. In addition, I had real and serious concerns about an independent counsel investigation that began with private business dealings 20 years ago. Dealings, I might add, about which an independent federal agency found no evidence of any wrong doing by me or my wife over two years ago.

The independent counsel investigation moved onto my staff and friends. Then into my private life. And now the investigation itself is under investigation. This has gone on too long, cost too much, and hurt too many innocent people. Now this matter is between me, the two people I love most, my wife and our daughter, and our God. I must put it right. And I am prepared to do whatever it takes to do so. Nothing is more important to me personally. But it is private. And I intend to reclaim my family life for my family. It's nobody's business but ours. Even presidents have private lives.

It is time to stop the pursuit of personal destruction, and to prying into private lives, and get on with our national life. Our country has been distracted by this matter for too long, and I take my responsibility for my part in all of this. That is all I can do. Now it is time in fact it is past time to move on. We have important work to do. Real opportunities to seize. Real problems to solve. Real security matters to face. And so tonight, I ask you to turn away from the spectacle of the past seven months. To repair the fabric of our national discourse. And to return our attention to all the challenges and all the promise of the next American century.

Thank you for watching and good night."[27]

The President received mixed reviews as to how well he did in his speech. Some felt he had come clean while others were upset with his attacks on the independent counsel Kenneth Starr. Let's examine the President's speech to see exactly what he told the American people.

The President starts out stating, "I answered their questions truthfully." This is a strong statement which is probably true. Most of the time when people tell us they did something, it is usually the truth. The President goes on to say, "Including questions about my private life. Questions no American citizen would ever want to answer." Now wait a second. I would answer those questions. Go ahead and ask me if I ever had sex in the Oval Office. I will without embarrassment give you an honest answer. There may be some Americans who would not want to answer some of the questions asked of the President. However, to say "no American citizen" is distorting reality.

The President described what happened by saying it was something "that was not appropriate." While this is a truthful statement, it is a very soft statement. It lacks specifics. The President does not want to tell us what happened. The President has admitted he exchanged gifts with Lewinsky. Some people may believe this is what he was referring to as not being appropriate. However, based on his previous statement that no American would want to answer these type of questions, we know that something very serious and very inappropriate occurred. The President tells us that in his Paula Jones deposition given in January 1998, his answers were "legally accurate" and that he "did not volunteer information." Notice the President did not say his answers were truthful. Instead they were "legally accurate." We have already witnessed that the President likes to play word games, and he chooses his words carefully. That is what he is telling us here. Even though he knew what information people were looking for, he "did not volunteer information." He gave what he felt were "legally accurate" answers. So, is the President being honest with us when he gave this speech, or is he being "legally accurate?"

"At no time did I ask anyone to lie, to hide or destroy evidence or to take any other unlawful action." This is probably a truthful statement. The President has always maintained he did not ask anyone to lie. Likewise, he probably did not ask anyone to hide or destroy evidence. However, it has been alleged he directly, or through someone else, told Lewinsky to return the gifts he had given to her. The theory being when the independent counsel requested the gifts, she could honestly state she does not have any gifts from the President. The President did not ask her to hide or destroy evidence, just give it back.

"I know that my public comments and my silence about this matter, gave a false impression. I misled people including even my wife. I deeply regret that." Again the President confirms that he chooses his words carefully. All along he has spoken the truth and been legally factual. However, he gave us "a false impression." He said he "misled people including even my wife." What is lacking is an apology. First to his wife and second to the American people, the voters who put him in office. He mentions he "misled" the first lady and "people." "People" could include the entire country. However, the word "people" probably refers to his advisors who stood up for him during the past seven months. The President doesn't acknowledge that he misled the entire country.

The President then attacked the independent counsel Kenneth Starr. "I had real and serious concerns about an independent counsel investigation." "The independent counsel investigation moved onto my staff and friends. Then into my private life." "This has gone on too long, cost too much, and hurt too many innocent people." Earlier the President told us he was "solely and completely responsible." Now he is shifting the blame onto the independent counsel. The reason for the ongoing investigation and the costs associated with it is because of the President's actions. Had he told us the truth and not some legal accuracy back in January, the investigation would have ended sooner. The reason people are being hurt is because of what the President did.

The majority of the President's speech deals with shifting the blame and shifting our attention away from the scandal. Instead of being completely honest with us and apologizing to us, he uses this address to make a political statement. Everyone is entitled to some privacy in their life. However, when you break the law, whether in private or in view of the public, an investigation is going to be conducted. Sexual harassment (Paula Jones case) is against the law. Lying under oath is against the law. Sometimes politics does play a part in all of this. However, the President found himself in this situation because of his own actions.

September 21, 1998

On September 21, 1998, President Clinton's videotaped grand jury testimony was released to the public. As I mentioned in chapter four, the independent counsel asked the President if he told the truth during his Paula Jones deposition. The President responded, "I swore an oath to tell the truth, and I believed I was bound to be truthful, and I tried to be."[28] The President clearly tells us he was not completely truthful when he testified in the Paula Jones deposition.

In his grand jury testimony, the President admitted he had an inappropriate physical relationship with Monica Lewinsky. The President would not go into details concerning the relationship. For anyone paying attention, it was quite obvious from the beginning that an affair did occur. By his own admission he misled people. While the President did not ask anyone to lie, it appears he may have tried to suppress evidence in order to spare himself any embarrassment. President Clinton gives us some good examples of having to pay close attention to what is being said.

Chapter 24

The Murder Of Marilyn Sheppard

Marilyn Sheppard was the wife of Dr. Sam Sheppard, an osteopath who practiced in Cleveland, Ohio in the 1950's. Dr. Sheppard, his wife Marilyn and their young son Sam lived in a two-story house near a lake in a Cleveland suburb. In July 1954, Dr. Sheppard and his wife were entertaining some neighbors at their house. As the evening progressed, the Sheppards put their seven-year-old son Sam to bed. The Cleveland Indians were playing baseball that night, so the men listen to the game on the radio. At around 12:30 a.m., the neighbors left the Sheppard house. Dr. Sheppard had fallen asleep on the couch, so Marilyn went upstairs to bed alone.

Sometime during the early morning hours, the doctor was awaken by the cries of his wife. He immediately ran upstairs to their bedroom. As he entered the bedroom, he saw what he described as a form in the room. Before he knew what was going on, he was struck from behind and fell to the floor unconscious. When he regained his senses he heard some commotion downstairs. Dr. Sheppard quickly ran downstairs and saw a form going out the backdoor of his house. Dr. Sheppard ran outside and chased the form which he would later describe as a bushy-haired man. Dr. Sheppard chased the man through the backyard and down to the lake located behind his house. On the shores of the lake, he struggled with the intruder. During the altercation, Dr. Sheppard received several blows which left him unconscious on the beach.

Later that morning, Dr. Sheppard was revived by the water washing ashore. He returned to his home and found his wife Marilyn lying in bed in a pool of blood. Marilyn Sheppard had been brutally murdered. His son was safe and still asleep in his bedroom. Sometime around 5:45 a.m., Dr. Sheppard telephoned his friend, Cleveland mayor, Spenser Houk. The mayor quickly arrived at the Sheppard residence. After seeing what happened to Marilyn, the mayor called the police.

At the start of their investigation, the police were suspicious of Dr. Sheppard's story. The house had been ransacked as if a burglar had entered the premises. What the police noticed is that it was a tidy ransacked house. Most burglars will remove a dresser drawer and dump its contents onto the floor. In the Sheppard house, the dresser drawers had been pulled open and had the appearance that someone had gone through them. However, they had not been emptied. The police found no sign of forced entry which accompanies most burglaries.

The police searched the area down by the lake where Dr. Sheppard said he fought with the bushy-haired man. The police found no evidence of a struggle. As the police searched the area around the Sheppard home, they found a small green bag. Inside the bag, they found several items that belong to Dr. Sheppard. One of the items was a bloodied wristwatch that had stopped at 5:00 a.m. The doctor said the intruder must have taken his watch. The question on the officer's mind was why didn't the burglar take his wallet.

When Dr. Sheppard fell asleep on the couch, he was wearing a t-shirt. When the mayor and the police arrived, he was not wearing the shirt. The police wanted to know where his t-shirt was. Dr. Sheppard could not explain what happened to his shirt. The police were now suspicious that Dr. Sheppard may have hidden his blood-soaked t-shirt and attempted to hide his blood-stained watch. The police were not able to find the shirt he was wearing that night. The police also did not have one other thing, a motive.

As the investigation continued, the police finally got their big break in the case. At the coroner's inquest, Dr. Sheppard testified under oath that he never had an extramarital affair. The police then found a 24-year-old woman who had worked with Dr. Sheppard. She stated that she and the doctor had a two-year affair. She also stated Dr. Sheppard was talking about getting a divorce. The police now had their motive.

As the winter of 1954 was approaching, Dr. Sam Sheppard went on trial for the murder of his wife Marilyn Sheppard. The defense pointed out that Marilyn Sheppard had two broken teeth. This indicated she probably bit her attacker. Dr. Sheppard had no open wounds on his body. The defense claimed the attack on

Marilyn was a sexual assault. The prosecution had to admit they never checked Marilyn Sheppard's body to see if she had been raped. Dr. Sheppard had on his body several bruises, including a fractured cervical vertebrae and a broken tooth. This would indicate he had been in a fight with someone. In the end, the prosecution's evidence was too great. On December 21, 1954, the jury found Dr. Sam Sheppard guilty of murder in the second degree. Dr. Sheppard was sent to prison for the rest of his life.

In November of 1959, the Sheppard murder case again attracted the public's attention. A man by the name of Richard Eberling was arrested for burglary in the Cleveland area. Found in his possession was a ring that had belonged to Marilyn Sheppard. Eberling stated he stole the ring from the home of Dr. Sheppard's brother, Richard Sheppard. Eberling denied he killed Marilyn Sheppard. During his interview with the police he made a startling statement. He claimed he was in Dr. Sheppard's house several days before Marilyn was murdered. Eberling said he had been hired to wash the windows in the Sheppard house. While removing a storm window, Eberling said he cut his finger and dripped blood in the house. Some people questioned why Eberling would account for his blood being in the house. This new information raised the possibility that Dr. Sheppard may be innocent and perhaps this window-washer was responsible for Marilyn Sheppard's death. The police and prosecutors felt they had convicted the right man. Dr. Sheppard remained in prison.

The Sheppard family believed the doctor did not kill his wife. Dr. Sheppard's brothers, Steven and Richard, were especially convinced of his innocence. It was through their efforts that in the early 1960's the family hired a young attorney to file an appeal of Dr. Sheppard's conviction. The attorney's name was F. Lee Bailey. Bailey argued that Dr. Sheppard did not receive a fair trial due to the pre-trial publicity. There was a considerable amount of media attention not only in the Cleveland area but throughout the country. The defense had asked for a change of venue, but the judge did not grant one. Bailey pointed out that the trial judge never instructed the jury not to read any news articles concerning the trial. The judge also did not sequester the jury. The press in the courtroom was allowed to get within several feet of the jurors who were seated in the jury box. The jurors could overhear any comments the press would make. Based on his arguments, a federal judge found that Dr. Sheppard did not receive a fair trial. In 1964, Dr. Sam Sheppard was released from prison. The prosecution, convinced that Dr. Sheppard was the killer prepared for a new trial.

The second trial of Dr. Sam Sheppard began in October 1966. The charge was second degree murder. After winning him a new trial, F. Lee Bailey stayed with the case as Dr. Sheppard's defense attorney. Bailey revisited some evidence that was brought out during the first trial which appeared to exonerate his client. However, Bailey's newest evidence for his client's innocence was quite clever and shocking. Mrs. Sheppard had received about 35 blows, mainly to the head area, with an unknown instrument. Bailey pointed out that none of these blows individually were fatal. He argued the reason the killer had struck Marilyn Sheppard so many times was because the killer was a weak person. Dr. Sheppard was a large and strong man. If he was the killer, it would only have taken one or two blows from him to end Marilyn's life. Bailey proffered that the killer may have been a woman. Bailey then released a bomb when a witness testified Marilyn Sheppard gave a house key to her friend, Mayor Spencer Houk. Mrs. Sheppard allegedly told the mayor not to tell Sam. Bailey suggested that Marilyn Sheppard was having an affair with the mayor. The mayor's wife found out about it, and the mayor's wife killed Marilyn Sheppard! There weren't many people who gave this theory much credence, but it did create a reasonable doubt in the juror's minds as to the guiltiness of Dr. Sheppard. The second jury found him not guilty.

Now a completely free man, Dr. Sheppard still had his problems. The ten years he spent in prison had taken its toll, and his health was declining. In 1970, at the age of 46, he died from liver failure. Though he was exonerated, many people then and today still believe Dr. Sam Sheppard killed his wife. His case has been memorialized with the television series and the movie "The Fugitive" which was loosely based on this murder. Today his son, Sam Reese Sheppard, is out to prove his father's innocence. In 1995, Sam Reese Sheppard along with Cynthia L. Cooper wrote a book titled *Mockery of Justice: The True Story of the Sheppard Murder Case.* In his book, Sam Reese Sheppard names window-washer Richard Eberling as the prime suspect in the death of his mother. In 1989, Eberling was convicted of murdering an elderly woman in 1984 and was sent to prison. Over the years Eberling has granted several interviews from prison. In October 1997, *The Learning Channel* broadcasted an interview in which Eberling was questioned about Marilyn Sheppard's death. In part of his response he said, "It's a very distasteful subject and I would like to move on. It's not true. Never was and I had no intention. I've never killed anybody. That's not my nature."[1]

In the first sentence, Eberling tells us he does not want to talk about the murder of Marilyn Sheppard. His reason for not wanting to talk about it is because, "It's a very distasteful subject." Distasteful means unpleasant. We have to ask ourselves, why is this subject unpleasant for him? There is no indication that he and Marilyn were close friends, or that her murder has created a loss in his life. If he didn't kill her, then he should be willing to talk about it and tell us he didn't do it. The murder of Marilyn Sheppard was a horrible crime. However, it should only be distasteful to a person who has a link to the victim. What is Richard Eberling's link to Marilyn Sheppard? Guilty people don't want to talk about the crimes they have committed and would rather, "move on."

Eberling goes on to say, "It's not true. Never was and I had no intention. I've never killed anybody. That's not my nature." Although Eberling tells us he has never killed anyone, in 1989 he was convicted of killing a woman. Our main focus on this part of his statement is the word "intention." When someone says he has no intention, he is telling us he has no plans. When used in the present tense, the person is telling us he doesn't want to do something. "I have no intention of going shopping with my wife." In this statement, the person is telling us he probably will not go shopping with his spouse. He is not telling us he won't go, but he is not planning on going. When the word "intention" is used in the past tense, the person is telling us he did something. "I had no intention of going shopping with my wife" tells us the husband went shopping even though he didn't want to go. Eberling uses the word "intention" in the past tense which tells us he did something even though he may not have planned to do it. He doesn't tell us what his intention was because he didn't finish his sentence.

Since the interview with Eberling dealt with the murder of Marilyn Sheppard, we can conclude his intention had something to do with Mrs. Sheppard. Therefore, we can complete the sentence for him with the following possibilities:

"I had no intention *of going to the Sheppard's house*."

"I had no intention *of witnessing Marilyn's murder.*"
"I had no intention *of killing Marilyn Sheppard.*"

Eberling's entire statement is an attempt to deny he killed Marilyn Sheppard, "It's not true. Never was." "I've never killed anybody. That's not my nature." Therefore, we can conclude his "intention" also had to do with Marilyn's death. "I had no intention *of killing Marilyn Sheppard.*" By saying he had no intention of killing her, he is telling us he did kill her. Why did the killer inflict so many blows to Marilyn Sheppard? F. Lee Bailey wanted the jury to believe the killer was a weak person perhaps a woman. Eberling is telling us it took approximately 35 blows because it was not his intention to kill Marilyn Sheppard. The crime scene did have the appearance of a sexual assault. In 1997, DNA testing was done on vaginal smears taken from Marilyn Sheppard's body at the autopsy. The test results showed there was a mixture of DNA. This means Marilyn Sheppard had sex with someone other than her husband. Was she having an affair or was she raped?

In September 1997, the NBC show *Dateline* interviewed Richard Eberling. When asked about his involvement with Marilyn's murder, Eberling responded, "I did not....You don't know that I killed anyone."[2] Again we have Eberling not finishing a sentence. "I did not...." is a denial but of what? He does not tell us what he did not do. He did not say, "I did not kill Marilyn Sheppard" which would have been a good answer. Richard Eberling could not say he did not kill Marilyn Sheppard.

"You don't know that I killed anyone" is not a denial that he has never killed anyone. We know he was convicted of murder in 1989. What Eberling is telling us is we do not have firsthand knowledge he has ever killed anyone. This is a true statement since the interviewer was not present at any of his killings. Eberling's statements only give the appearance he did not commit this murder. Even though he has the opportunity, Richard Eberling does not tell us he did not kill Marilyn Sheppard.

With the acquittal of Dr. Sam Sheppard at the second trial, the murder of Marilyn Sheppard remains officially open and unsolved. In 1997, DNA testing was done on the blood found in Marilyn's bedroom. The test results showed a third person was in Marilyn's room the night she was murdered. DNA testing of Richard

Eberling's blood, to see if there is a match with the blood found at the murder scene, showed he could not be excluded as a suspect. In 1998, Eberling died in prison not having confessed to Marilyn's murder. Based on Eberling's statements and lack of denials, we can be certain he was involved in the death of Marilyn Sheppard.

Chapter 25

The JonBenet Ramsey Murder

JonBenet Ramsey was the six-year-old daughter of John and Patsy Ramsey. In 1996, the Ramsey family resided in Boulder, Colorado. At the time of her death, John Ramsey was the president and CEO of Access Graphics, a small company he helped build. Patsy Ramsey was a former Miss West Virginia. JonBenet was following in her mother's footsteps. At the age of six, she was already a child beauty queen.

On December 26, 1996, Patsy Ramsey woke up around 5:45 a.m. She was usually the first one in the family to get up in the morning. As she walked down the stairs to the first floor, she found a three-page, handwritten note at the bottom of the staircase. The note was addressed to "Mr. Ramsey"[1] and stated that JonBenet had been kidnapped. After reading that her daughter had been kidnapped, Patsy Ramsey ran to JonBenet's bedroom to find she was missing. She then awakened her husband and called the police.

The Boulder Police arrived shortly after the 911 call. The police and the family did a cursory search of the Ramsey residence. Nothing seemed to be missing except for JonBenet. Because of the ransom note, everyone was treating this as a kidnapping. The ransom note demanded $118,000.00 in cash. The note stated, "I will call you between 8 and 10 am tomorrow to instruct you on delivery."[2] The police were checking on any leads they had and were waiting for the kidnappers to call.

At around 1:00 p.m., a detective at the house asked John Ramsey and one of his friends to check the house to see if anything had been taken or was out of place. The two men started their search in the basement. John Ramsey opened the door to a small room and turned on the lights. There he found JonBenet on the floor. Her wrists were tied above her head. A piece of duct tape was covering her mouth and a cord was wrapped around her neck. John Ramsey removed the duct tape from her mouth and picked up her body. He quickly carried her upstairs and emergency medical services were called. The discovery of JonBenet was too late. She had been dead for several hours.

The police now had on their hands a homicide. The initial investigation, at the time Patsy Ramsey reported JonBenet's disappearance, showed there was no forced entry into the house. There appeared to be no footprints leading to and from the house. The police had no suspects. Because of the recent publicized Susan Smith case in which Smith murdered her two children, suspicion was cast on John and Patsy Ramsey.

On January 1, 1997, John and Patsy Ramsey gave their first interview which aired on CNN. CNN correspondent Brian Cabell conducted the interview. The following are excerpts from the interview:

Cabell: "Why did you decide you wanted to talk now?"

J. Ramsey: "Well we have been pretty isolated, totally isolated for the last five days, but we've sensed from our friends that this tragedy has touched not just ourselves and our friends but many people. And we know that there's many people that are praying for us that are grieving with us. And we want to thank them, to let them know that we are healing, and that the grieving that we all have to do is for ourselves and for our loss, but we want to thank those people that care about us."

P. Ramsey: "We have just been overwhelmed by the cards and letters and visits and people we haven't seen for years have come to call and be supportive in their — many of them are parents, and they know and can feel our grief."

J. Ramsey: "But the other, the other reason is that for our grief to resolve itself we now have to find out why this happened."[3]

When you look at the Ramsey's answer to this question, you find they use the pronouns "we" and "us" repeatedly. "And we know that there's many people praying for us." "We want to thank those people that care about us." "We have just been overwhelmed." The focus is on themselves and the grief they are experiencing. The loss of a child will sadden any parent and there will be a period of mourning. However, ask yourself how you would answer this question, "Why did you decide you wanted to talk now?" Sure you would want to thank people for their support, and you would want to let everyone know you are okay. However, there is one other thing you would stress at every opportunity. You would tell people, "We need to find out who did this." The Ramseys never mention this in responding to this question. I thought John Ramsey was going to address this when he commented a second time saying, "the other reason is," but he went on to talk about themselves again, "for our grief to resolve itself." The Ramseys are only concerned with their grief and thanking people. They have not shown a great interest in finding the killer of their daughter. In a later interview, John Ramsey comments on the CNN interview saying, "We primarily felt the need to thank people. And that was the principle reason we did that interview."[4] The principle reason for giving the interview was "to thank people." My reason for giving an interview would be to appeal to the public for help in finding the killer.

Cabell:	"There has been some question as to why you hired a defense attorney."
J. Ramsey:	"I know. Well, we were fortunate from almost the moment that we found the note to be surrounded by friends, our minister, our family doctor, a personal friend of mine who is also an attorney, and we relied on their guidance almost from that moment on and my friend suggested that it would be foolish not to have knowledgeable counsel to help both us and with the investigation."
P. Ramsey:	"And if anyone knows anything, please, please help us. For the safety of all of the children, we have to find out who did this."
J. Ramsey:	"Not because we're angry, but because we have got to go on."

P. Ramsey:	"We can't — we can't—"
J. Ramsey:	"This — we cannot go on until we know why. There's no answer as to why our daughter died."⁵

Patsy Ramsey does say, "we have to find out who did this." The reason why they need to find out the identity of the killer is "for the safety of all of the children." That is a very good reason for wanting to find the killer. However, another reason that would be on most people's minds is because they want justice. The Ramseys don't mention this. John Ramsey states, "Not because we're angry, but because we have got to go on." I think most parents would be angry and this would cause them to say "we need to find out who did this." The Ramseys do not have to be sobbing and acting hysterical during the interview, but they should let the public know they are upset. Again, they appear to be more concerned with themselves, "but because we have got to go on" "we cannot go on until we know why." In the previous excerpt, John Ramsey stated, "we now have to find out why this happened." They are more interested in finding out "why our daughter died" than finding out who killed her.

On May 1, 1997, the Ramseys gave another interview to seven members of the media. Before answering questions, John Ramsey gave an opening statement. He concluded his statement with the following remarks:

"Um, to those of you who may want to ask, let me address very directly: I did not kill my daughter JonBenet. There have also been innuendos that she has been or was sexually molested. I can tell you those were the most hurtful innuendos to us as a family. They are totally false. JonBenet and I had a very close relationship. I will miss her dearly for the rest of my life."⁶

In the minds of many people, the Ramseys were suspects in the death of their daughter. The Ramseys knew this so John Ramsey addresses this issue by saying, "I did not kill my daughter JonBenet." This is a very strong denial. If his other statements support this denial, we should believe he is telling the truth. He then talks about the innuendos she may have been sexually molested. He responds to these innuendos by saying, "I can tell you those were the most hurtful innuendos to us as a family. They are totally false." The rumors were not only that JonBenet may have been sexually molested at the time of her death, but that her father, John Ramsey, may have been sexually molesting her. John Ramsey chooses not to specifically address this issue. Unlike the killing of JonBenet, he never denies molesting her. He never says, "I did not molest JonBenet."

Patsy Ramsey also gave an opening statement. In part of her statement she said, "I'm appalled that anyone would think that John or I would be involved in such a hideous, heinous crime. But let me assure you that I did not kill JonBenet. I did not have anything to do with it. I loved that child with my whole of my heart and soul."[7]

Patsy Ramsey also denies killing JonBenet. However, she adds to her denial "I did not have anything to do with it." John Ramsey does not mention this in his denial. Therefore, it is possible he did not kill JonBenet but had something to do with it. Patsy Ramsey refers to JonBenet as "that child." We would expect a parent to say, "I loved *her* or I loved *JonBenet* with my whole of my heart and soul." The term "that child" is used when one is referring to a child whom one does not know or does not like. There is also a difference between the phrase "that child" and "this child." The word "that" means distance while "this" indicates closeness. "That child" is an impersonal term which indicates there was not a close relationship.

After giving their opening statements, they allowed the media to ask questions. The following are excerpts from the media interview:

Question:	"Mr. Ramsey, what do you want to say to the killer of your daughter?"
J. Ramsey:	"We'll find you. We will find you. I have that as a sole mission for the rest of my life."
Question:	"Pasty?"
P. Ramsey:	"Likewise. The police and investigators have assured us that this is a case that can be solved. You may be eluding the authorities for a time, but God knows who you are and we will find you."[8]

Ask yourself what you would say to the killer. You would probably tell him he will not get away with this, that he will be caught. You would probably also tell him to turn himself into the authorities. After all, that is what you would want. You would want him to surrender to the authorities so this crime is solved. The murderer would be off the street, and the judicial process and the healing process could begin. The Ramseys never ask for the killer to turn himself in.

In searching for the killer, John Ramsey says, "I have that as a sole mission for the rest my life." We would expect him to say something like, "I will not stop looking for you until you are found" or "I will search for him for the rest of my life if that's what it takes." John Ramsey tells us he will be looking for the killer for the rest of his life. How does he know that it will take him the rest of his life to find the killer? What if the killer was caught the very next day? His mission would then be over. However, if he knows who the killer is and does not want to turn that person in, then he knows he will be searching for the rest of his life.

Question:	"If I may follow up— what does it do to you, to hear these comments and reports from profilers, investigators, rampant speculation in public that somebody close to you may have been in your home and done this to your daughter?"
J. Ramsey:	"As a person, I think it makes you very much more guarded, uh...We felt we lived in a safe community. We still do. We weren't terribly concerned about security, privacy, but certainly those issues come right up to the top of your priority list when something like this happens, regardless of ultimately who might have done it."[9]

Someone once broke into my next-door neighbor's house while they were on vacation. It turned out to be kids who only stole a piggy bank full of change. The idea that someone had broken into my neighbor's house was unsettling for the entire neighborhood. My neighbor was even more upset and concerned, so he immediately bought a security system for his house. When someone breaks into your home, you feel violated. It causes you to raise your guard. John Ramsey does not tell us with certainty this incident caused him to be more guarded because he said "I think it makes you very much more guarded." John Ramsey may not have his guard up because nobody broke into his house.

John Ramsey also said, "We felt we lived in a safe community. We still do." Even after someone has entered their house and killed their daughter, John Ramsey can say they still live in a safe community. This doesn't make sense. After a tragedy like this, you may not feel like your community has gone to hell, but you definitely would not feel safe. I wonder how safe the rest of the community was feeling at this time. However, if no one broke your house, and it wasn't a stranger who killed your daughter, then you could have the feeling your community is still safe.

Question:	"John, would you recommend the death penalty for the person convicted of killing JonBenet?"
J. Ramsey:	"I would absolutely want the most severe penalty to be brought."
Question:	"Patsy?"
P. Ramsey:	(Nods silently with tears in her eyes.)[10]

John Ramsey gives a strong answer to this question. However, he does not answer the question. He does tell us he wants the death penalty for the person convicted of killing JonBenet. Why didn't he say "Yes" or "Absolutely, I want the death penalty?" It is possible John Ramsey does not believe in capital punishment. He is now faced with a dilemma with the murder of his daughter. Personal convictions will not allow him to ask for the death penalty. Public opinion will not allow him to say he does not want the death penalty. So, he doesn't answer the question.

Another possible reason why John Ramsey did not answer the question is because he knows who the killer is and he doesn't want this person to be put to death. Remember, when people do not answer a question they are withholding information. We get this same impression from Patsy Ramsey who answers the question by only nodding her head. Why doesn't she vocally proclaim she wants the death penalty for the person who killed her child?

Question:	"What would you like to say to people who are watching this about you, and about this?"
J. Ramsey:	"We think we are a normal American family that loves and values their children, much like most of the families in this country......."[11]

The Ramseys want us to believe they are an average, normal, all American family. The problem is John Ramsey does not tell us that. He states "we think" which shows us he is uncertain if they are a normal family.

After their May 1, 1997 interview, the Ramseys went into seclusion as far as granting interviews. The next interview I saw with them was on March 17, 2000, on the ABC news show *20/20 Friday*. The interview was conducted by Barbara Walters and coincided with the release of the Ramsey's book *The Death of Innocence*. Barbara Walters begins the interview with some direct questions.

Walters:	"Mr. And Mrs. Ramsey, did either of you have anything to do with the death of your daughter?"
J. Ramsey:	"No."
P. Ramsey:	"No."
Walters:	"Mr. Ramsey, did you kill JonBenet?"
J. Ramsey:	"No, I did not."
Walters:	"Mrs. Ramsey, did you kill your daughter?"
P. Ramsey:	"No, I did not kill my daughter."[12]

The Ramseys strongly deny involvement in the death of their daughter. We must remember that almost three years have passed since their last interview. Since that time, there have been many accusations about their role in JonBenet's death. We expect them to be fully prepared to answer this type of question. Even so, we can believe them as long as they give us a consistent statement. In the very next question posed to them, we see a problem.

Walters:	"How do you feel when I ask you these questions?"

P. Ramsey:	"Insulted, pain, hurtful. How can I tell you how much I love my daughter? I love her from the depths of my being. It's just unimaginable."[13]

In talking about loving her daughter, Patsy Ramsey speaks in the present tense, "I love my daughter." "I love her." Patsy Ramsey can still have love for her daughter. However, most people would refer to this love in the past tense if their daughter had been deceased for over three years. Patsy Ramsey speaks as if JonBenet has not died. If that is what she believes, perhaps on a subconscious level, then maybe this is why she can say she did not kill her daughter.

Walters:	"The note said if you do anything - if the police come, if FBI come - your daughter will die. You called 911."
J. Ramsey:	Yes I did. (Pause) It would have been impossible to sit there and wait by ourselves."
Walters:	You also called friends to come over. Was that wise?"
J. Ramsey:	"Your daughter is gone..."
P. Ramsey:	(Overlap) "We were desperate, desperate."
J. Ramsey:	"She's in the hands of a madman, and, and you reach out for any help you can get. Um. (Pause) If I have a regret it's I didn't get more help...that morning."[14]

Remember to ask yourself how you would answer a question, and then compare your answer with the interviewee's answer. Why would you call 911? Probably to get help in finding your missing daughter. John Ramsey says the reason he called 911 is because, "It would have been impossible to sit there and wait by ourselves." It would appear his first concern is being comforted during this tragedy.

After Walters asked about calling friends to come over, John Ramsey does mention reaching out for help. However, there are three points we need to consider.

1. Order is important. First he says he called 911 because they did not want to be by themselves. Second on his mind was getting help.

2. He does not specify why he needed help. He does not state, "You reach out for any help you can get *in order to find her.*" The help he is referring to could be a comforting help for him and his wife.

3. Look at the pronouns. He states that "you" reach out for help. He did not say that "I" or "we" reached out for help.

The crime scene photos showed that in the Ramsey's basement there was an opened window that had a suitcase sitting under the window. Some believe this is how the killer left the house. He used the suitcase to boost himself up and through the window. Others believe the Ramseys planted the suitcase to support the intruder theory. Walters asks about finding the suitcase.

Walters:	"So you thought perhaps..."
J. Ramsey:	(Overlap) It was ..."
Walters:	"...the kidnapper had gone through that window."
J. Ramsey:	"I... that was my first impression, yes."[15]

John Ramsey tells us he had a "first impression." This means he also had a second impression as to why the suitcase was sitting beneath the window. We should ask him what are the other possible explanations for the suitcase being below the window.

Walters:	"During the day that your child was found and in the days following, Mr. Ramsey, there were reports from the police that you didn't seem distraught and you weren't sobbing. You seemed stoic. It was said you two rarely talked to each other. To them this made it look as if you were guilty."
J. Ramsey:	(Pause) "I've heard that. And I find that, uh... unbelievable. Uh... I've lost two children and for some one to tell me that I didn't act right, uh, I don't accept."[16]

People can express their grief and sorrow in different ways. Some people are more open than others. John Ramsey may be a private person. However, he does not tell us he was distraught or that he was devastated. All he states is he finds these comments about him "unbelievable." We see a similar noncommital answer later on in the interview.

Walters: "And Linda Arndt said she felt then from your expression that the killer was in the house, and she was afraid of you."

J. Ramsey: "Well the question I would ask Linda Arndt, has she ever looked before in the eyes of a father who has just been told his six-year-old daughter is dead? Lying there on the floor in front of him? I don't know what I looked like. I'm sure I was in agony. I'm sure I went into shock. Uh. (Pause) Linda Arndt's ability to look in someone's eyes and determine they were a killer is a remarkable talent."[17]

Note that John Ramsey did not tell us he was in agony or that he went into shock. He only said he was "sure" he was in agony. The word "sure" can mean with absolute certainty. For example, "With this evidence, I am certain (sure) he is innocent." The word "sure" can also show confidence as in "He is confident (sure) he will win." With this usage, it is not a certain thing. Is John Ramsey saying he is certain he went into shock or he is confident he went into shock? A better statement would have been "I went into shock."

Walters: "Okay. But on December 26th there are some indications that your daughter was sexually molested."

J. Ramsey: (Overlap) Well that's..."

Walters: (Overlap) "Therefore here's the motive um. You were doing it. Maybe you'd done it before. Maybe you just did it that night. Um. Perhaps your wife discovered you. Whatever it was, JonBenet cried out... you killed her."

J. Ramsey: "Well that's (Pause) fits right in the category of it could have been done by an alien as well.

It makes no sense. There is no history. A person doesn't go throughout their lives a normal human being. One night turn into a monster. Slaughter their daughter. Go to bed and get up and act normal from there on. That doesn't happen. In these kinds of cases, virtually all of 'em I suspect, where there is child abuse in a family there's a long history. And that's not the case in our family."[18]

Barbara Walters states that one of the theories to this murder is that John Ramsey was sexually molesting his daughter. He responds by saying that makes no sense because there is not a history of sexual abuse in their family. What we do not see is a denial he never molested his daughter. This would be the perfect time to state he never did such a thing. This is the same thing we saw during the March 1, 1997 interview when all he said was the innuendos that JonBenet had been sexually molested were hurtful.

Walters: "This is a very brutal murder, and yet some of the authorities have said that you staged this. Um, that you loosely tied your daughter's hands. That you put the noose, the garrote, to make it look as if some terrible person had done this. That this whole... picture was staged."

J. Ramsey: "Well, that's absurd. This was done by a terrible person. The garrote... was deeply embedded in JonBenet's throat. Her hands were tightly bound, I couldn't get the knot untied, I tried to get untied, even before I brought her upstairs. The fundamental issue is no logic has been applied to any of this case.........."[19]

Again we have no denial. Walters states "YOU staged this" "YOU loosely tied" "YOU put the noose" and yet John Ramsey does not deny it he only tries to explain the irrationality of such a theory.

Walters: "What has this done to your marriage?"

J. Ramsey:	(Pause) "I think it's strengthened our love. Uh. For each other."
P. Ramsey:	"I can't imagine... what I would do without John to lean on."
Walters:	"Did either of you ever considered suicide?"
J. Ramsey:	"I have to admit that yes I did."
Walters:	"You did too?"
P. Ramsey:	"Yes. But we have other children. They need us now more than ever. So we have to be strong for them. That's the only reason... that we have to go on."[20]

John Ramsey said he "thinks" this tragedy has strengthened their marriage. Since he does not tell us this with certainty, we cannot believe their marriage is stronger.

Patsy Ramsey states the only reason they have to live is because they have other children. We would expect her to say that one of the reasons to go on would be to find out who killed their daughter. If they know who killed JonBenet, then this would no longer be a reason for living.

At the end of the interview, Barbara Walters played a video tape of Colorado governor Bill Owens who on October 27, 1999, challenged the Ramseys to stop hiding behind their attorneys and work with the police to find the killer. Walters asked the Ramseys how they would respond to the governor. After John Ramsey gave his response, Patty Ramsey then gave her reply.

P. Ramsey:	"The Boulder police would like this to go away. They would like to just close the books on it, pretend that none if it ever happened. But we are not going away. We are going to be their worst nightmare. Patsy and John Ramsey are hanging in there, until the day we die we'll be looking for the person that murdered our daughter."[21]

In their May 1, 1997 interview, John Ramsey stated that in looking for the killer, "I have that as a sole mission for the rest of my life." Three years later, Patsy Ramsey affirms that the killer will never be found during their lifetime. "Until the day we die we'll be looking for the person that murdered our daughter." How do they know it will take that long to find the killer? What if the killer was found tomorrow? This is a clear indication they know who killed JonBenet and that they will not reveal that person to us.

The next interview of the Ramseys was with Katie Couric. The five-part series of their interview was aired on NBC's *Today* show on March 20 - 24, 2000.

Couric: "Did you all lock the doors and turn the alarm system on when you left?"
J. Ramsey: "We normally did not use the alarm system. It was a very ... it was an older alarm system that was put into the house by the previous owner. And it had this huge siren inside the house. It was an ear-piercing siren. So we didn't – sadly we didn't use it."[22]

John Ramsey tells us they did not use the alarm system. However, he did not answer the question as to whether they locked all of the doors. Katie Couric asked a compound question which allowed him to get away with not answering one of the questions.

Couric: "Tell me what happened once you got her home."
P. Ramsey: "We put her to ... John carried her up to bed and then I, you know, kind of got her undressed and pulled her pajama pants on. They were kind of some long underwear pants around her - pajama drawer. She was sound asleep. Tucked her in bed, kissed her good night, said her prayers."
Couric: "You said your prayers."
P. Ramsey: "I said my prayers over her and tucked her in bed."[23]

On the night of JonBenet's death, the Ramseys had dinner at a friends house. They stated that while returning home, JonBenet fell asleep in the car. Patsy Ramsey tells us that after her husband carried JonBenet to bed, "I, you know, kind of got her undressed." When a person uses the phrase "you know" it shows a lack of commitment to their statement. She is not saying she definitely got her undressed. She is saying you know I did it. We do not know what she did until she tells us what she did. The words "kind of" qualify her statement. Did she get her undressed or did she not get her undressed? As an interviewer, we would want to explore this area. We also see a lack of the pronoun "I." "Tucked her in bed, kissed her good night, said her prayers." She does not tell us she (I) did this.

Couric:	"One problem which we've heard about repeatedly is that the crime scene was contaminated."
J. Ramsey:	"Mmm-hmm." (affirmative)
Couric:	"That's because you removed the duct tape, because you took JonBenet in your arms and took her upstairs."
J. Ramsey:	"But what would you have done? If you had just found your daughter in the basement, in a ... grimy room in a cellar? If the police expected me to say, 'Opps, I better not touch this, this is a crime scene,' they're crazy. That was my daughter. I found her. I wanted to – take her back in my arms."[24]

In talking about contaminating the crime scene, Katie Couric mentions that John Ramsey removed the duct tape from JonBenet's mouth and held her in his arms. John Ramsey focuses on the latter not addressing the removal of the duct tape. We would expect him to say the reason he contaminated the crime scene (removed the duct tape) was because he wanted to see if she was alive. Why did he not mention this? Is it because he already knew she was dead?

Couric:	"Do you in your hearts believe that this crime will one day be solved?"
P. Ramsey:	"Yes, I do."
J. Ramsey:	"I do."
P. Ramsey:	"We've been told that we can find the killer. That's what we're living for."[25]

In their March 17, 2000 interview with Barbara Walter, Patsy Ramsey said the only reason for living was because they had other children. "We have to be strong for them. That's the only reason that we have to go on." Now she says they are living for the day that they find the killer. Why the change? Perhaps it was pointed out to her what she had said in her previous interview.

The Ramseys continued to make the talk show circuit. They next surfaced on March 27, 2000 on the *Larry King Live* show which aired on CNN. Larry King asked them what happened the morning they discovered JonBenet was missing.

P. Ramsey:	"Then I go down the spiral staircase, and there on one of the runs of the stair is the three-page ransom note."
King:	"And no one has entered the house. The door isn't open. You read the note."
P. Ramsey:	"I don't know."
King:	"What did you do?"
P. Ramsey:	"Well, I hurriedly read it, you know, and didn't take long to understand what was happening. And I ran back upstairs and pushed open her bedroom door, and she was gone."[26]

At the time of this interview, Patsy Ramsey knows that the note left on stairs was a ransom note. However, as she tells her story from memory, she should not refer to the three-page note as a ransom note. Put yourself in her shoes. You are retelling the story of walking down the stairs and you see three pieces of paper lying on the steps. You do not know what they are until you read them. In previous interviews, she did refer to it as a three pieces of paper. In this interview, she calls it a ransom note before she ever picks it up.

She tells us she "hurriedly read it, you know." The phrase "you know" shows a lack of commitment to the statement. Patsy Ramsey uses this phrase a lot during all of her interviews. For some people this may be an idiosyncrasy. They are always saying "you know." However, when Patsy Ramsey talks about JonBenet competing in the pageants and how much fun she was, she doesn't use the phrase "you know." It only appears when she is asked sensitive questions.

After reading the ransom note, Patsy Ramsey runs upstairs, goes into JonBenet's room and tells us that "she was gone." There is a difference between saying "she was gone" and "she wasn't there." Saying that someone is "gone" can be used to refer to one who has passed away. It can also be used to describe that a person is no where to be found. The Ramseys lived in a very big house. How did Patsy Ramsey know that JonBenet was not somewhere else in the house? She didn't tell us she wasn't there in her bed. She told us "she was gone."

King:	"Well, this is hard. When was the first time you saw your daughter? After all of this, you got the note, how long after this did you see JonBenet?"
J. Ramsey:	"You mean, when did they find her?"
King:	"Yes."
J. Ramsey:	"Well, they found her later that morning."[27]

John Ramsey uses the pronoun "they." Who is he talking about? The police? John Ramsey is the one who found JonBenet's body in the basement. It was he who open the basement door, turned on the light and found her body on the floor. He should have said, "when did I find her?" Changing pronouns is an indication of deception.

King:	"What are you going through at this point?"
J. Ramsey:	"Your daughter is in the hands of a monster. You don't know where. You don't know if she's cold, if she's – you just don't know. It's a horrible feeling for..."[28]

John Ramsey does not finish his sentence "if she's - you just don't know." It would appear he probably was going to say "if she's alive." The reason he didn't say this may be because as a grieving father this would be difficult to say. It could also be he knew JonBenet was dead so he couldn't bring himself to say "You don't know if she's alive." Also note that he says "you don't know" instead of "I don't know."

Later in the interview, King asked John Ramsey if he knew JonBenet was dead when he found her. Ramsey does state he did not know she was dead.

> J. Ramsey: "No, I didn't. I had this rush of just, thank God, I found her. She - her hands were tied. She had tape over her mouth. I removed the tape immediately. I could feel that her skin was cool, and I feared the worst, but I still held out hope that she would be okay."[29]

Note that John Ramsey "held out hope" vs "had hope." The word "had" shows definite possession. "I had hope that she would be okay." The phrase "held out" is not as personal and somewhat distant.

> J. Ramsey: "There is a dangerous killer loose, we believe. This killer, if he's still alive, will kill again. It's time to get on with that."
> King: "You're worried for your other boy?"
> P. Ramsey: "Yes, I am worried."
> King: "Worried for the neighbors?"
> P. Ramsey: "I'm worried for the entire country. There is a killer walking around out there someplace. Lou Smits tells us that we can ..."[30]

This response seems to be in contrast to their May 1, 1997 interview in which John Ramsey said they still live in a safe community.

> King: "Well, living with this, Patsy, you know the truth. But you don't know who did it."
> P. Ramsey: "I don't know."
> King: "But you know you didn't."
> P. Ramsey: "I did not."
> King: "And you know you didn't."
> J. Ramsey: "That's one the one thing we know with absolute certainty that's a fact in this case is that we did not kill our daughter."[31]

The Ramseys do deny killing their daughter. Keep in mind though that no question was posed to them. Larry King told them "You know you didn't." This makes it easier for a person to deny by confirming what the interviewer has stated.

King:	"A couple of things before we take another call. Some people ask why you didn't search the house right away, run through the whole house right away."
J. Ramsey:	"We thought we were dealing with a kidnapping. We really did."[32]

John Ramsey uses the word "really" to convince us they thought this was a kidnapping. This is one of those words that indicates deception.

On the following night, March 28, 2000, The Ramseys returned to the *Larry King Live* show.

King:	"Patsy, what do you make of a ransom note? Why would a kidnapper write a ransom note when they've killed someone and left that someone in the house? What would be the point of a ransom note, do you think?"
P. Ramsey:	"I don't know, but I hope to ask the killer one of these days."
King:	"Can you guess?"
P. Ramsey:	"I think it was a ruse to throw us off."
King:	"From what? I mean, unless he's in the house."
J. Ramsey:	"We did two things in the book..."
King:	"By the way, the book is "The Death of Innocense." I should have mentioned that right at the beginning of the show. The book is now on sale everywhere. The book is "The Death of Innocence." Our guests are the Ramseys. I'm sorry John."
J. Ramsey:	"We spent a considerable amount of time describing as best we could what we think happened, and we think the killer wrote the note before we came home that night. We

	think he was in the house while we were out four to five hours. The note was written before the crime."
King:	"He intended then to kidnap you?"
J. Ramsey:	"We think it was a kidnapping."
King:	"Gone awry?"
J. Ramsey:	"And something went terribly wrong. That's what seasoned investigators have told us."[33]

Over the years, the Ramseys have stated several times they believe this was a kidnapping that turned into a murder. John Ramsey reaffirms this belief, "We think it was a kidnapping....and something went terribly wrong." However, when Larry King asked Patsy Ramsey what would be the point of a ransom note when JonBenet's body was left in the house, she responds "I don't know." Why didn't she say she thought this was a kidnapping? That the kidnapper wrote the note, but then for some reason killed JonBenet before he left the house? She goes on to say, "I think it was a ruse to throw us off." She is now supporting the theory that JonBenet was intentionally murdered, and the murderer left the note to confuse the police. If she firmly believed this was a kidnapping that went bad, she should have stated that. Either she believes this may not have been a kidnapping, or she knows this was not a kidnapping.

Later on in the show Larry King took telephone calls from his viewers.

Caller:	"Hello. I'd like to know, John and Patsy, why is December 25th the date of death on JonBenet's tombstone, not December 26th?"
J. Ramsey:	"Well, that's a question we've been asked, and I have - I chose that date, and I'll tell you why. And I debated that, because I didn't know for sure when she died. But I picked December 25th because I wanted the world to remember what happened to my daughter on Christmas day. I can't imagine a more horrible crime than a child being murdered on Christmas night. That was the main reason I picked December 25th. I knew we'd be

criticized. I knew it would raise suspicions, but I wanted the world to remember what was done to my daughter on Christmas night."[34]

A lot of people believe that JonBenet was killed some time after midnight. Her death would then have occurred on December 26th. John Ramsey knows that by putting the date of December 25th on her tombstone, it would draw suspicion that perhaps they know the exact time of her death. He tells us the main reason for picking the 25th is because he wants the world to remember what happened on that Christmas day. Look at the words he uses. The key word is "main." He didn't say "the reason," but stated "the main reason." John Ramsey clearly tells us there is another reason why he selected December 25th. However, he chose to keep that reason to himself. Perhaps he does know the date JonBenet died.

Two months later on May 31, 2000, the Ramseys once again appeared on the *Larry King Live* show. Also appearing on the show was former Boulder Colorado police detective Steve Thomas. Thomas resigned from the Boulder Police Department in 1998 after being frustrated with how the JonBenet murder investigation was proceeding. He admittedly believes Patsy Ramsey was involved in her daughter's death. The majority of the interview has the Ramseys squaring off against Thomas. Larry King acts as the referee. Both sides refuse to answer some questions and there is a lot of crosstalk between them. Amidst their bickering two things jump out at us.

King: "All right. Patsy, he asked a fair question."
P. Ramsey: "How many overtures have been made to them, including one on the table right now, for us to come and talk with them, and bring our detectives and our investigators and share information and work together..."
King: "You're making that offer to them now."
P. Ramsey: "... put pride and prejudice aside, Mr. Thomas, and work to find the killer of this child?"[35]

Patsy Ramsey refers to JonBenet as "this child." As I mentioned earlier the word "this" indicates closeness whereas the word "that" shows distance. However, we do not see a personal closeness because Patsy Ramsey did not use the pronoun "our." She did not refer to JonBenet as "our child."

Toward the end of the interview, we find the following exchange:

Thomas: "Do you support the death penalty for the person who is ultimately convicted of this crime?"
J. Ramsey: "I do not support the death penalty because of the horrible flaws I've seen in our justice system. There are many, many innocent people on death row today because of people like Steve Thomas."
Thomas: "Patsy?"
P. Ramsey: "I concur."[36]

On May 1, 1997, the Ramseys were asked an almost identical question. Let's compare their answers.

Question: "John, would you recommend the death penalty for the person convicted of killing JonBenet?"
J. Ramsey: "I would absolutely want the most severe penalty to be brought."
Question: "Patsy?"
P. Ramsey: (Nods silently with tears in her eyes.)[37]

I had mentioned that when asked this question on May 1, 1997, John Ramsey did not answer the question. Therefore, he is withholding some information. He is either against the death penalty, or he knows who killed JonBenet and doesn't want that person to be executed. Based on his answer on May 31, 2000, it would appear he opposes the death penalty. The problem is why didn't he tell us this on May 1, 1997? Maybe he felt that public opinion right after the murder would not allow him to say that. Still, in 1997 he said he would want the most severe penalty to be brought. If the most severe penalty is a death sentence, then he is stating he does support the death penalty. There is also the possibility that in May 1997 John Ramsey was in favor of the death penalty. By May 2000 he opposed it.

In the 1997 interview, Patsy Ramsey did not verbally answer this question. She only nodded her head. Three years later she still has very little to say about whether the person responsible for her daughter's death deserves the death penalty. She only replied, "I concur."

In March 2000, John and Patsy Ramsey's book, *The Death Of Innocence*, published by Thomas Nelson Publishers was released. The Ramseys give us insight as to what they experienced with the death of their daughter. They also tell us what they believe happened to JonBenet on that fateful night. Let's take a look at some excerpts from their book.

After finding the ransom note, John and Patsy checked to see if their son Burke was okay. Patsy writes:

> "Both of us race to Burke's room at the far end of the second floor and find him apparently still asleep."[38]

We find in this statement an unnecessary word; "apparently." Instead of telling us that Burke was asleep, Patsy Ramsey states he "apparently" was asleep. She qualifies her statement allowing for the possibility that Burke was not asleep. In their first interviews with the police, the Ramseys said Burke was asleep when they discovered JonBenet was missing. There were reports that on the tape of Patsy Ramsey's call to 911, Burke's voice can be heard in the background. This was supposed to be evidence they were lying to the police. Perhaps this is why she will not definitely state Burke was asleep.

John Ramsey describes what is was like the morning of the kidnapping. The police were at their house and everyone was waiting with anticipation for the kidnappers to call. Sometime that morning he remembered that earlier in the year he was locked out of his house. In order to get in, he had to break a basement window so he could reach in and release the latch. With that thought, he rushed to the basement to find the window pane still broken and the window open. Under the window was a Samsonite suitcase. It was his belief that maybe this is how the kidnapper entered and left their house. What is amazing is that John Ramsey then went back upstairs, but he did not tell the police about finding the open window!

In 1992, John Ramsey's daughter Beth died in an automobile accident. In comparing her death with that of JonBenet's, he writes, "But JonBenet was murdered. Someone had entered our home while we were asleep."[39] Later in the book, the Ramseys state they believe the killer entered their house not while they were asleep, but while they were out visiting with friends.

The ransom note was written on a pad of paper that was in the Ramsey residence. The police also found a practice ransom note on one of the pads. Speculation was that either John or Patsy had written the ransom note. John Ramsey comments on this and writes "The police immediately saw this evidence as supporting the theory of our guilt."[40] He could have stated this evidence supported the theory *that we killed JonBenet* or *that we were guilty*. Instead he chose the words "our guilt." He is not talking about anyone else's guilt. He is talking about John and Patsy Ramsey's guilt. Later on, Patsy Ramsey would write about how the media would misprint a story, and this "further convinced the public of the certainty of our guilt."[41] Pronouns give us responsibility. The Ramseys are telling us they are guilty of something. When John Ramsey writes about a documentary that showed Geraldo Rivera pointing the finger at the Ramseys, John Ramsey states, "The documentary presented a clip from his show where he was seen proclaiming our guilt."[42] Geraldo Rivera cannot proclaim their guilt. He can proclaim they are guilty. Only John and Patsy Ramsey can proclaim their own guilt, and this is what they have done when they use the phrase "our guilt."

Chapter 33 is the last chapter of their book. It is titled *The Murderer*. In describing what they believed happened that night, John Ramsey writes,

> "What do we believe actually happened the night of December 25, 1996? I believe the killer came into our house while we were at the Whites' for dinner that evening."[43]

> "I believe he entered our house during our absence and was hiding when we returned, possibly in the basement."[44]

Look at the pronouns. John Ramsey repeats a question that apparently has been asked of them, "What do we believe." However he does not tell us what they believe. He tells us what he believes, "I believe." This explains why Patsy Ramsey couldn't tell Larry King on March 28, 2000, why a kidnapper would leave a ransom note. Despite what John Ramsey said during that interview, "We think he was in the house while we were out four to five hours,"[45] he tells us in their book that this is his theory and that his wife may have a different theory as to what happened that night.

In describing a possible scenario of the crime, John Ramsey makes several references to his house in chapter 33 in the following order:

> "I believe the killer came into our house..."
> "He could have entered our home..."
> "The killer could have easily watched our house..."
> "(He) could have been in a car near the front of our house..."
> "I believe he entered our house..."
> "The killer was familiar with the house..."
> "Our home had been opened to the public..."
> "Two thousands visitors streamed through our house..."
> "Our house had been vacant..."
> "A trespasser could have entered the house..."
> "(The killer had time) to get a layout of the house..."
> "He familiarized himself with the house..."
> "The fact that it was written in our home..."
> "The man cleverly waited in our home..."[46]

Ten times he refers to their residence as being "our house" or "our home." However, four times he refers to it as being "the house." We know that when a person goes from "our house" to "the house," he is not taking possession of the house. He is distancing himself from the house. But why create such distance? Why doesn't John Ramsey continually refer to it as their house? We also know that changing pronouns is an indication of deception.

We also find the following passage in this last chapter:

> "Of course, we don't know exactly what time JonBenet was murdered, but it had to be sometime after we went to sleep

around ten o'clock and before we awoke early the next morning around 5:30 a.m."[47]

We can consider the words "of course" as being unnecessary words. Without these words the sentence still makes sense and it is actually a much stronger denial, "We don't know exactly what time JonBenet was murdered." The words "of course" mean we are to take it for granted they do not know the time of her death. We do not take anything for granted but believe what they tell us. They haven't clearly told us they do not know the time of JonBenet's death.

At the end of their book the Ramseys have a message for the killer.

"Patsy and I and our families want you to know that we will be after you until we find you."[48]

During their May 1, 1997 interview, John Ramsey told us he would be searching for his daughter's killer for the rest of his life. Three years later during their interview with Barbara Walters, Patsy Ramsey told us that until the day she dies she will be looking for the person that murdered her daughter. However, in their book we have a change of language. They now tell us they will be after the killer "until we find you." For some reason, they have now decided it may not take them an entire lifetime to find the killer. Perhaps someone mentioned to them their previous statements were a bit incriminating. Maybe they decided to reword their statement. We must also remember an editor was probably used to make their book more readable. It may be an editor recognized what they were really saying and changed the wording.

The last thing I want to point out about their book has to do with the order in which the Ramseys refer to Burke and JonBenet. There is always a reason why one name gets mentioned before another name. When parents lists their children's names, they will usually mention them according to their age. Since the eldest child has been around longer than his siblings, he or she gets mentioned first. The next in line get mentioned second. Of course, if a parent is talking about a particular child, they should mention him or her first. Let's look to see how John and Patsy Ramsey refer to their children.

Seventeen times Patsy Ramsey mentions the names of her two children in the same sentence. On fifteen of those occasions, she refers to them as "Burke and JonBenet." We would expect this since Burke is the oldest. Only twice does she mention JonBenet's name first and Burke's second. One time is in reference to getting a dog. JonBenet and Patsy went to a pet store where JonBenet picked out a dog. About three weeks later, the dog wasn't acting right. A visit to the veterinarian revealed the dog was dying. Patsy did not want to tell her kids about the dog's condition. So, she went back to the pet store and traded dogs for the same kind of puppy. "The new dog was a month younger, so he was smaller. But I hoped we could pull the transfer off without JonBenet and Burke knowing."[49] She then goes on to say that JonBenet noticed the dog was different. She never tells us about Burke's reaction. We can clearly see why she deviates from her normal language and mentions JonBenet's name first. Even though the dog was a family dog, JonBenet selected him. In a sense, it was her dog. She probably played with the dog more than Burke did. So, when Patsy talks about the dog and her kids, she mentions JonBenet's name first, Burke's second.

The other time she mentions JonBenet's name first may not be as innocent. In talking about being in the hospital, Patsy Ramsey writes, "Everyone who came into my room wore a surgical mask - and I wore one myself. JonBenet and Burke could stand at the doorway of my room, but I couldn't hug them as I desperately wanted to do."[50] When Patsy Ramsey talks about hugging her kids, she mentions JonBenet's name first. Other times in their book when she talks about missing her kids, and her kids visiting her in the hospital, she always refers to them as "Burke and JonBenet." The one time she talks about wanting to have physical contact with her kids, JonBenet is mentioned first. This probably means she physically felt closer to JonBenet than to Burke. We must remember that someone had such severe physical contact with JonBenet that it caused her death.

John Ramsey mentions the names of both of his kids in the same sentence ten times. He starts out as we would expect listing Burke's name first and JonBenet's name second.

> "Our nine-year-old son, Burke, and six-year-old daughter, JonBenet."
> "Burke and JonBenet knew how to work the system."

"Burke and JonBenet were very excited about the trip."
"Patsy, Burke, JonBenet, and I planned to meet Mike Archuleta, our pilot, at Jeffco in the morning for a 7:00 departure."[51]

John Ramsey then talks about how he is a certified pilot, but he prefers to have Mike Archuleta fly with them as a copilot. He goes on to say, "Besides, Mike was like part of the family; he and his wife, Pam, had no children of their own, so he really took up with JonBenet and Burke when he was with us."[52] This is the first time John Ramsey mentions JonBenet's name first and Burke's second. He does this when talking about the relationship Mike Archuleta had with his children. Apparently in John Ramsey's eyes, Mike gave more attention to JonBenet than he did to Burke. Therefore, he lists JonBenet's name first.

From this point on, John Ramsey always mentions JonBenet's name first and Burke's second. It doesn't matter in what context he is talking about them, JonBenet comes first. This is a change from the first four times he mentioned their names. We can see why he started out listing Burke's name first. On page one, he refers to Burke and JonBenet by their ages. Since Burke is the oldest, he mentions his name first. Apparently this set the tone for the next five pages and three references. On pages one through six, he mentions Burke's name first and JonBenet's name second. However, during the next 376 pages of their book, he lists JonBenet's name first. We have to wonder why he changed his language. Everything a person says has a meaning. It is possible that John Ramsey liked JonBenet more than he did Burke. I am sure he would disagree with that. Maybe he did love both of them equally. However, there is absolutely a reason why he put JonBenet's name first and Burke's second.

Perhaps the biggest piece of evidence that we have in solving this murder is the ransom note. The police as well as the Ramseys believe that whoever wrote the note is probably the killer. If the police can match the handwriting in the ransom note to a suspect's handwriting, the case is solved. The problem has been they have not found a match. Even without a positive match, the ransom note is still the key to solving this crime.

Using Statement Analysis we can examine this ransom note and determine if it is a legitimate ransom note. Was it the intention of the writer to extort money from the Ramseys, or was the note written as a ploy after JonBenet was killed? Determining the veracity of the ransom note is important. If the note is legitimate, then we know we have a kidnapping that went bad. This would exclude the Ramseys as possible suspects. Why would they kidnap their own child and demand money from themselves? If the note is fraudulent, then we know this was a murder made to look like a kidnapping. Anyone could be a possible suspect. Let's examine the ransom note left at the Ramsey residence.

"Mr. Ramsey.

Listen carefully! We are a group of individuals that represent a small foreign faction. We respect your bussiness but not the country that it serves. At this time we have your daughter in our posession. She is safe and unharmed and if you want her to see 1997, you must follow our instructions to the letter.

You will withdraw $118,000.00 from your account. $100,000 will be in $100 bills and the remaining $18,000 in $20 bills. Make sure that you bring an adequate size attache to the bank. When you get home you will put the money in a brown paper bag. I will call you between 8 and 10 am tomorrow to instruct you on delivery. The delivery will be exhausting so I advise you to be rested. If we monitor you getting the money early, we might call you early to arrange an earlier delivery of the money and hence a earlier pick-up of your daughter.

Any deviation of my instructions will result in the immediate execution of your daughter. You will also be denied her remains for proper burial. The two gentlemen watching over your daughter do not particularly like you so I advise you not to provoke them. Speaking to anyone about your situation, such as Police, F.B.I., etc., will result in your daughter being beheaded. If we catch you talking to a stray dog, she dies. If you alert bank authorities, she dies. If the money is in any way marked or tampered with, she dies. You will be scanned for electronic devices and if any are found, she dies. You can try to deceive us but be warned that we are familiar with Law enforcement countermeasures and tactics. You stand a 99% chance of killing your daughter if you try to out smart us.

Follow our instructions and you stand a 100% chance of getting her back. You and your family are under constant scrutiny as well as the authorities. Don't try to grow a brain John. You are not the only fat cat around so don't think that killing will be difficult. Don't underestimate us John. Use that good southern common sense of yours. It is up to you now John!

Victory!
S.B.T.C"[53]

One of the first things we notice is that this is a very long ransom note. Most ransom notes are short and to the point. "We have your kid and she is safe. It will cost you $400,000 to get her back. Do not call the police. We will be contacting you." This ransom note was written on three pieces of paper. This is our first clue this note may be bogus.

As we read the ransom note, we find it doesn't make much sense. "We are a group of individuals that represent a small foreign faction." What exactly does the writer mean by "group of individuals?" Every group is comprised of individuals. That's what makes it a group. Is the writer telling us despite being a group, they maintain their individuality? Most of the year they live separate lives, but everyone once in a while they come together as a group?

The writer states they "represent a small foreign faction." The use of the word "foreign" doesn't make sense. Even if to us they are foreigners, they wouldn't call themselves foreigners. They are not foreigners to themselves. They would tell us, "We are the Islamic Jihad." Remember you can learn a lot if you ask yourself how you would state something. Then compare your statement with the suspect's statement. If you went to Iran and kidnapped someone, it is doubtful you would leave a note stating you are a foreigner.

The writer goes on to say, "We respect your bussiness but not the country that it serves." Are we to believe that JonBenet was kidnapped and then murdered because someone has a hatred for the United States? Most people would agree this crime is not an international incident.

The writer misspells two common words, "business" (bussiness) and "possessions" (posessions). However, the writer correctly spells the words "deviation" and "attache" even including the accent on the word "attache." This leads us to believe the writer purposefully misspelled these two words to try to make it look like an uneducated person or a foreigner wrote this note. The two misspellings occur in the first paragraph. After that, the writer uses correct grammar except for using the article "a" when he should have written "an." This is further indication the misspellings were done on purpose. The writer showed his true writing skills and forgot to misspell words throughout the note.

The writer says, "You will withdraw $118,000.00 from your account.....Make sure that you bring an adequate size attache to the bank." The kidnapper may know the Ramseys are wealthy, but how does he know they have $118,000 in the bank. Most kidnappers would simply state get the money. They don't care where you get it from just get it. They also would not remind you to bring an adequate size case to hold the money.

The ransom note is addressed to "Mr. Ramsey." However, towards the end of the note three times the writer refers to John Ramsey as "John." If this was a foreign group, they would continually use the term "Mr. Ramsey." Referring to him by his first name is too personal for an unknown kidnapper.

Also remember that everyone has an internal dictionary. Certain words mean certain things. If the kidnapper saw John Ramsey as being "Mr. Ramsey" then he should always refer to him as "Mr. Ramsey." When he changes his language and calls him "John" there has to be a justification for the change. I do not see a justification. Therefore, the writer is not speaking from the heart but is making up the story.

In examining the pronouns, we find this crime was not committed by "a group of individuals that represent a small foreign faction." If you are writing for a group, then your language will reflect there are several people involved. Throughout the ransom note, the writer uses the plural pronouns "we," "us" and "our" because he wants to give the impression that a group is responsible for the kidnapping. In paragraph one we find the statements, "<u>We</u> are a group of individuals." "<u>We</u> respect your business." "<u>We</u> have your daughter." "Follow <u>our</u> instructions." Towards the end of the letter the write states, "Follow <u>our</u> instructions and you stand a 100% chance of getting her back." However, the writer slips up and the truth comes out when he uses the pronoun "my." In the second paragraph, we have the statement, "Any deviation of <u>my</u> instructions will result in the immediate execution of your daughter." If this was truly a group effort, the writer would have a group mentality and would consistently use the plural pronouns. In paragraph two, we have the phrases "I will call you" and "we might call you." Again we have the shift from singular to plural. We see deception in this ransom note with the changing pronouns. This kidnapping was not the work of a terrorist group. One person wrote this ransom note. One person and perhaps an accomplice committed this crime. This of course does not prove the ransom note is a fake. It could still be a kidnapping committed by one person. However, since the writer is being deceptive about the number of people involved, we have to wonder if the entire ransom note is a lie.

In the third paragraph, we have an unnecessary word. "The two gentlemen watching over your daughter." Unnecessary words are words that can be taken out of the sentence, and yet the sentence still makes sense. The writer could have stated, "The two gentlemen watching your daughter." By including the extra word, the writer is including extra information.

What is the difference between watching someone and watching over someone? The best example I can think of is in reference to God. If I say that God is watching over me, I visualize God keeping his distance. He sees me, but he also see the entire world at the same time. He can see me because I am part of the world. While He is watching over me He is also watching over others. The word "over" means God is spreading His watchful eye upon the earth. However, if I say that God is watching me it becomes more personal. Even though He can see the entire world, He is focusing His attention on me. Another example would be if a friend asked you to "watch over" his house while he was out of town. In this case he probably wants you to stop by every once in a while and make sure everything is okay. Maybe you will pick up his mail and water his plants. However, if he asked you to "watch" his house he probably wants you to housesit. He wants you to be there where you can keep a close eye on things.

In a kidnapping, the kidnappers should be "watching" the abductee. They will want to keep a close eye on her. They want to make sure she doesn't escape or alert someone that she needs help. They will want to make sure she doesn't harm herself if her being alive is dependent upon them receiving the ransom. When the writer of the ransom note said they were "watching over" JonBenet, he was telling us they were not keeping a close eye on her. There are only two reasons why you would not closely watch your hostage: 1. If you knew for certain she was alright and could not escape; 2. If you knew she was dead. Since a dead body isn't going anywhere, it is something you "watch over." Based on the language used, it appears the writer knew JonBenet was dead when he wrote the ransom note.

The writer's own words tell us this ransom note was not written with the intent to obtain money. The length of the note is an indication this is not a true ransom note. Most kidnappers would not tell you where to get the money from, and they would ask for a lot more than $118,000. There is deception in the language, pronouns, and misspelled words. Calling John Ramsey by his first name is too personal for a kidnapper. The writer's internal dictionary involving the words "Mr. Ramsey" and "John" reveal this note was a fabrication. The word "over" shows us the note was written after JonBenet had been killed.

Since the ransom note was written as a ruse, we can conclude this was not a kidnapping that turned into a murder, but a murder made to look like a kidnapping. This means we cannot exclude the Ramseys as possible suspects. Since this was a murder, why would the killer write a bogus ransom note? The only reason I can think of is he wanted to confuse the police. If an intruder committed this murder, a ransom note may buy him some time to leave the area. The police would not be searching for a murderer. They would not be searching the bus, train or airport terminals. They would not be looking for a body. They would be sitting in the Ramsey's house waiting for a telephone call while he is effecting his escape. In essence, that is what happened since JonBenet's body wasn't discovered for several hours. However, this theory does not make sense based on the crime scene evidence. The killer placed JonBenet's body on the floor in a small room located in the basement. If the police would have performed a proper cursory search they would have immediately found her body. Open the door to the room and there she is. Quickly finding her body means the killer's plans would have been foiled. If the killer wanted to make it look like a kidnapping, he would have hidden her body. Place her body in a basement closet and she may not be found for quite some time. This would have given him plenty of time to escape.

Writing a ransom note but not concealing the body does not add up to an intruder committing this crime. Therefore, we are left with only one other plausible possibility. Someone within the Ramsey residence killed JonBenet and wrote the ransom note. Let's look at what evidence ties John and Patsy Ramsey to the ransom note.

1. The ransom note was written on a pad of paper that was in the Ramsey's residence. Likewise, the pen that was used to write the note also came from their residence.

2. The killer placed a nylon cord made into a garrote around JonBenet's neck and strangled her. A broken paintbrush belonging to Patsy Ramsey was used to make the garrote.

3. Immediate family members submitted handwriting samples which were compared to the ransom note. Patsy Ramsey is the only immediate family member who has not been ruled out as a possible match.

4. The kidnapper demanded $118,000 from the Ramseys. This is a very unusual amount. Kidnappers are greedy. Most people would ask for a much larger amount. There is a reason why the writer chose $118,000. Even John Ramsey agrees that the number 118 is significant to the killer. It has been reported that in 1996 John Ramsey received a bonus of $118,000. Is this a coincidence? When the writer had to think of a number, $118,000 was on his mind.

5. At the end of the second paragraph, the writer states, "If we monitor you getting the money early, we might call you early to arrange an earlier delivery of the money and hence a earlier pickup of your daughter." The word "hence" is not a common word. When was the last time you used that word in a sentence? We should look to see if this word appears in any writings of John or Patsy Ramsey. Well, it does. On December 14, 1997 the First United Methodist Church in Boulder, Colorado held a memorial service for JonBenet. In the program there was "A Christmas Message from the Ramsey Family." This

message was also posted on the Ramsey Family's Web site. In the message, we find the statement, "Had there been no birth of Christ, there would be no hope of eternal life, and, hence, no hope of ever being with our loved ones again."[54]

6. The word "hence" is a transition word. You do not have to use the word "and" with it. For example, "There would be no hope of eternal life, hence, no hope of ever being with our loved ones again." The writer of the ransom note used the same phrase "and hence." In their Christmas Message, the Ramseys used this exact same phrase. In their book, Patsy Ramsey addresses the use of the phrase "and hence."

"Actually, I have no idea why we used that phrase. Maybe we'd seen it so many times in reading the ransom note - and having to write it over and over again for the police - that it became a part of our subconscious vocabulary. Who Knows? Then again, maybe people everywhere use the phrase 'and hence' everyday of the week, because it's a normal part of the English language."[55]

Like I said, when was the last time you used that phrase? It is not part of the normal English language. Patsy Ramsey does not tell us why they used that phrase. She only says "maybe" it is because they saw it in the ransom note and had to write it several times for the police. She then asked a question, "Who knows?" She is trying to sweep this under the carpet as if it is no big deal. However, this is a very big deal. We have the same phrase that is in the ransom note, appearing in their writings.

7. When we look at the original ransom note we find the writer had crossed out a word. The note actually reads: "If we monitor you getting the money early, we might call you early to arrange an earlier delivery of the money and hence, a earlier delivery pickup of your daughter." The writer realized that a kidnapper would not deliver JonBenet to her parents. So, the writer crossed out the

word "delivery" and wrote "pickup." It is doubtful that a kidnapper would make this mistake. His mind set would always be "Give me the money and I will show you where your daughter can be found." However, a person trying to make this look like a kidnaping and trying to think like a kidnapper might make this mistake.

This crossed out word also gives us insight into the author's writing style. We find that whatever comes before the phrase "and hence" comes after the phrase "and hence." "If we monitor you getting the money early, we might call you early to arrange an earlier <u>delivery</u> of the money and hence, a earlier ~~delivery~~ pickup of your daughter."

We see this same writing style in the Ramsey's Christmas Message. "Had there been no birth of Christ, there would be <u>no hope</u> of eternal life, and, hence, <u>no hope</u> of ever being with our loved ones again."

8. Finally, the pronouns in the ransom note show us this murder was not committed by a group. One person wrote the ransom note and one or two people were responsible for JonBenet's death.

From the beginning of the investigation, John and Patsy Ramsey were suspects in the murder of their daughter. Statistics say that someone within the residence committed this crime. The majority of the evidence indicates that a stranger did not kill JonBenet. The killer spent so much time in the house it would appear he had no fear of being discovered. The ransom note appears to have been staged to divert attention away from the Ramseys. Based on what the Ramseys have said and what they have not said, the police should continue to focus their investigation on John and Patsy Ramsey.

Notes

Chapter 2
Liar Liar Pants On Fire

1. *The Atlanta Journal-Constitution*, by Kathy Scruggs and Ron Martz, "Hero denies planting bomb," July 31, 1996.

2. *Lubbock Avalanche-Journal*, October 26, 1996.

3. *The Atlanta Journal-Constitution*, by Ron Martz, "Jewell breaks silence for 60 Minutes," September 20, 1996.

Chapter 3
Watch How You Phrase Your Questions

1. CNN Interactive transcript, *Larry King Live Weekend, The Saga of James Earl Ray*, April 12, 1997.

2. Transcript of LAPD's interview with O.J. Simpson, June 13, 1994. Provided by Bruce Spielbauer.

3. *TIME*, April 15, 1996.

Chapter 4
Look At The Language

1. Videotape of President Clinton's Grand Jury testimony on August 17, 1998

2. The *Atlanta Journal-Constitution*, July 31, 1999.

3. Transcript, *CBS News 60 Minutes*, January 26, 1992.

4. Ibid.

5. *U.S. News & World Report*, April 14, 1997.

6. Barbara Walters interview of Marv Albert, *ABC 20/20*, November 1997.

7. *The Brunswick News*, May 21, 1997.

8. Transcript, *CBS News Eye to Eye with Connie Chung*, February 10, 1994.

9. Ibid.

10. Ibid.

11. *The State*, Columbia, S.C., November 18, 1999.

12. *The Daily Reflector*, January 4, 2001.

13. *Walker Texas Ranger*, September 7, 2000, *USA Network*.

14. *Law And Order*, March 30, 2001, *A & E*.

Chapter 5
Examine All Of The Pronouns

1. O. J. Simpson, *I Want To Tell You*, 1995, page 11.

2. *Court TV* Library transcript of the conversation between O.J. Simpson and detective Tom Lange on June 17, 1994.

3. Ibid.

4. Ibid.

5. Video tape of a statement made by Susan Smith on November 2, 1994.

6. *Herald-Journal*, Spartanburg, S.C., November 23, 1994.

7. Obtained from a copy of the published ransom note.

8. Ibid.

9. Ibid.

10. Ibid.

11. Ibid.

Chapter 6
Check The Verb Tenses

1. *The Washington Post*, November 5, 1994.

2. *The Washington Post*, July 26, 1995.

3. *The Brunswick News*, June 10, 1992.

Chapter 9
Words And Phrases That Indicate Deception

1. Videotape, *CBS News 60 Minutes*, March 18, 2001.

2. *The Brunswick News*, July 22, 1995.

Chapter 10
Did The Subject Answer The Question?

1. *Newsweek*, July 3, 1995.

2. Transcript, *CBS News 60 Minutes*, November 22, 1992.

3. *TIME*, April 15, 1996.

4. Rocky Mountain News Online transcript of the John and Patsy interview conducted on May 1, 1997.

5. Videotape, *CBS News 60 Minutes*, June 18, 2000.

6. *The Washington Post*, January 28, 1998.

7. Transcript, *CBS News 60 Minutes*, May 11, 1997.

Chapter 11
Did The Subject Answer The Question With A Question?

1. Transcript, *CBS News 60 Minutes*, November 22, 1992.

2. Transcript, *CNN Larry King Live*, October 24, 2000.

Chapter 12
Did The Writer Cross Out Any Words?

1. Obtained from a photostatic copy of the letter.

Chapter 13
Look For Unnecessary Words

1. Obtained from a photostatic copy of the ransom note.

Chapter 14
Internal Dictionary

1. O. J. Simpson, *I Want To Tell You*, 1995, page 13.

2. Ibid., page 25.

Chapter 16
What Hasn't The Subject Told You?

1. Steven Truscott, *The Steven Truscott Story*, 1971, page 54.

Chapter 17

A Quick Review

1. Obtained from a videotape of the show *Unsolved Mysteries*. The date the show aired is unknown.

2. Ibid.

Chapter 18
The Oklahoma City Bombing

1. *Newsweek*, July 3, 1995.

2. Ibid.

3. Ibid.

4. *Time*, April 15, 1996.

5. Ibid.

6. Ibid.

7. Ibid.

Chapter 19
The Nicole Brown Simpson And Ronald Goldman Murders

1. Transcript, *OJ Simpson's Statement to the LAPD*, June 13, 1994.

2. Ibid.

3. Ibid.

4. Ibid.

5. Ibid.

6. Ibid.

7. Ibid.

8. Ibid.

9. *Court TV* Library transcript of the conversation between O.J. Simpson and detective Tom Lange on June 17, 1994.

10. Ibid.

11. Obtained from a photostatic copy of the letter.

12. Faye Resnick, *Nicole Brown Simpson, The Private Diary Of A Life Interrupted*, 1994, page 25.

13. O.J. Simpson, *I Want To Tell You*, 1995, page xv.

14. Ibid., page 3, 10.

15. Ibid., page 15.

16. Ibid., page 14.

17. Ibid., page 14 - 15.

18. *Webster's New World Dictionary*.

19. O.J. Simpson, *I Want To Tell You*, 1995, page 43.

20. Ibid., page 93.

21. Ibid., page 94.

22. Ibid., page 161.

23. Ibid., page 54.

24. Ibid., page 24.

25. Ibid., page 167.

26. Transcript, *Black Entertainment Television, O.J. Simpson: Beyond The Verdict, The Interview*, January 24, 1996.

27. Ibid.

28. Transcript, *ESPN, UpClose, Conversation with O.J. Simpson*, part I, January 15, 1998.

29. Ibid.

30. Transcript, *Black Entertainment Television, O.J. Simpson: Beyond The Verdict, The Interview*, January 24, 1996.

31. Ibid.

32. Transcript, *Granada TV*, May 13, 1996.

33. Ibid.

34. Transcript, *Court TV Case Files*, November 22, 1996.

35. Transcript, ESPN, *UpClose, Conversation with O.J. Simpson*, part I, January 15, 1998.

36. Ibid.

37. Ibid.

38. Ibid.

39. Ibid.

Chapter 20
Sexual Molestation Allegations Against Michael Jackson

1. Transcript, *ABC's Prime Time Live*, June 14, 1995.

2. Ibid.

3. Ibid.

4. Ibid.

5. Ibid.

6. Ibid.

7. Ibid.

Chapter 21
The Assassination Of Dr. Martin Luther King, Jr.

1. Transcript, *ABCNEWS Saturday Night*, March 22, 1998, quoting Andrew Young.

2. Transcript, *State of Tennessee versus James Earl Ray*, March 10, 1969.

3. Ibid.

4. Ibid.

5. Ibid.

6. Ibid.

7. James Earl Ray, *Who Killed Martin Luther King Jr.? The True Story by the Alleged Assassin*, 1992, second edition, pages 130 -131.

8. Ibid., page 131.

9. Ibid.

10. Ibid., page 132.

11. Transcript, *State of Tennessee versus James Earl Ray*, March 10, 1969.

12. Ibid.

13. Ibid.

14. Ibid.

15. Transcript, *ABCNEWS Saturday Night*, March 22, 1998, quoting Louis Stokes and James Earl Ray.

16. Ibid.

17. James Earl Ray, *Who Killed Martin Luther King Jr.? The True Story by the Alleged Assassin*, 1992, second edition, page 191.

18. Transcript, *ABCNEWS Saturday Night*, March 22, 1998, quoting Louis Stokes and James Earl Ray.

19. James Earl Ray, *Who Killed Martin Luther King Jr? The True Story by the Alleged Assassin*, 1992, Second edition, page 120.

20. Ibid, page 270

21. *CNN Interactive, Ray tells M.L. King's son he didn't kill his father*, March 27, 1997.

22. Ibid.

23. *CNN Interactive* transcript, *Larry King Live Weekend, The Saga of James Earl Ray*, April 12,1997.

24. Transcript, *ABCNEWS Saturday Night*, March 22, 1998, quoting Louis Stokes and James Earl Ray.

25. *CNN Interactive, Ray tells M.L. King's son he didn't kill his father*, March 27, 1997.

26. James Earl Ray, *Who Killed Martin Luther King Jr.? The True Story by the Alleged Assassin*, 1992, second edition, page 120.

27. *CNN Interactive* transcript, *Larry King Live Weekend, The Saga of James Earl Ray*, April 12,1997.

28. Ibid.

29. Ibid.

30. Ibid.

31. Transcript, *State of Tennessee versus James Earl Ray*, March 10, 1969.

32. *CNN Interactive* transcript, *Larry King Live Weekend, The Saga of James Earl Ray*, April 12, 1997.

33. Ibid.

34. James Earl Ray, *Who Killed Martin Luther King Jr? The True Story by the Alleged Assassin*, 1992, Second edition, page 179.

35. *CNN Interactive* transcript, *Larry King Live Weekend, The Saga of James Earl Ray*, April 12, 1997.

36. Ibid.

37. Ibid.

38. Ibid.

Chapter 22
The Lindbergh Kidapping
And The Trial Of Bruno Richard Hauptmann

1. Lindbergh Archives.

2. Transcript of Bruno Richard Hauptmann's interview, September 19, 1934, New York.

3. Ibid.

4. Ibid.

5. Transcript of Bruno Richard Hauptmann's interview, September 20, 1934, New York.

6. Ibid.

7. Ibid.

8. Ibid.

9. Ibid.

10-19. *The Trial Of Bruno Richard Hauptmann*, Sidney B. Whipple, 1934.

20-30. *Why Did You Kill Me?*, Bruno Richard Hauptmann, date unknown.

Chapter 23
President Clinton and Monica Lewinsky Scandal

1. Transcript of Jim Lehrer's January 21, 1998 interview, as reported by the *Washington Post.com*, February 6, 1998.

2. Ibid.

3. Transcript of *National Public Radio's* January 21, 1998 interview, as reported by the *Washington Post.com*, February 6, 1998.

4. Transcript of Jim Lehrer's January 21, 1998 interview, as reported by the *Washington Post.com*, February 6, 1998.

5. Ibid.

6. Videotape of *ABC's Prime Time Live*, January 21, 1998.

7. Transcript of remarks at a photo opportunity with Chairman Yasser Arafat, January 22, 1998, as reported by the *Washington Post.com*, February 6, 1998.

8. Transcript of remarks at the After-School Program Event, January 26, 1998, as reported by the *Washington Post.com*, February 6, 1998.

9. Transcript, *CBS News 60 Minutes*, January 26, 1992.

10. *USA Today*, March 31, 1992.

11. *The Washington Post*, January 28, 1998.

12. *USA Today*, February 18, 1998.

13. Ibid.

14. Exhibit #1, *Deposition Of William Jefferson Clinton*, March 13, 1998.

15. Transcript, *Deposition Of William Jefferson Clinton*, March 13, 1998.

16. Videotape, *CBS News 60 Minutes*, March 15, 1998.

17. Ibid.

18. *The Brunswick News*, March 16, 1998.

19. Ibid.

20. Ibid.

21. Ibid.

22. Ibid.

23. Ibid.

24. *The Brunswick News*, March 17, 1998

25. Ibid.

26. Videotape, *CBS News 60 Minutes*, March 15, 1998.

27. Transcript, President Clinton's address to the nation, August 17, 1998.

28. Videotape, *William Jefferson Clinton's Grand Jury Testimony*, August 17, 1998.

Chapter 24
The Murder Of Marilyn Sheppard

1. Videotape, *The Learning Channel*, October 1997.

2. Videotape, *NBC News Dateline*, September 1997.

Chapter 25
The JonBenet Ramsey Murder

1. Obtained from a photostatic copy of the ransom note.

2. Ibid.

3. Transcript, *CNN Interactive, Interview With Parents of Slain Child Beauty Queen*, aired January 1, 1997.

4. Ibid.

5. Ibid.

6. Transcript, *Rocky Mountain News Online, The JonBenet Ramsey Case*, May 1, 1997

7. Ibid.

8. Ibid.

9. Ibid.

10. Ibid.

11. Ibid.

12. Transcript, *ABC News 20/20*, March 17, 2000.

13-21. Ibid.

22. Transcript, *NBC's Today Show*, aired March 20, 2000.

23. Ibid.

24. Transcript, *NBC's Today Show*, aired March 21, 2000.

25. Transcript, *NBC's Today Show*, aired March 24, 2000.

26. Transcript, *CNN Larry King Live*, March 27, 2000.

27. Ibid.

28. Ibid.

29. Ibid.

30. Ibid.

31. Ibid.

32. Ibid.

33. Transcript, *CNN Larry King Live*, March 28, 2000.

34. Ibid.

35. Transcript, *CNN Larry King Live*, May 31, 2000.

36. Ibid.

37. Transcript, *Rocky Mountain News Online, The JonBenet Ramsey Case*, May 1, 1997

38. *The Death of Innocence*, John & Patsy Ramsey, 2000, page 11.

39. Ibid, page 26.

40. Ibid, page 101.

41. Ibid, page 105.

42. Ibid, page 280.

43. Ibid, page 365.

44. Ibid, page 366.

45. Transcript, *CNN Larry King Live*, March 28, 2000.

46. *The Death of Innocence*, John & Patsy Ramsey, 2000, pages 365 - 367.

47. Ibid, page 366.

48. Ibid, page 385.

49. Ibid, page 96.

50. Ibid, page 84.

51. Ibid, pages 1 - 6.

52. Ibid, page 6.

53. Photostatic copy of the ransom note. The ransom note is printed on pages 11 -12 of the Ramsey's book. However, in their book they correctly spell the words the kidnapper misspelled.

54. Obtained from the Ramsey's web site www.ramseyfamily.com, November 6, 1999.

55. *The Death of Innocence*, John & Patsy Ramsey, 2000, page 235.